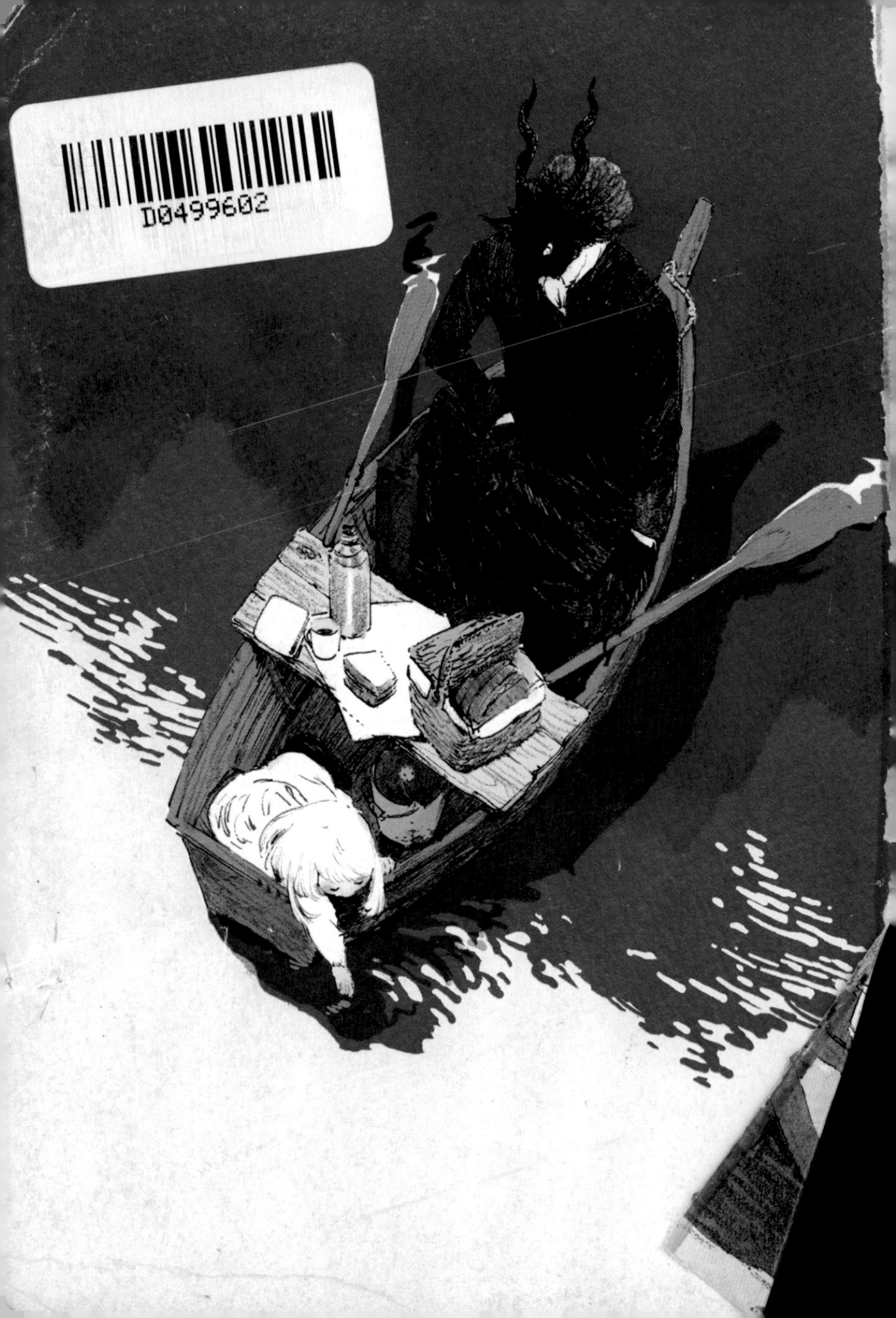

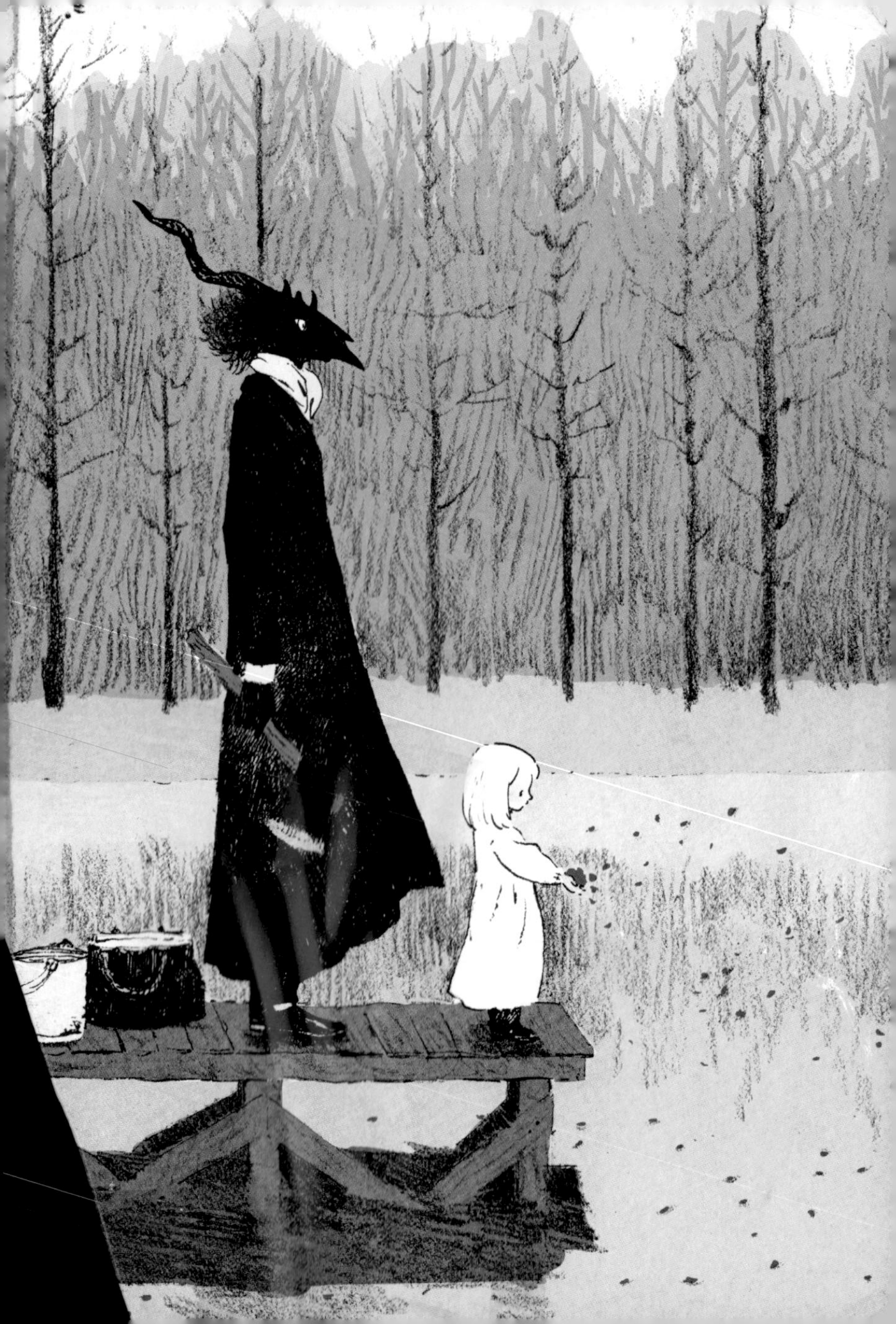

Chapter 6

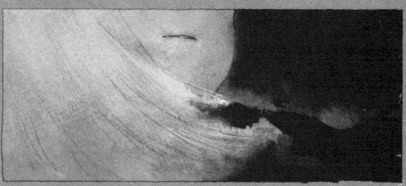

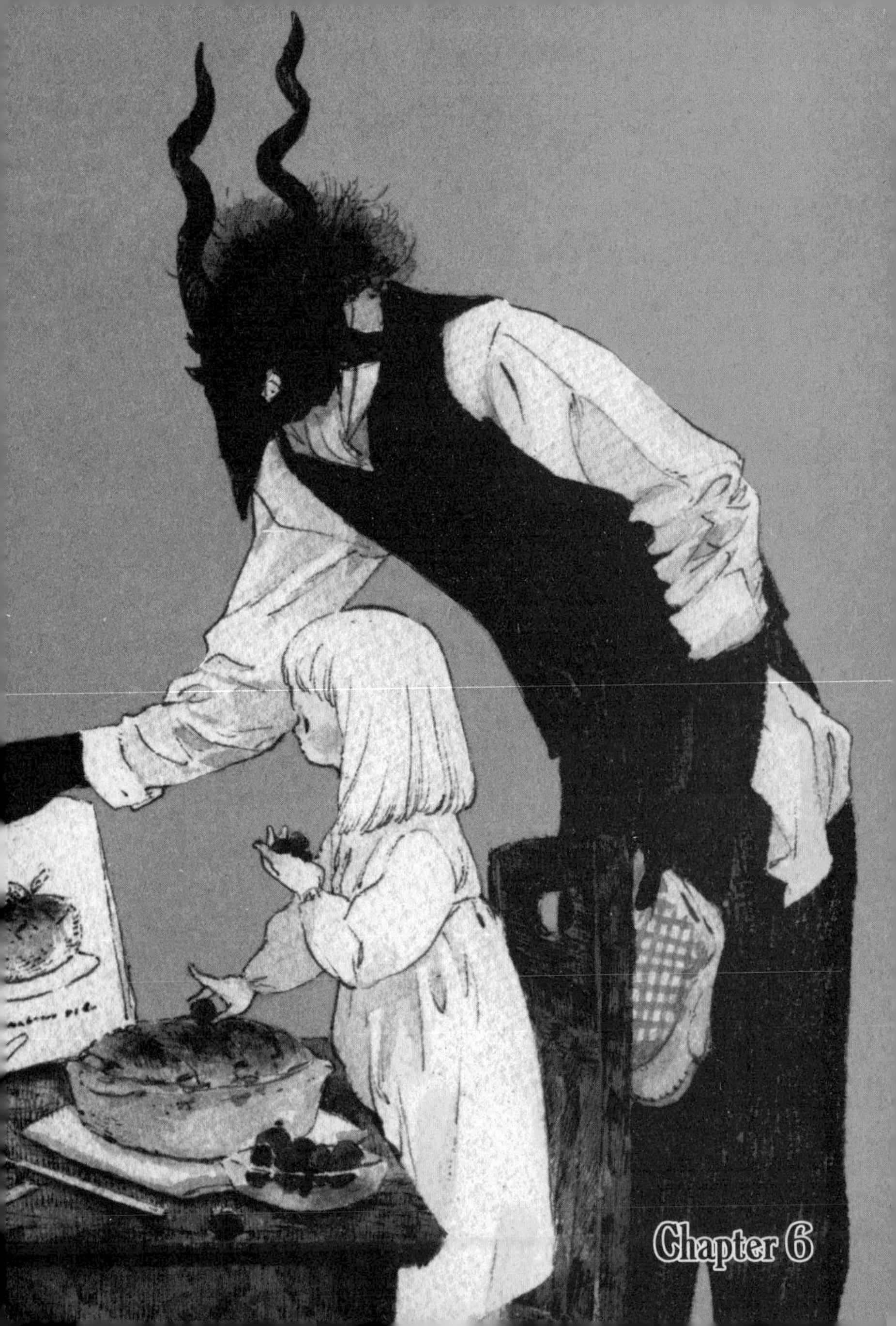
Chapter 6

Siúil, a Rún
The Girl from the Other Side

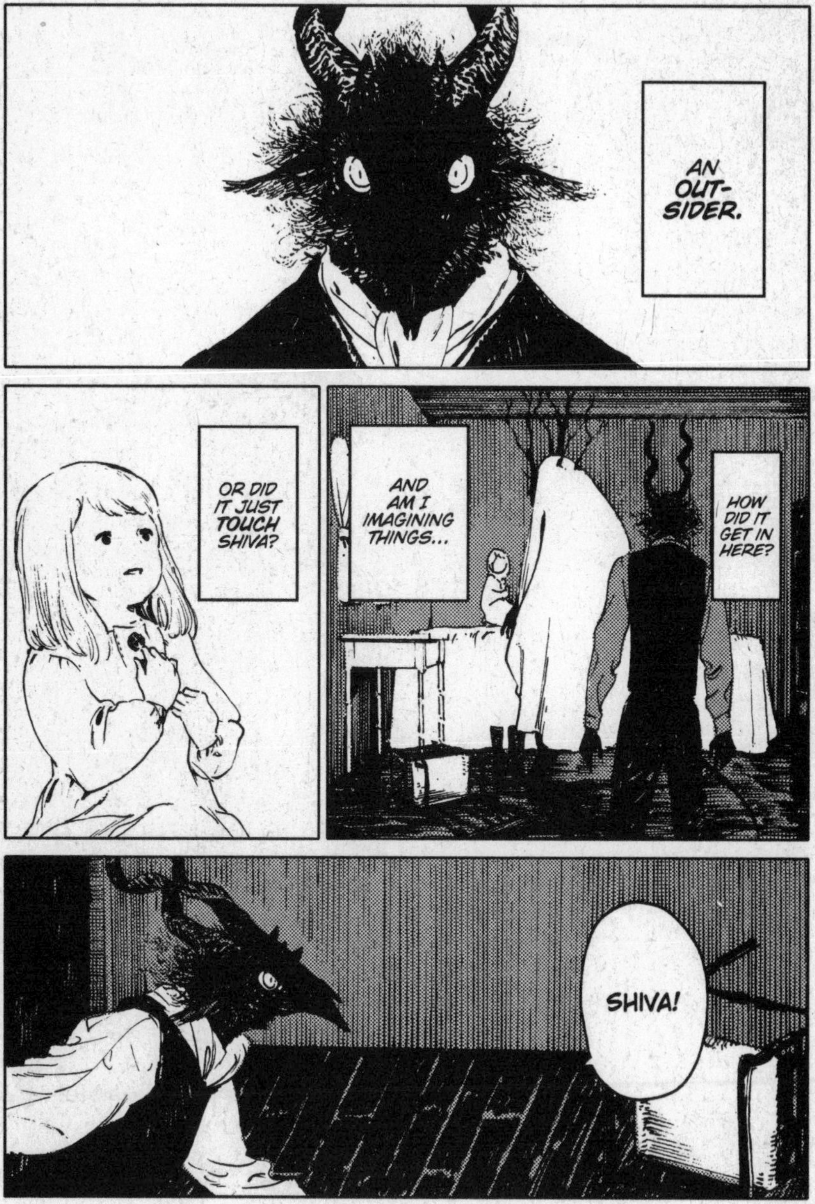
AN OUTSIDER.
HOW DID IT GET IN HERE?
AND AM I IMAGINING THINGS...
OR DID IT JUST TOUCH SHIVA?
SHIVA!

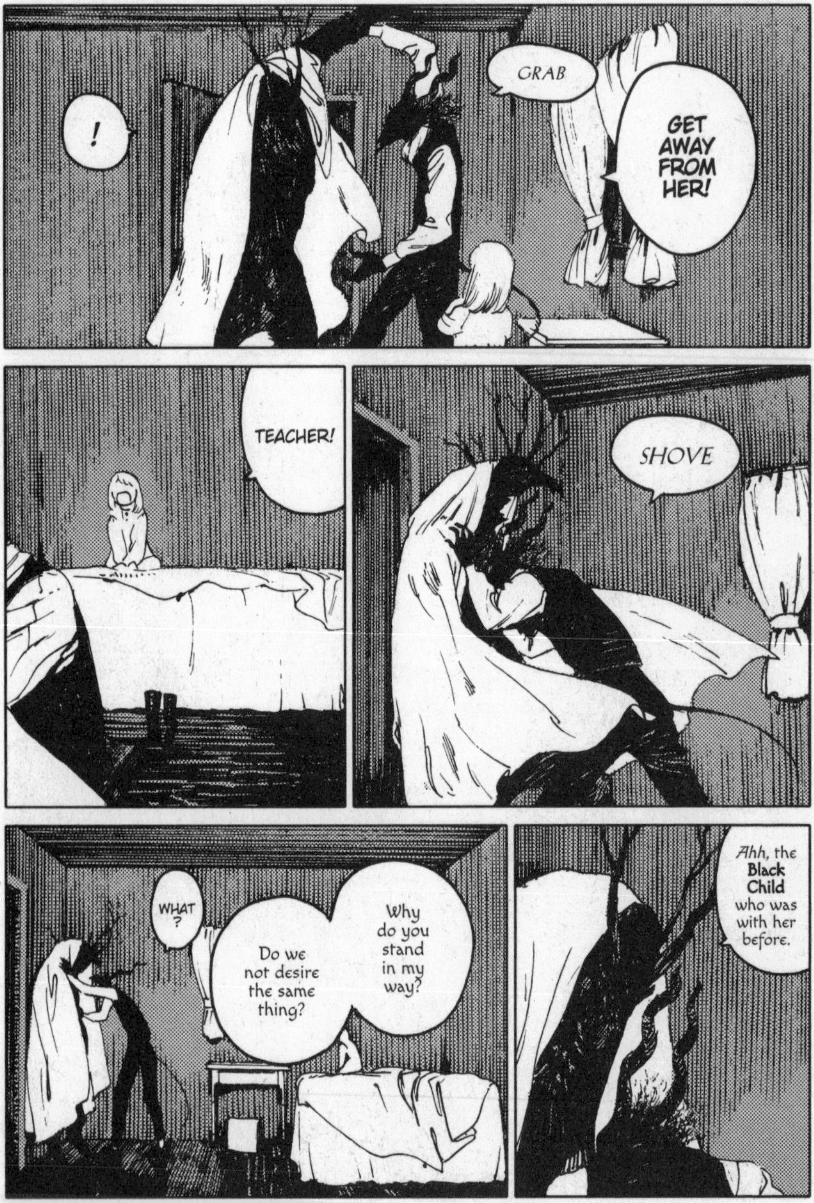

GET AWAY FROM HER!
GRAB
!
SHOVE
TEACHER!
Ahh, the **Black Child** who was with her before.
Why do you stand in my way?
Do we not desire the same thing?
WHAT?

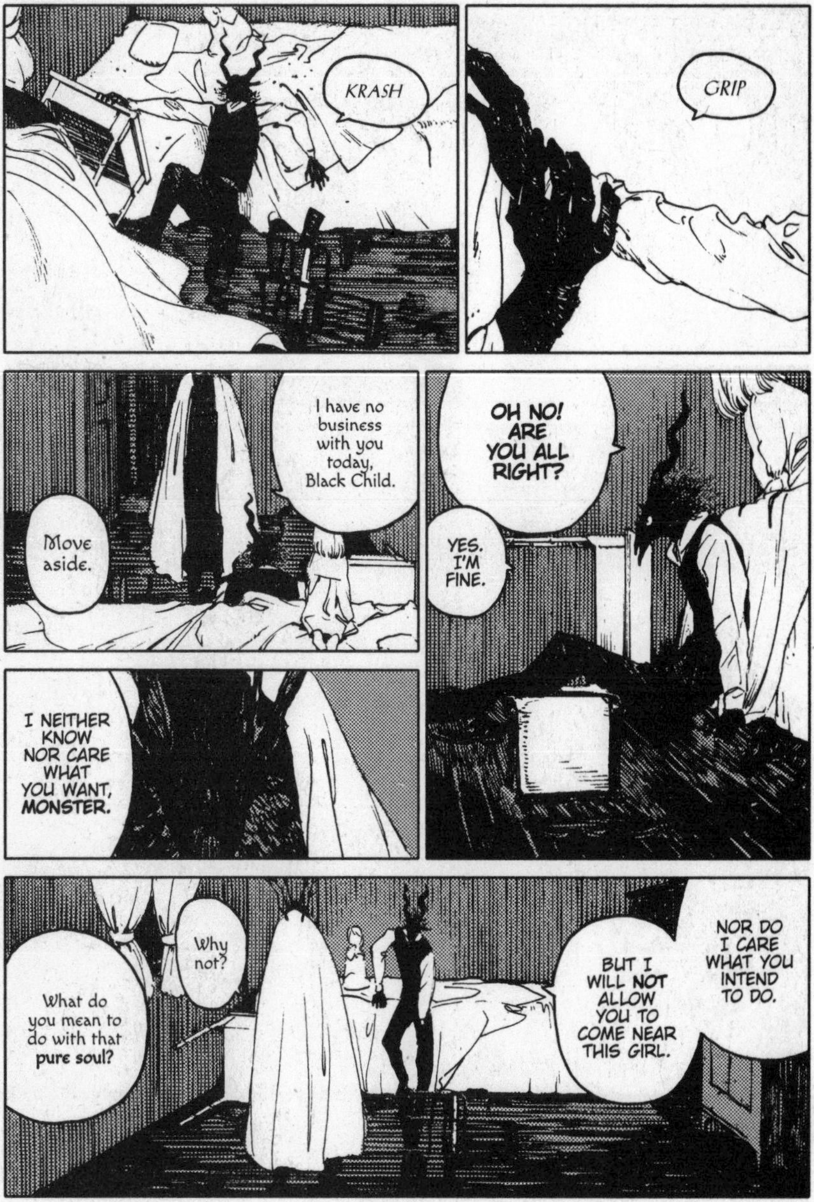
GRIP
KRASH
OH NO! ARE YOU ALL RIGHT?
YES. I'M FINE.
I have no business with you today, Black Child.
Move aside.
I NEITHER KNOW NOR CARE WHAT YOU WANT, MONSTER.
NOR DO I CARE WHAT YOU INTEND TO DO.
BUT I WILL NOT ALLOW YOU TO COME NEAR THIS GIRL.
Why not?
What do you mean to do with that pure soul?

Keep it for *yourself...?*

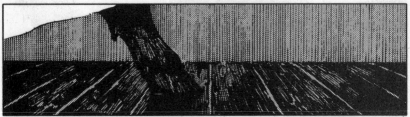

CURSED ONE--!

Move.

KLUNK

DMP

THUNK

THMP

LEAVE US BE!

Release me.

THUD

BUMP

CLUTCH

STOP!

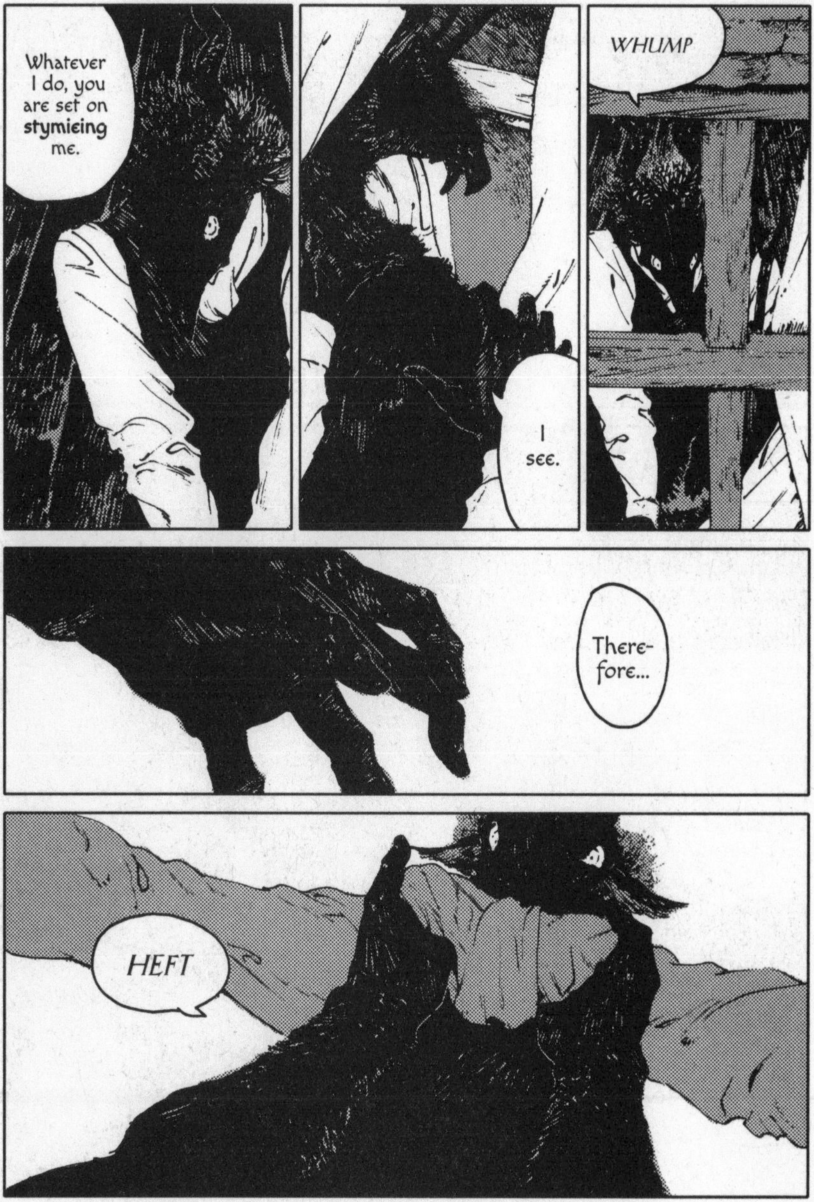
WHUMP
I see.
Whatever I do, you are set on stymieing me.
There-fore...
HEFT

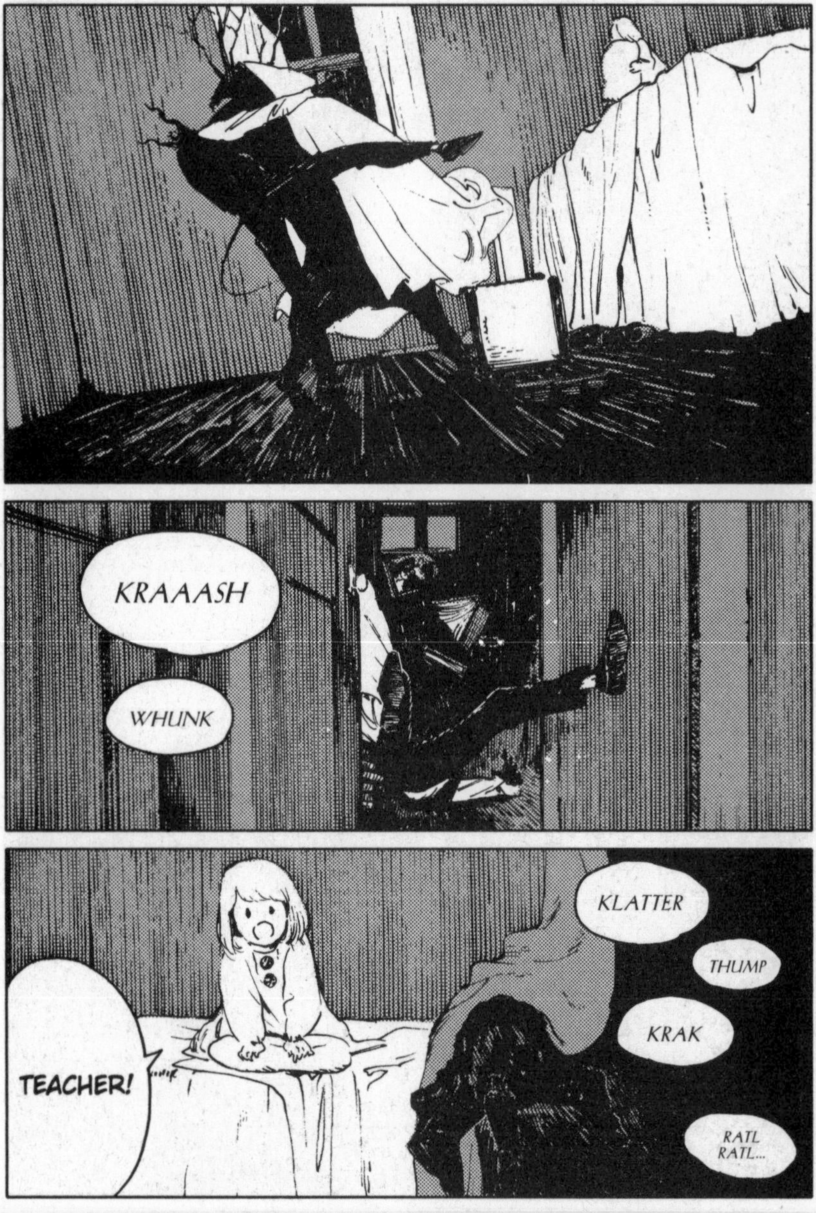
KRAAASH
WHUNK
KLATTER
THUMP
KRAK
RATL RATL...
TEACHER!

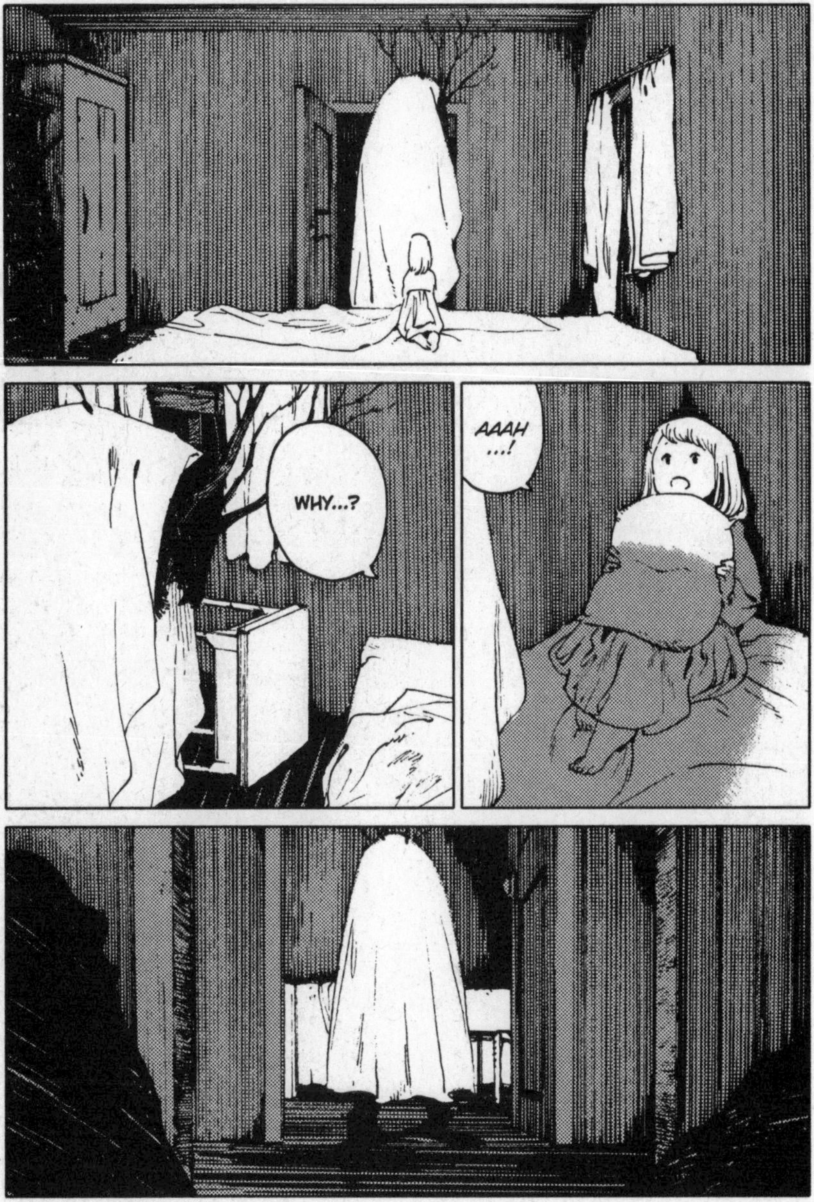
AAAH ...!
WHY...?

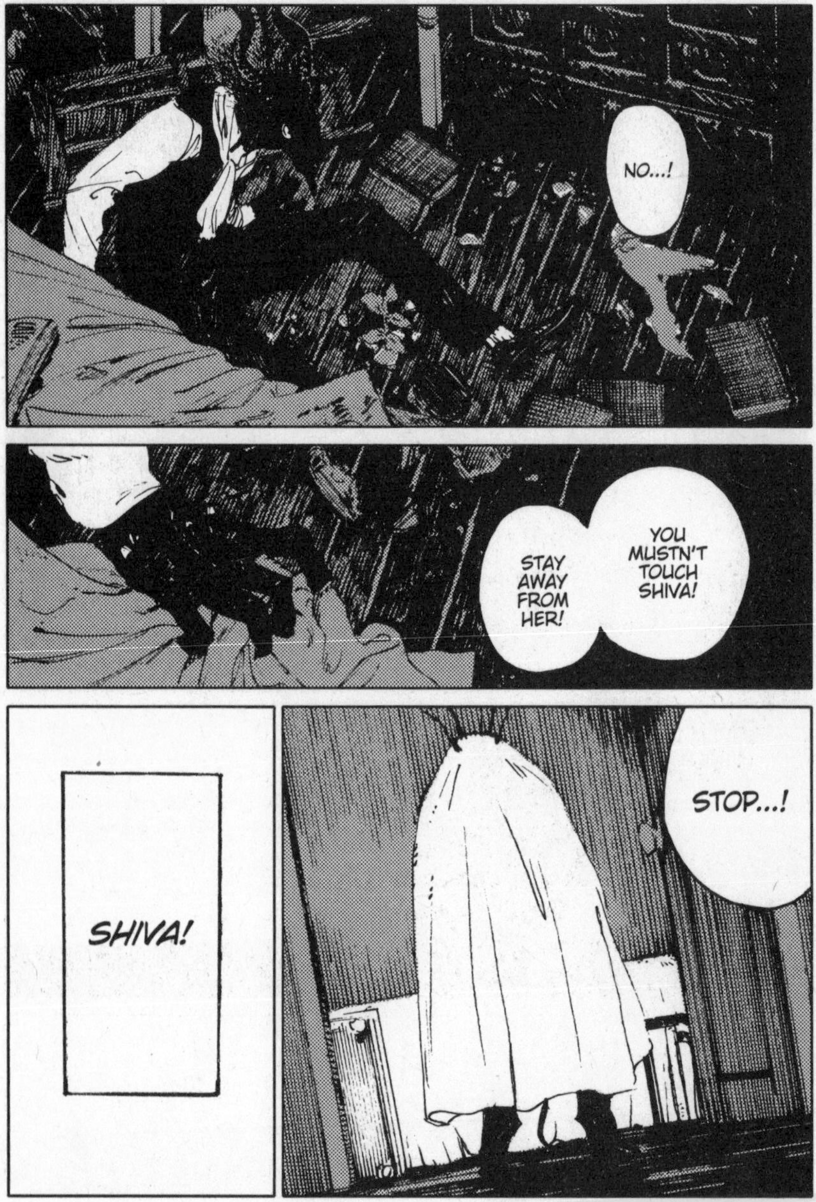
NO...!
YOU MUSTN'T TOUCH SHIVA!
STAY AWAY FROM HER!
STOP...!
SHIVA!

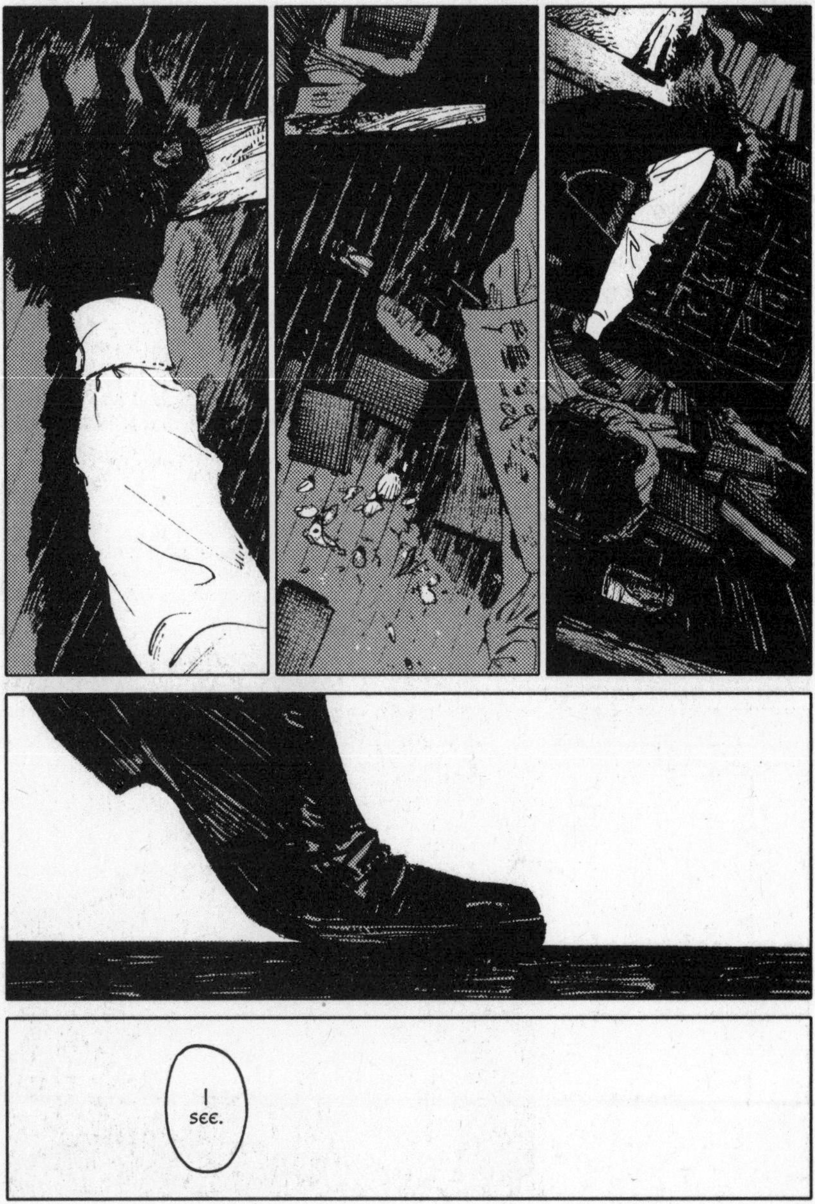
I see.

You still do not under-stand.
No matter.
Come. Let's go home.
I DON'T KNOW YOU.
WHO ARE YOU?
THE THING YOU SAID... IS IT TRUE?

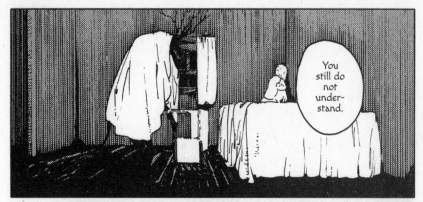

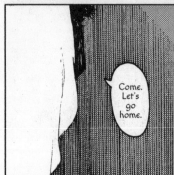

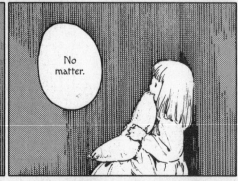

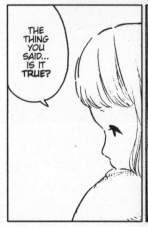

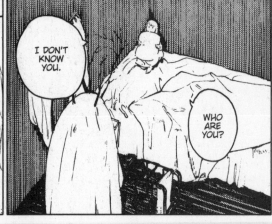

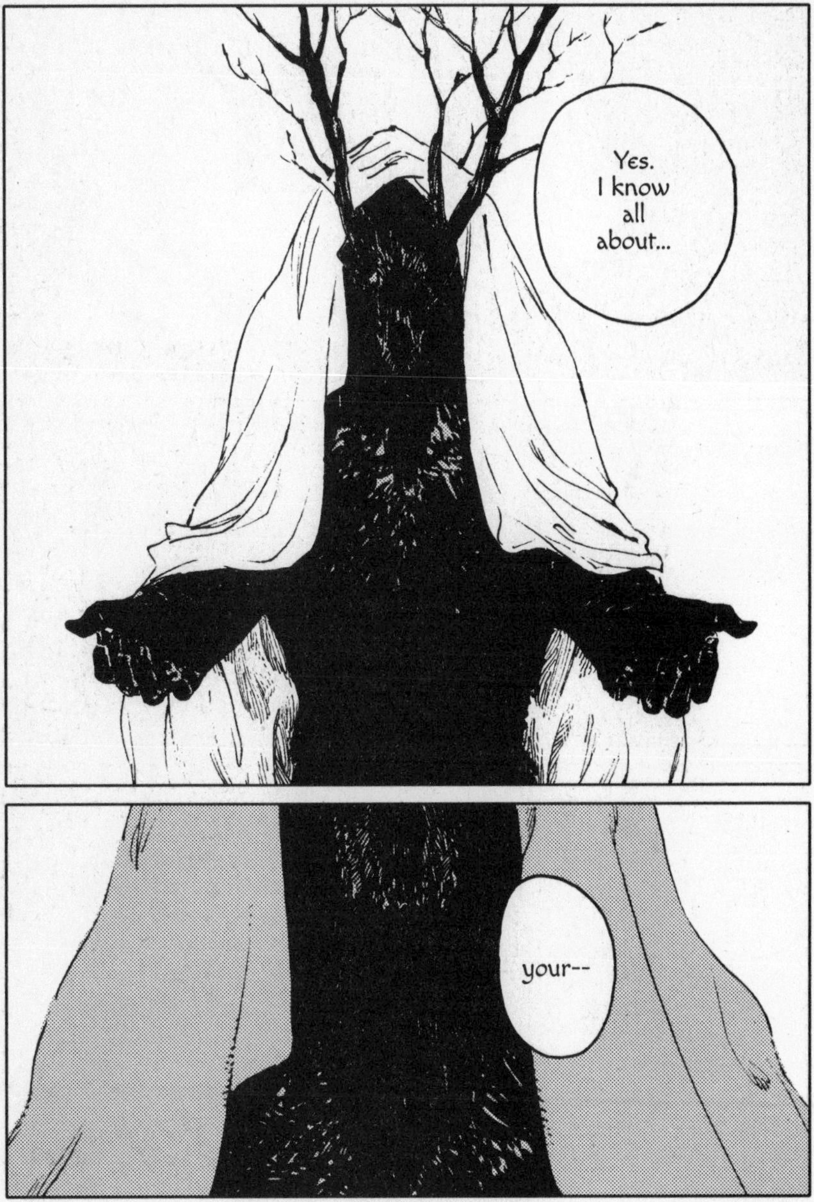
Yes. I know all about...
your--

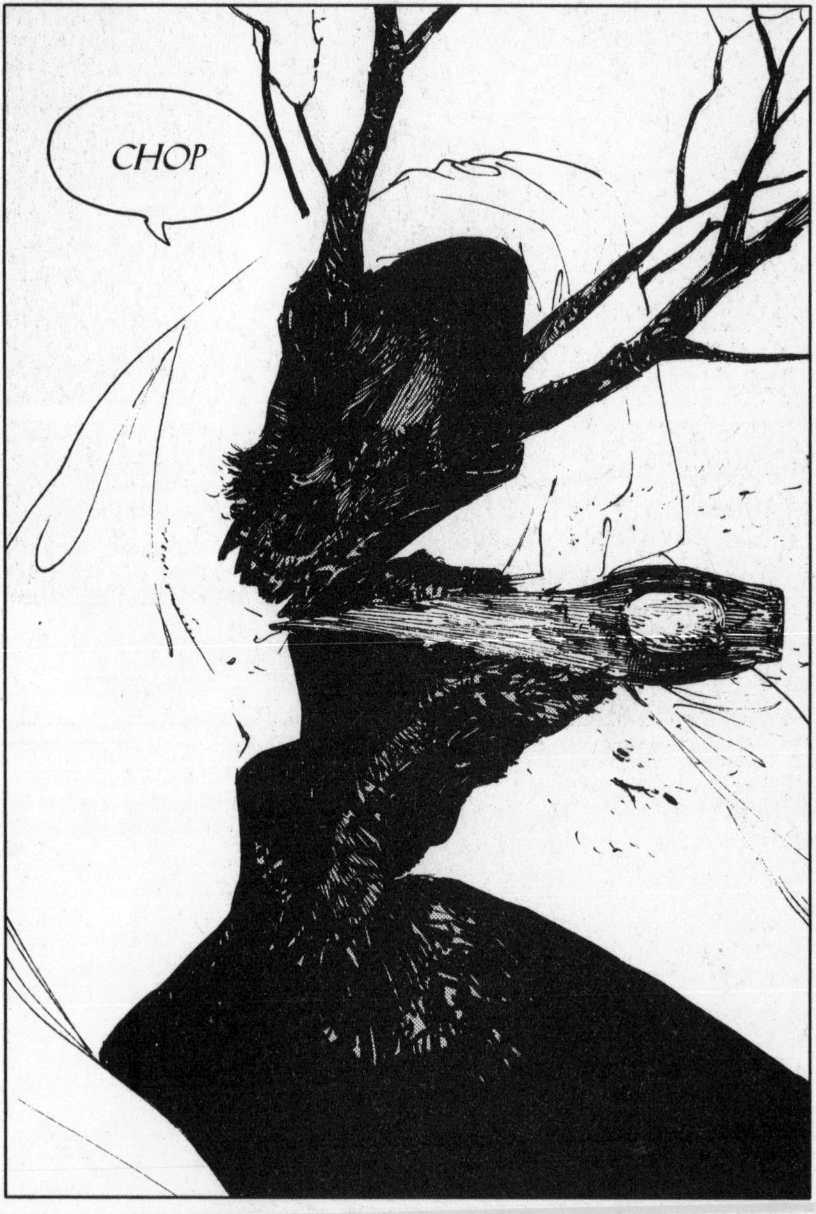
CHOP

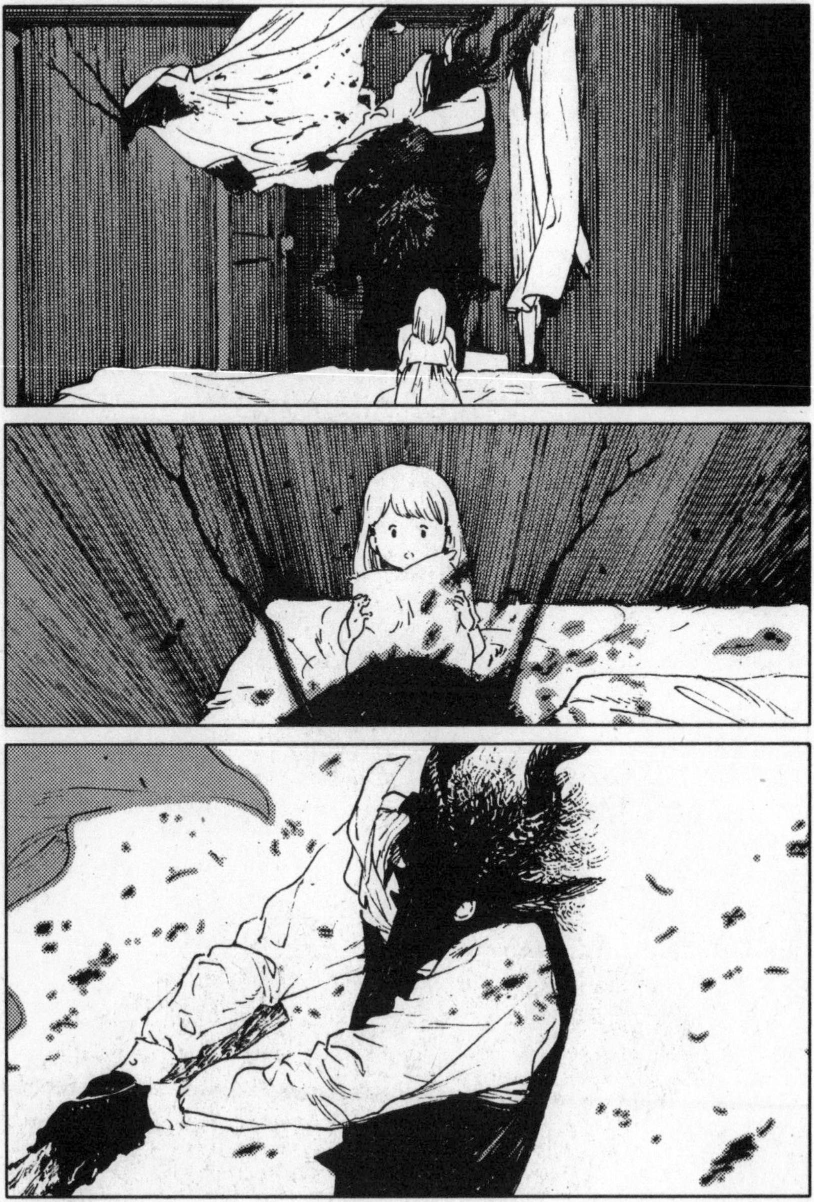

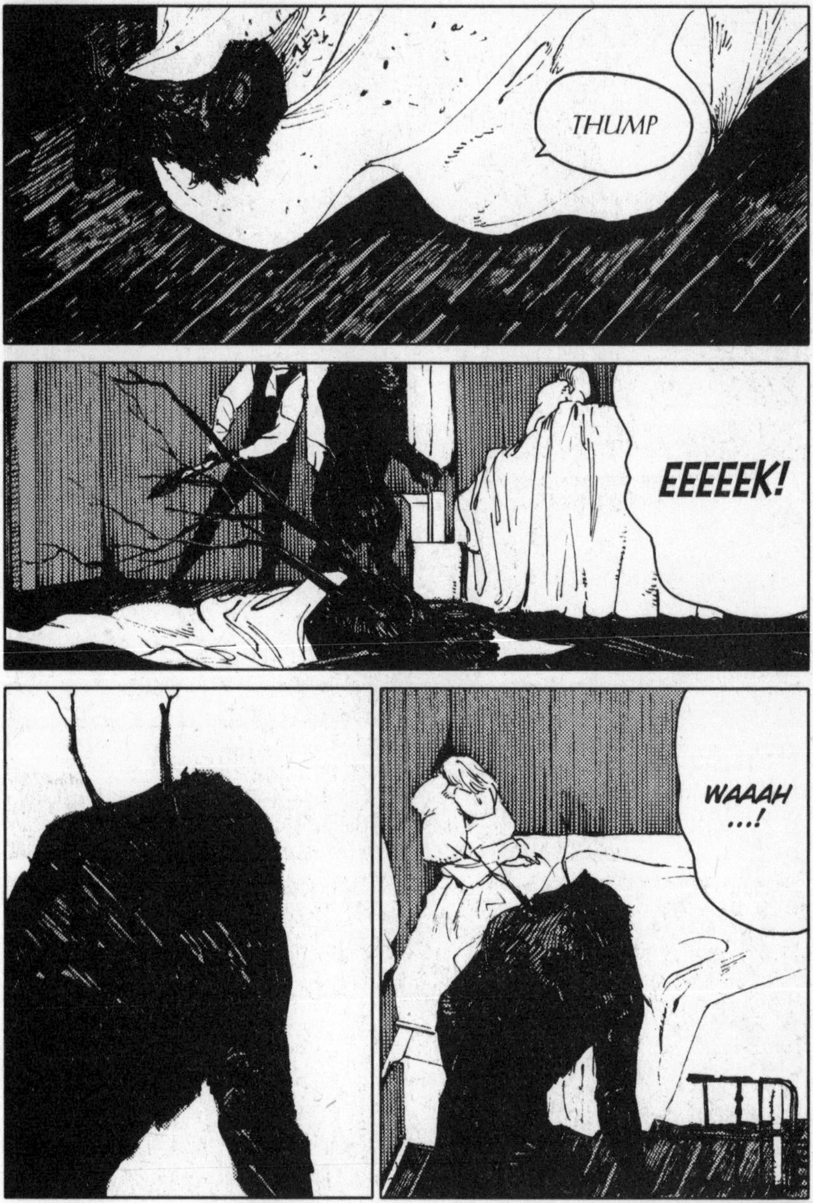
THUMP
EEEEEK!
WAAAH ...!

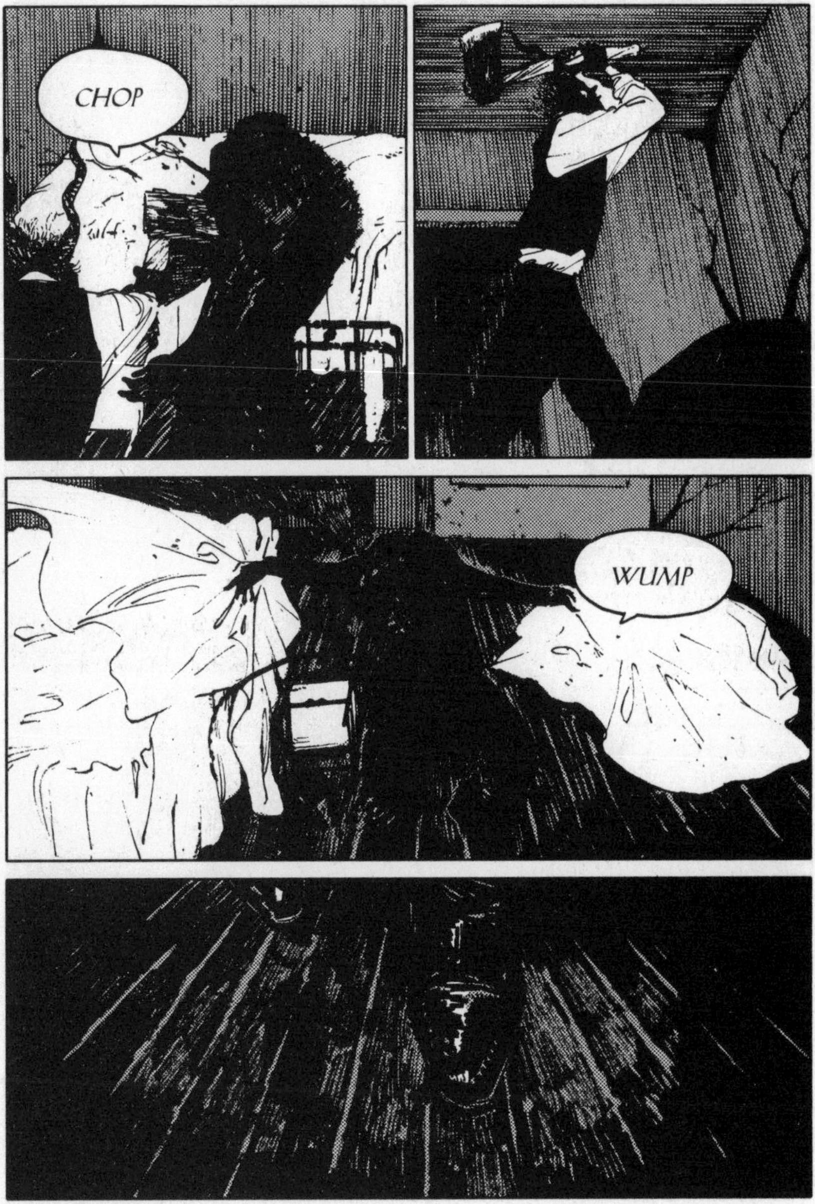
CHOP
WUMP

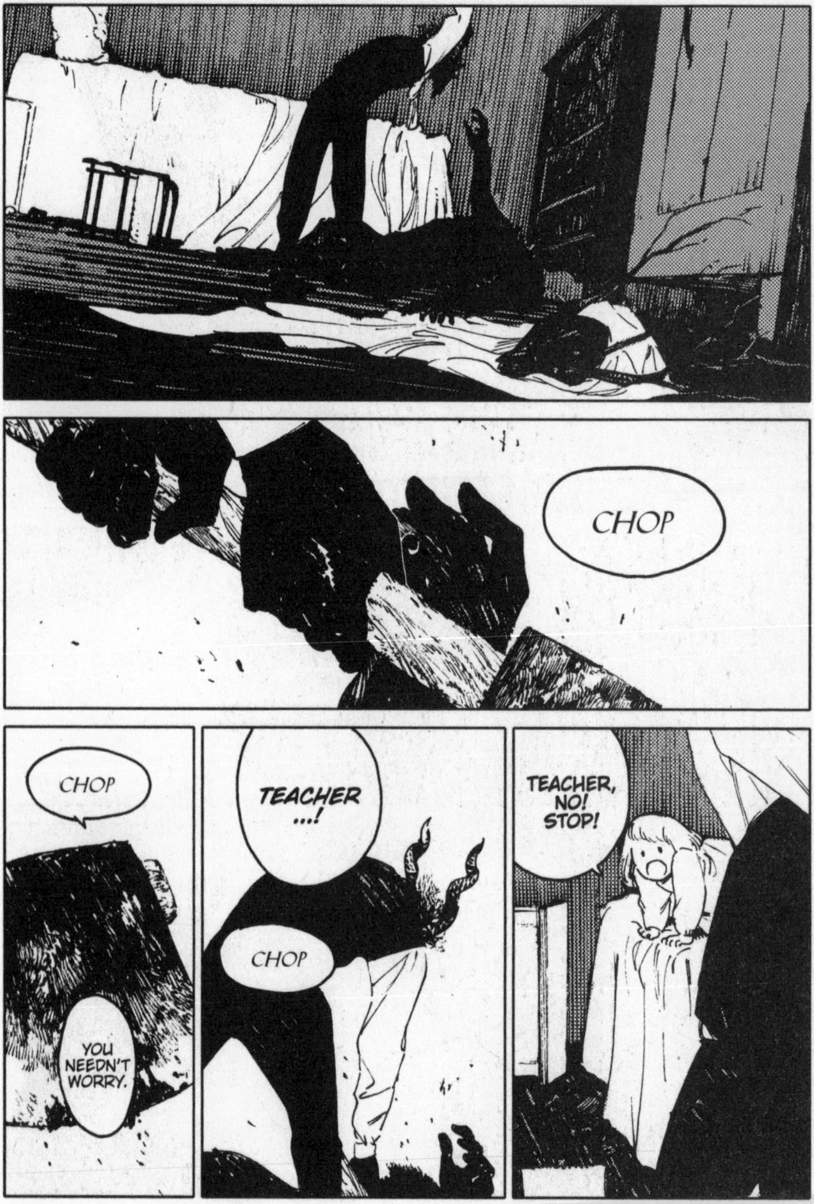
CHOP
TEACHER, NO! STOP!
TEACHER ...!
CHOP
CHOP
YOU NEEDN'T WORRY.

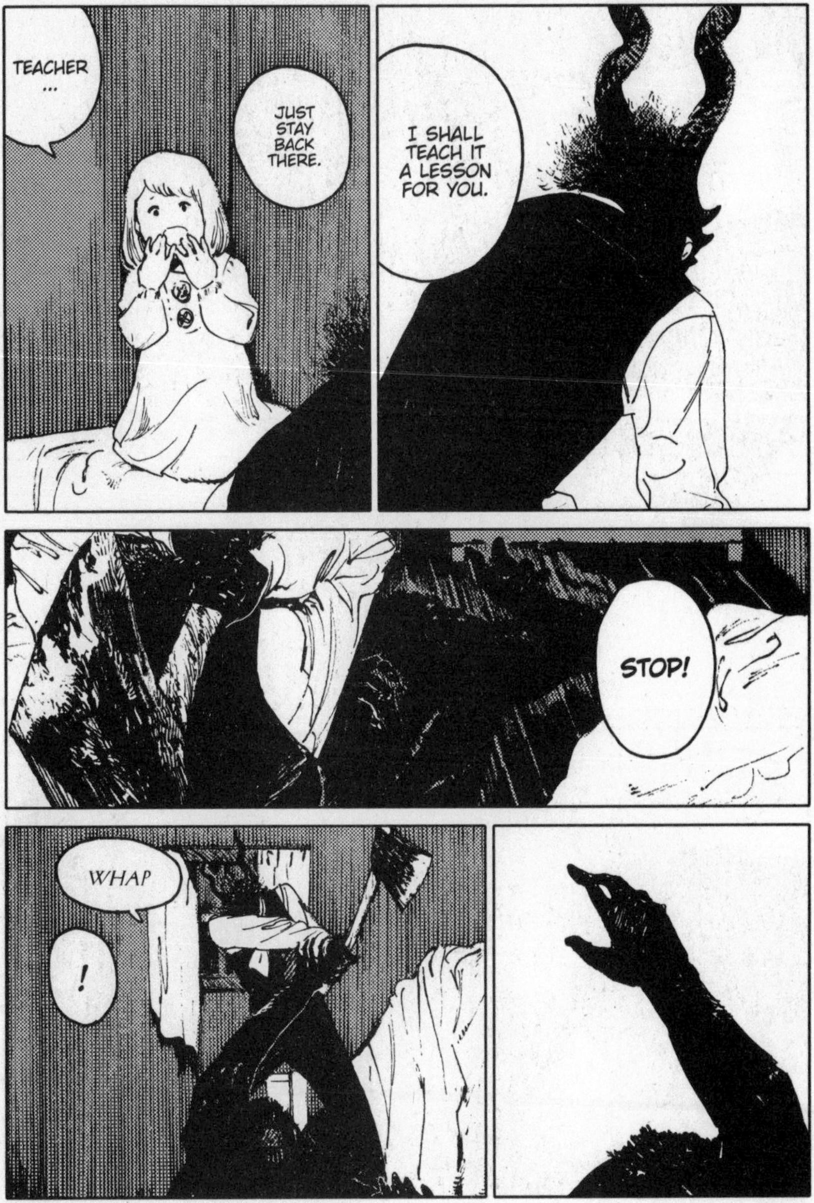
I SHALL TEACH IT A LESSON FOR YOU.
TEACHER ...
JUST STAY BACK THERE.
STOP!
WHAP
!

WUNK
CURSES!
TUMP
GRIP
STOP! STOP!
STOP! PLEASE!
THUMP

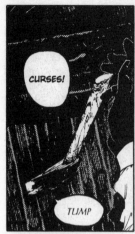

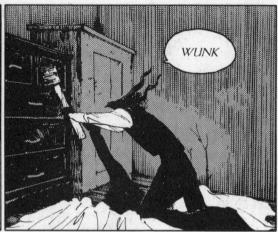

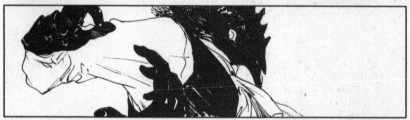

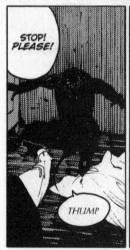

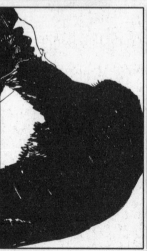

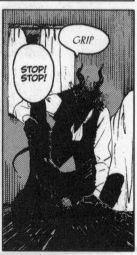

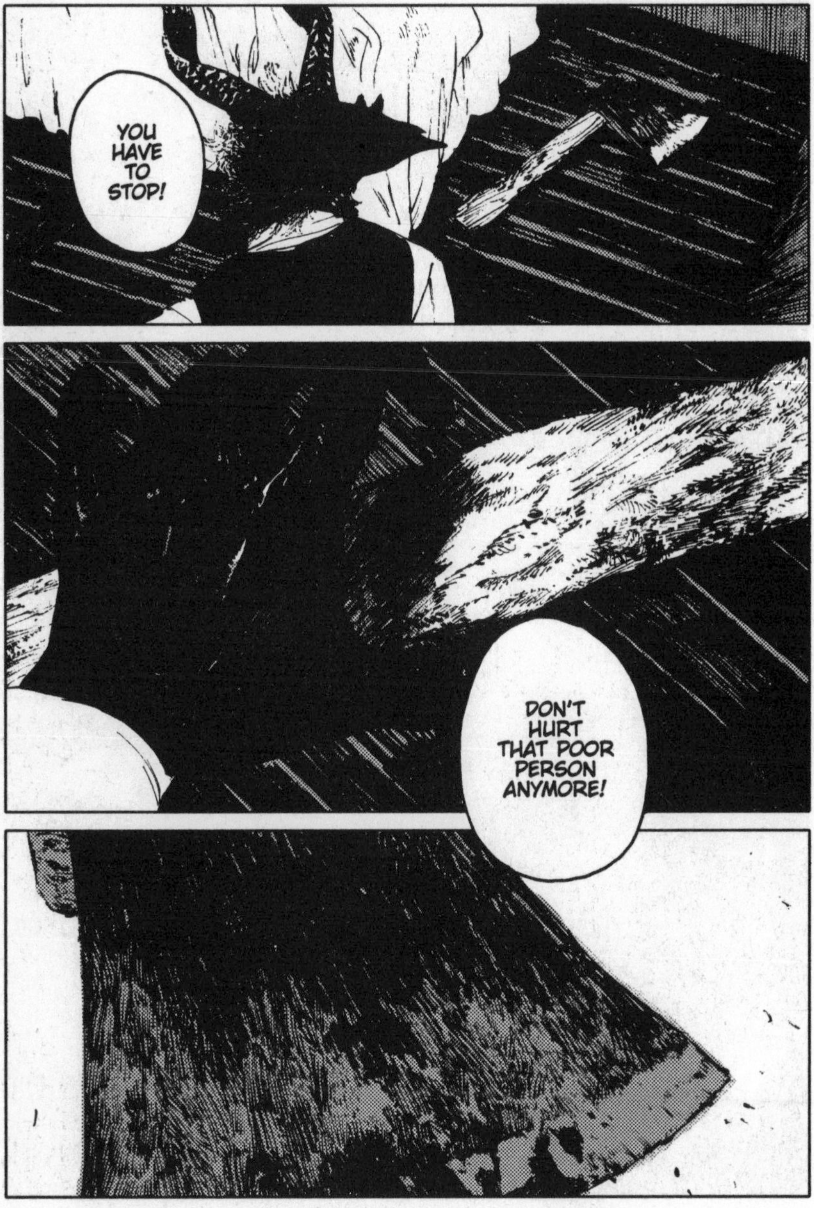
YOU HAVE TO STOP!
DON'T HURT THAT POOR PERSON ANYMORE!

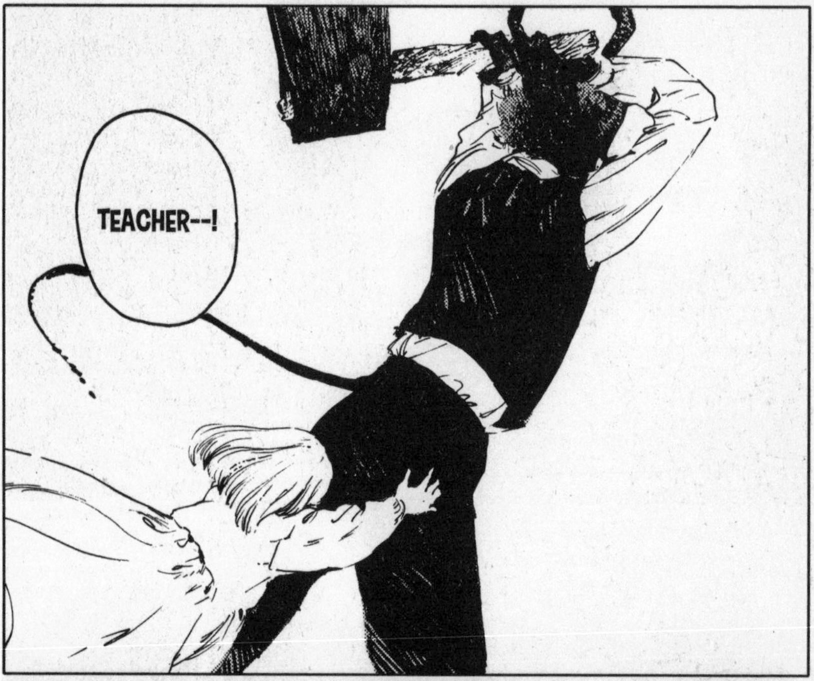
TEACHER--!
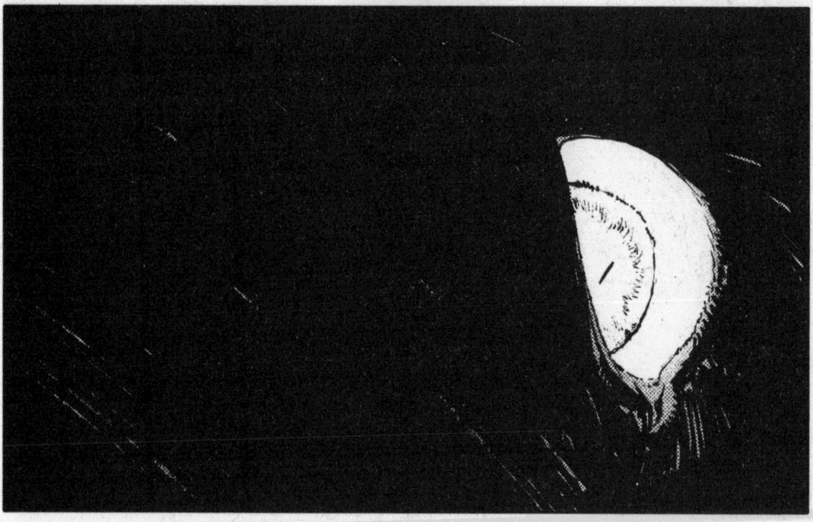

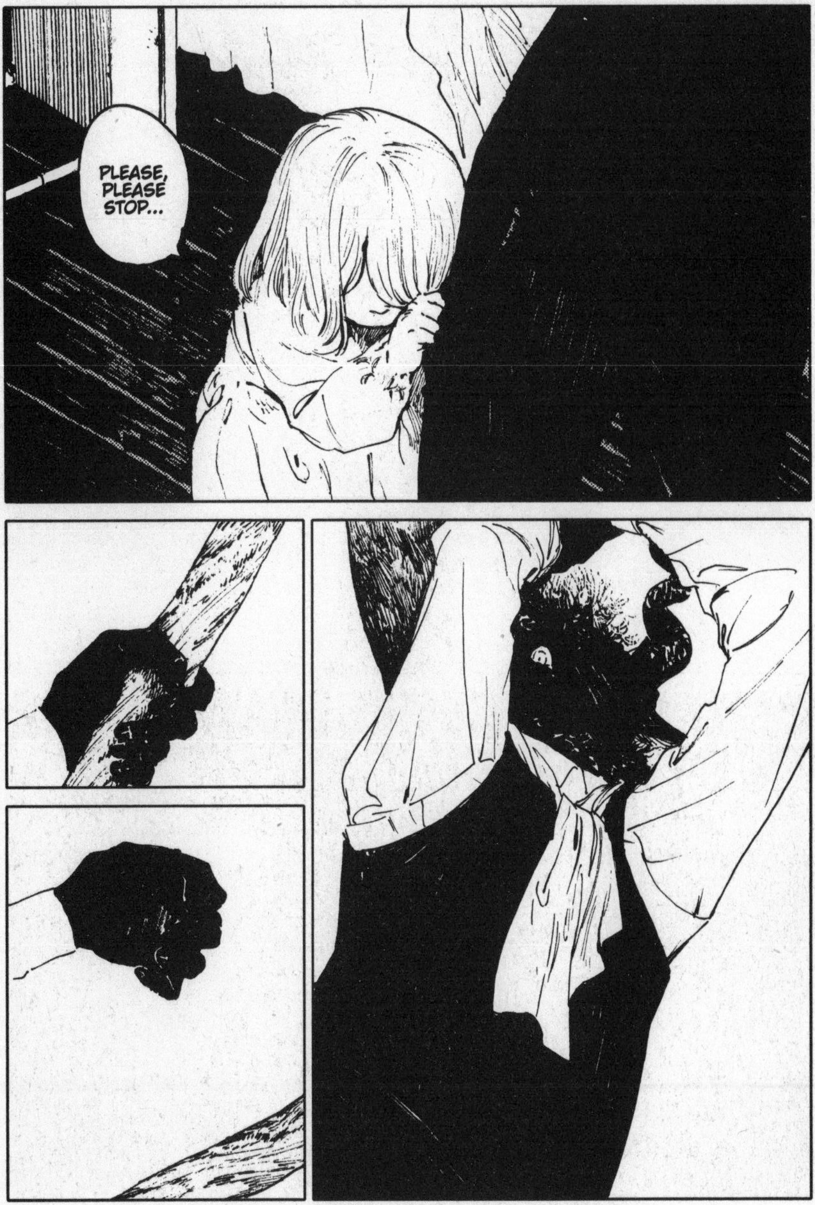
PLEASE, PLEASE STOP...

KLUNK

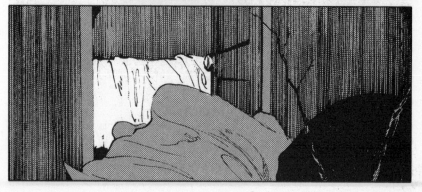

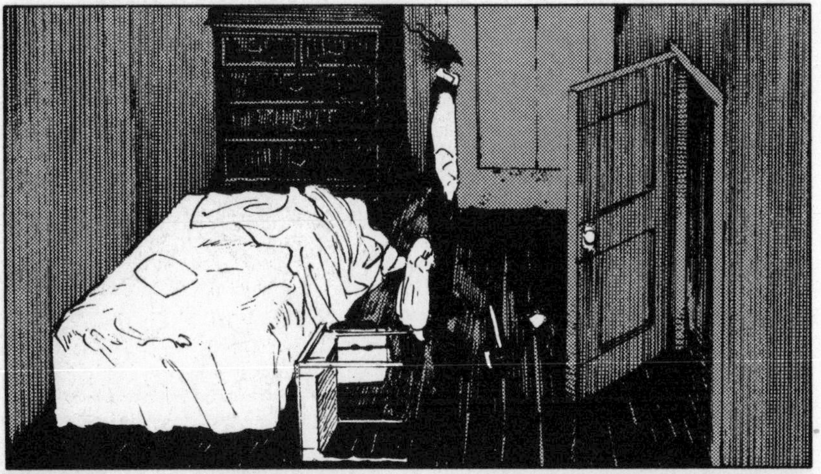

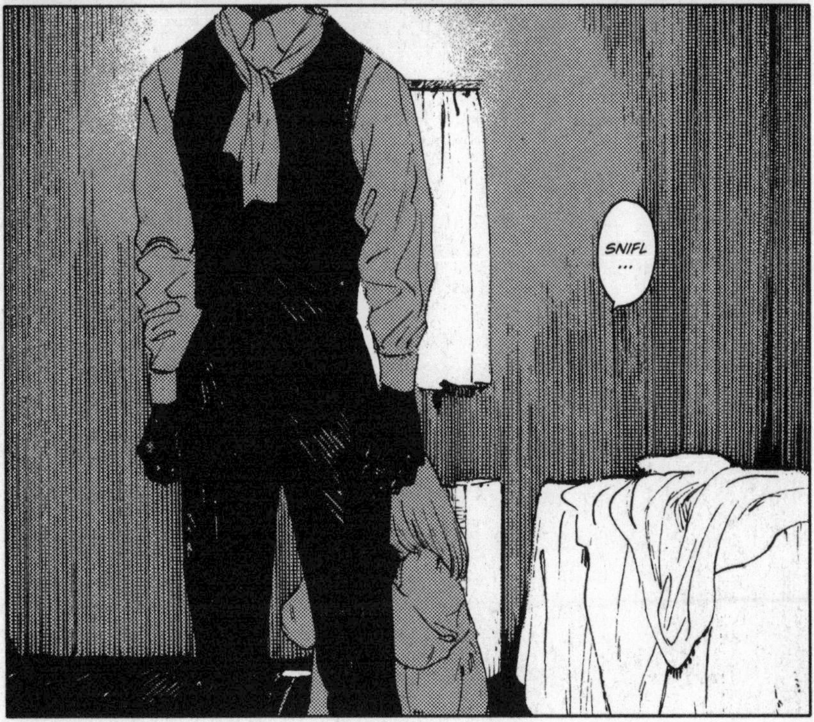
SNIFL
...

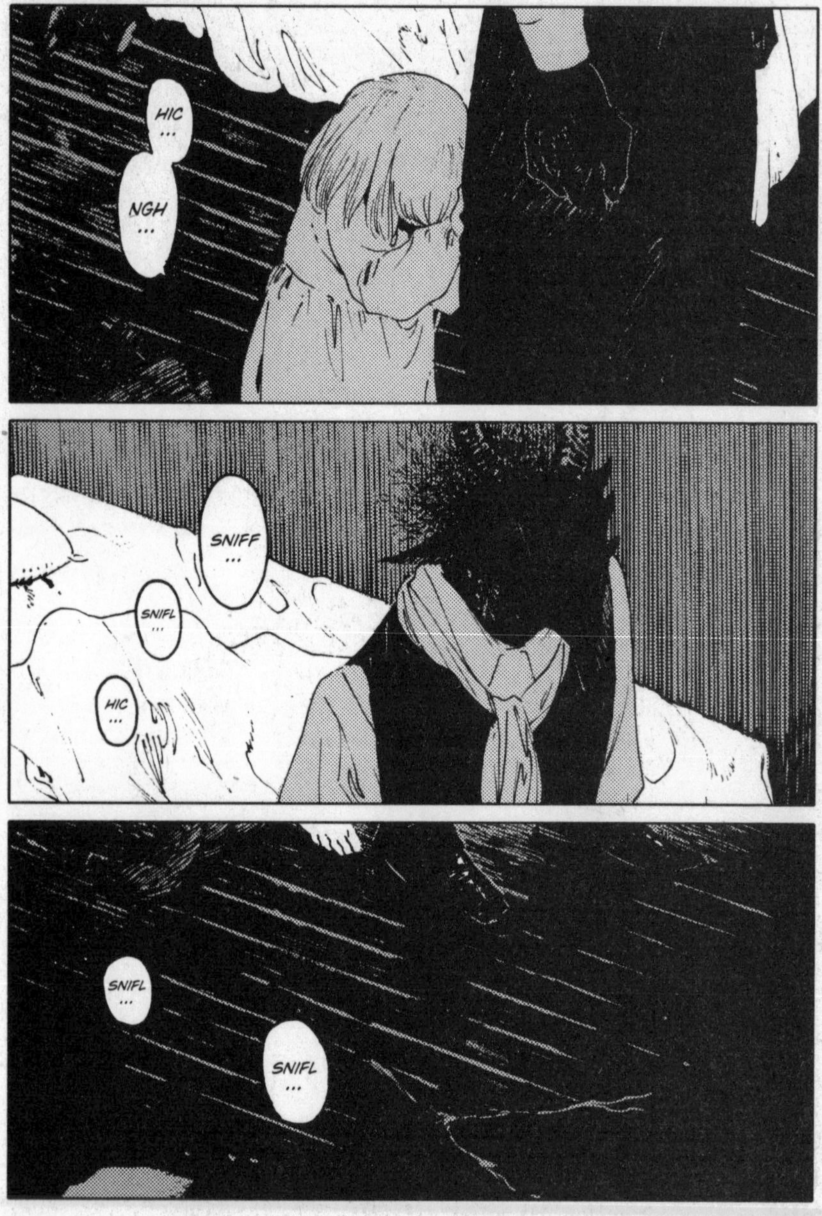
HIC ...
NGH ...
SNIFF ...
SNIFL ...
HIC ...
SNIFL ...
SNIFL ...

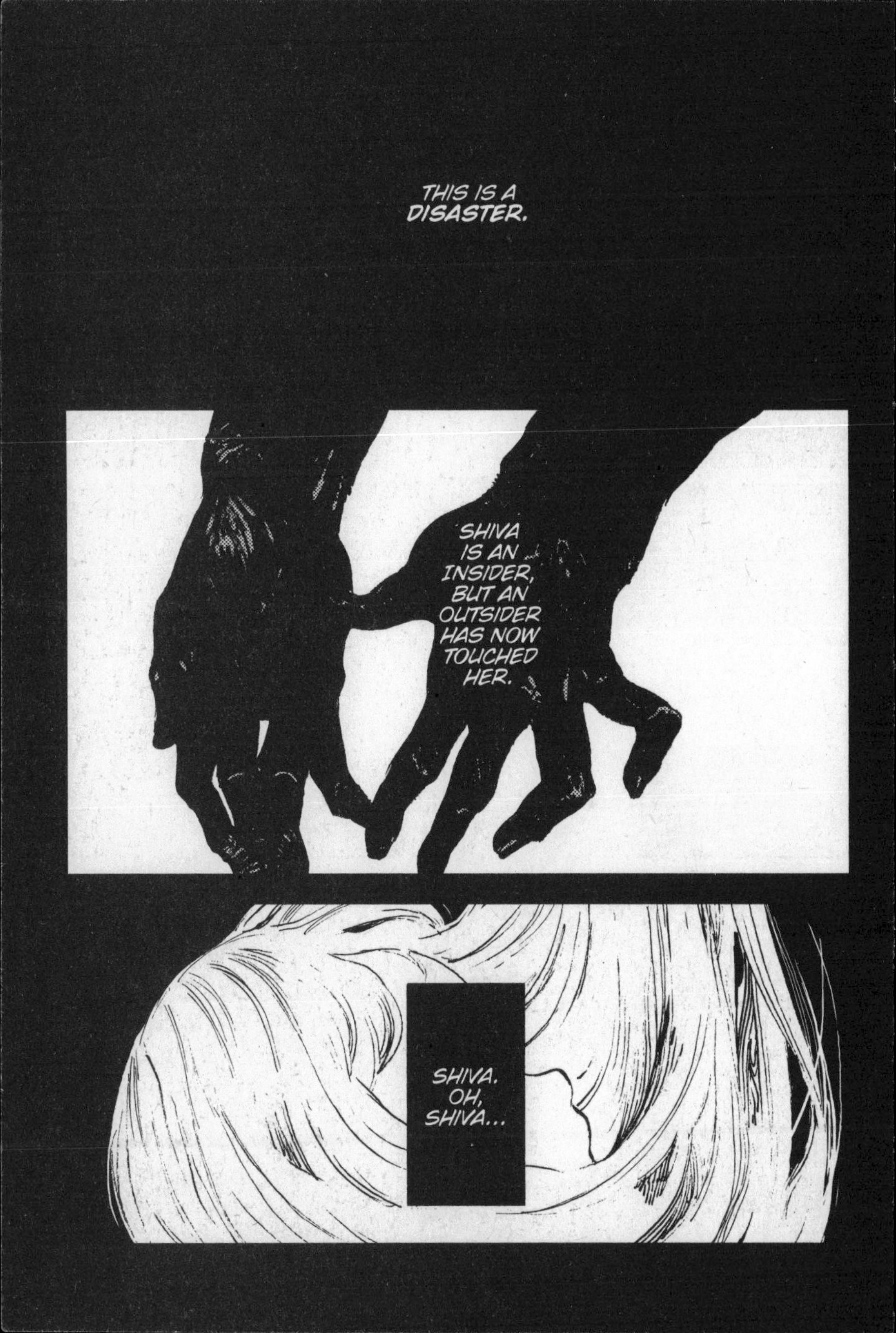
THIS IS A DISASTER.
SHIVA IS AN INSIDER, BUT AN OUTSIDER HAS NOW TOUCHED HER.
SHIVA. OH, SHIVA...

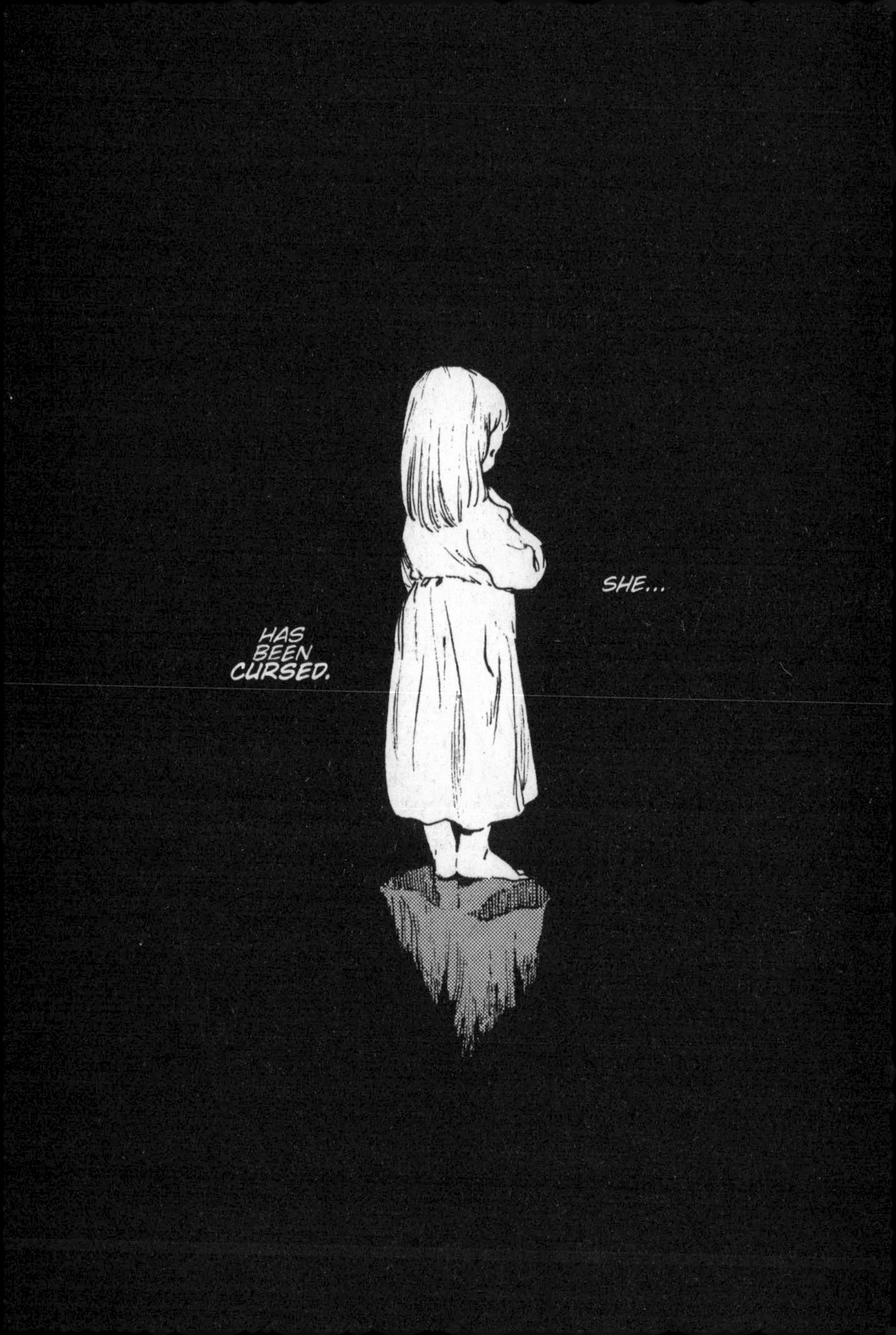
SHE...
HAS BEEN CURSED.

I
found
it.

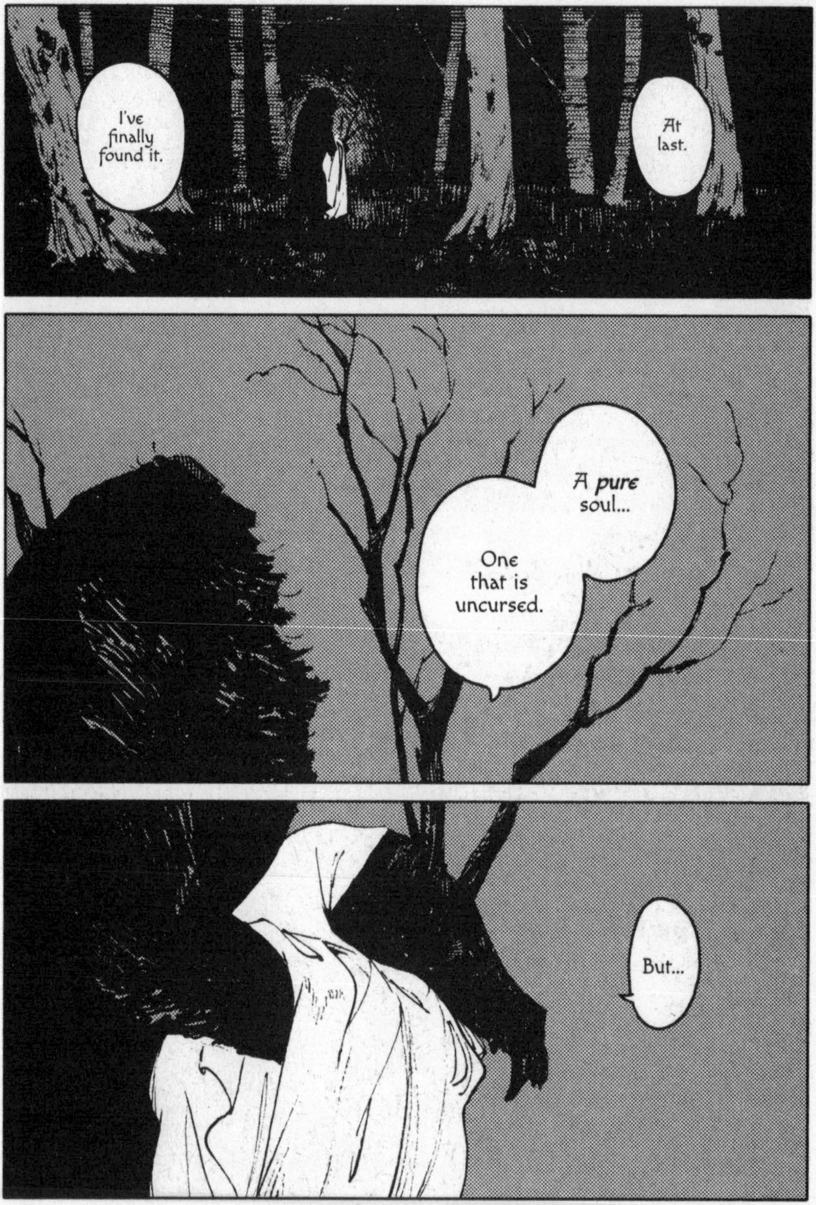
At last.
I've finally found it.
A *pure* soul...
One that is uncursed.
But...

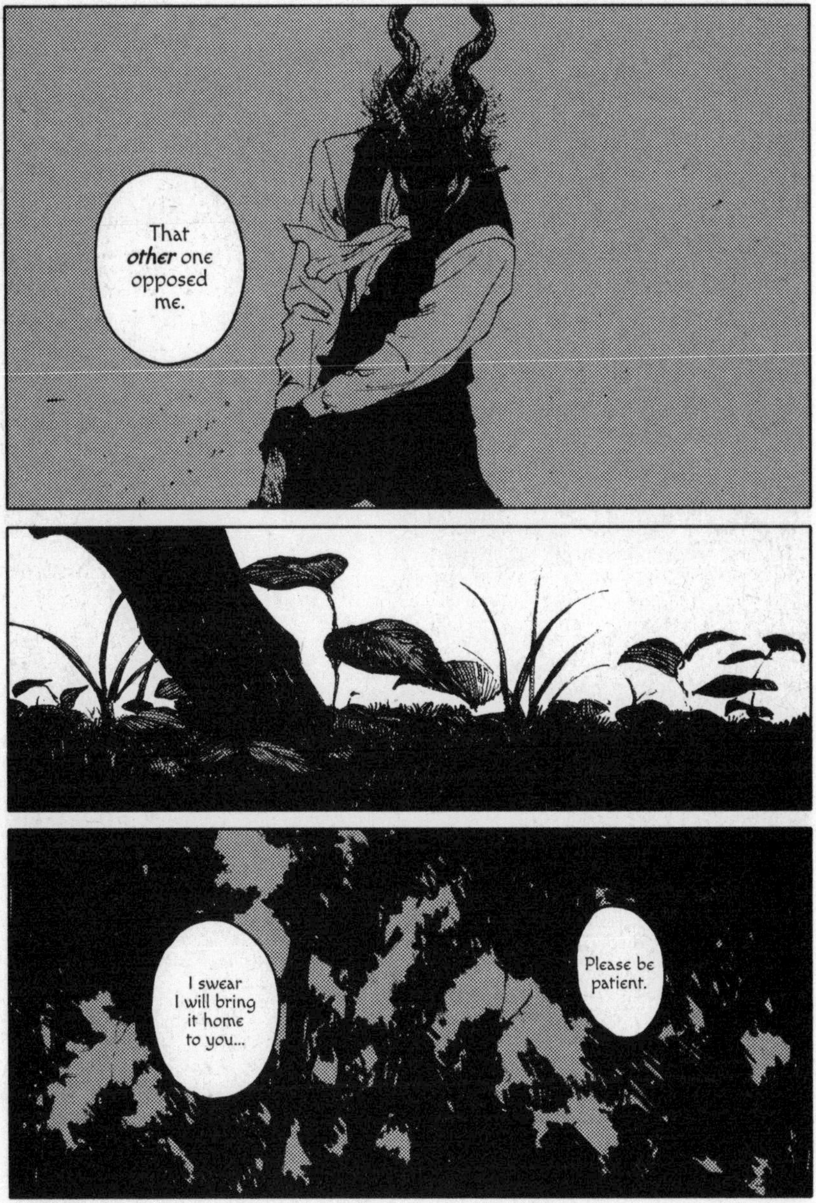
That *other* one opposed me.
Please be patient.
I swear I will bring it home to you...

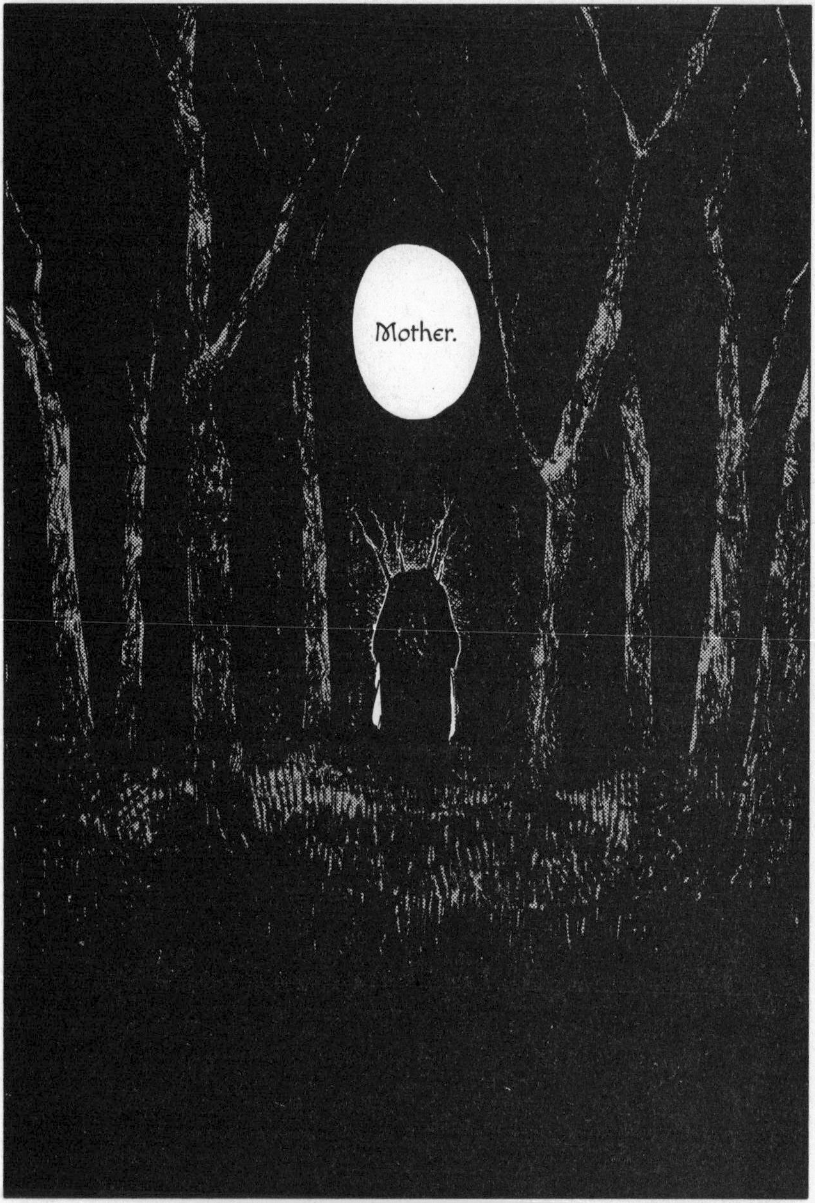
Mother.

Chapter 7

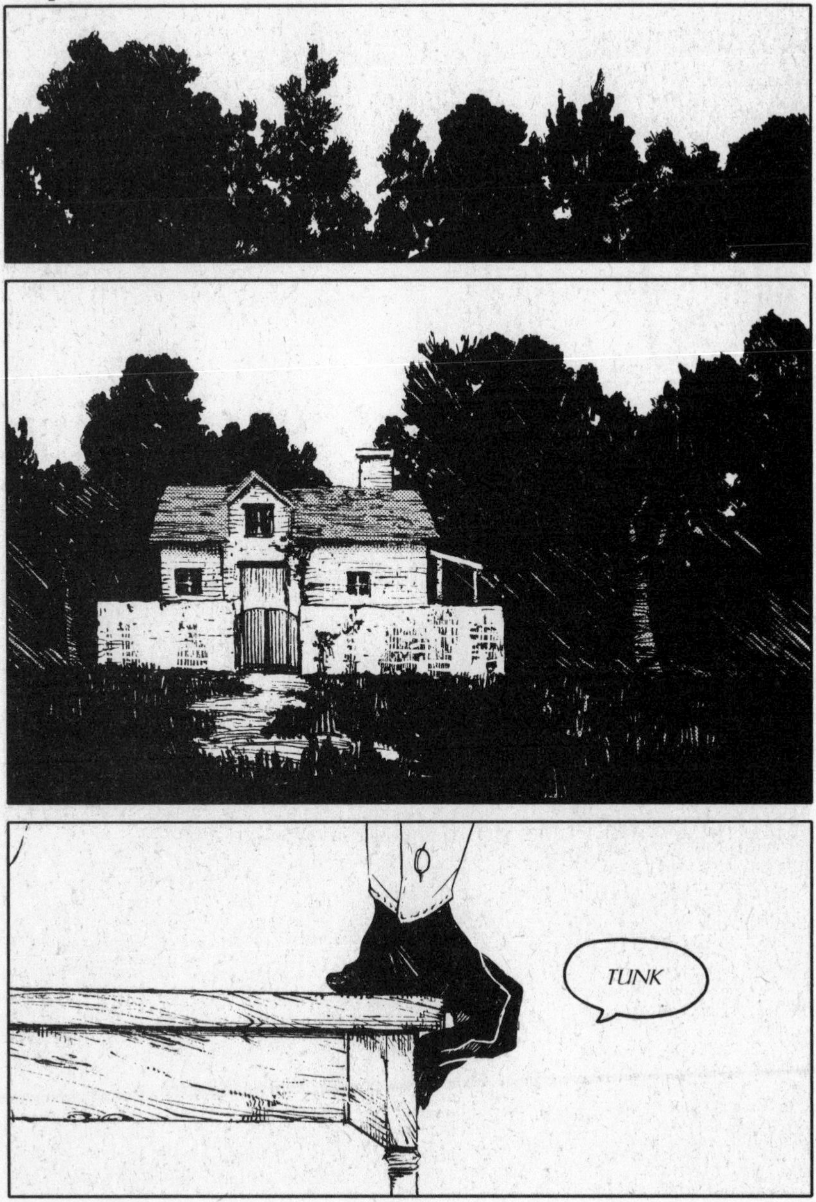
TUNK

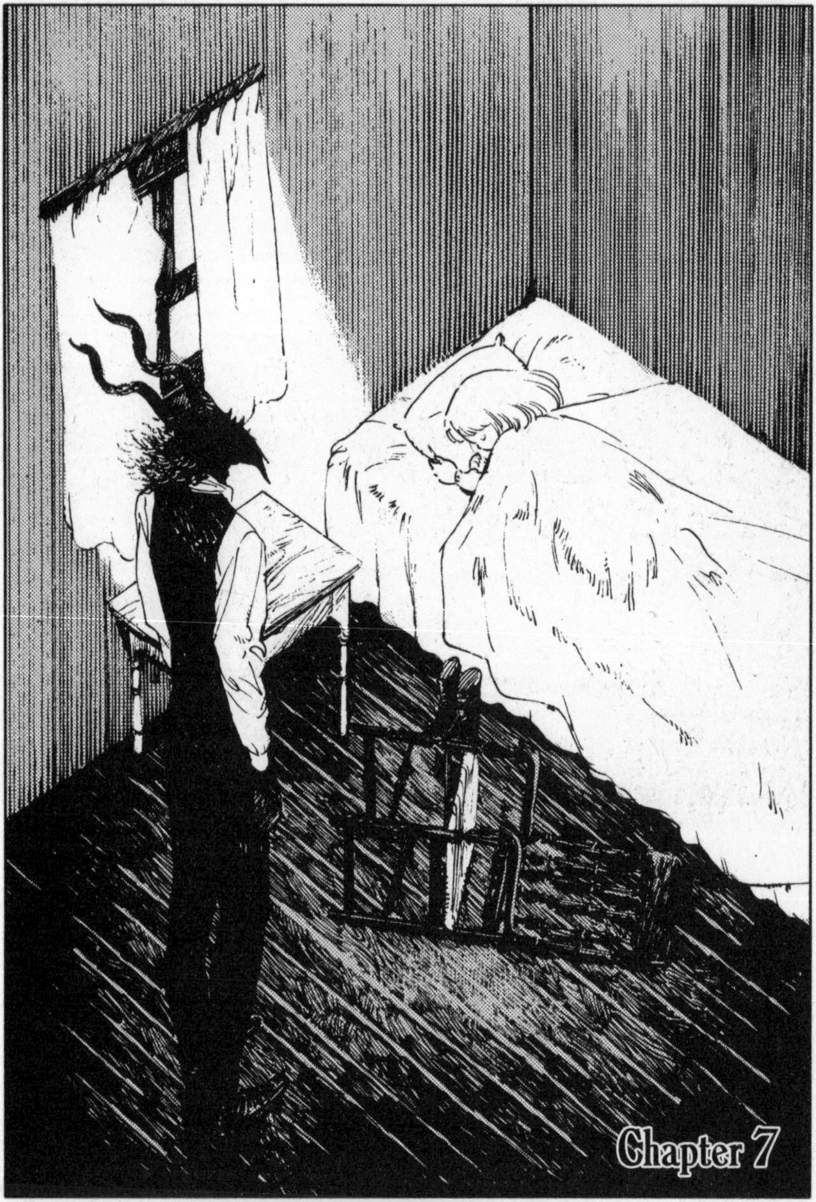
Chapter 7

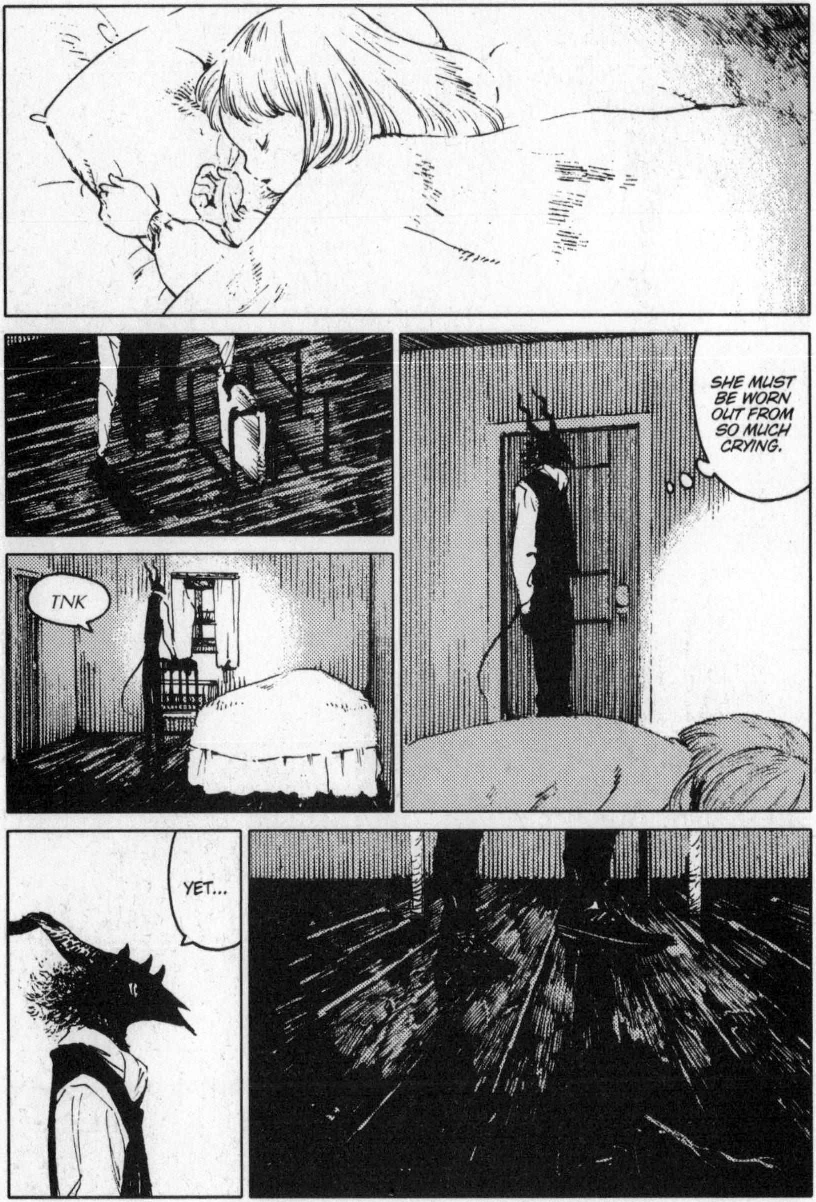
SHE MUST BE WORN OUT FROM SO MUCH CRYING.
TNK
YET...

PAT

IT'S LIKE A WAKING NIGHT-MARE.

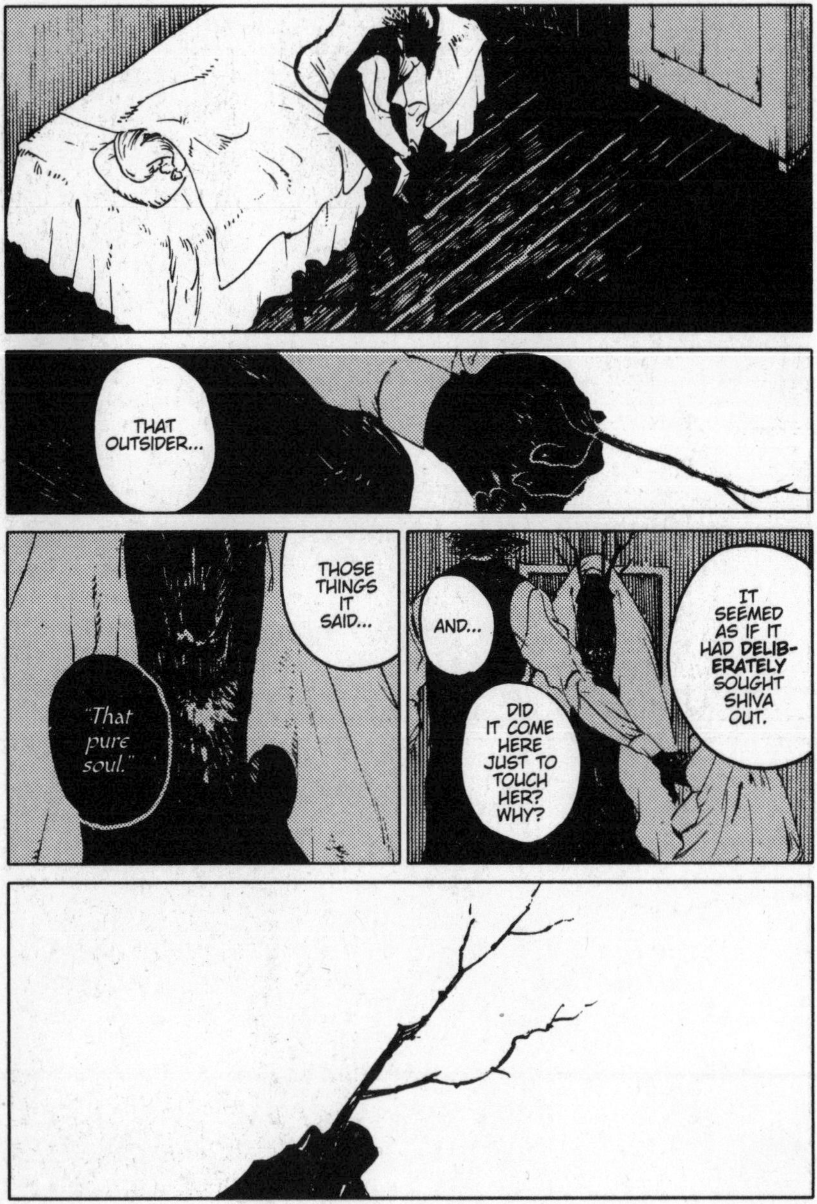
THAT OUTSIDER...
IT SEEMED AS IF IT HAD DELIBERATELY SOUGHT SHIVA OUT.
AND...
DID IT COME HERE JUST TO TOUCH HER? WHY?
THOSE THINGS IT SAID...
"That pure soul."

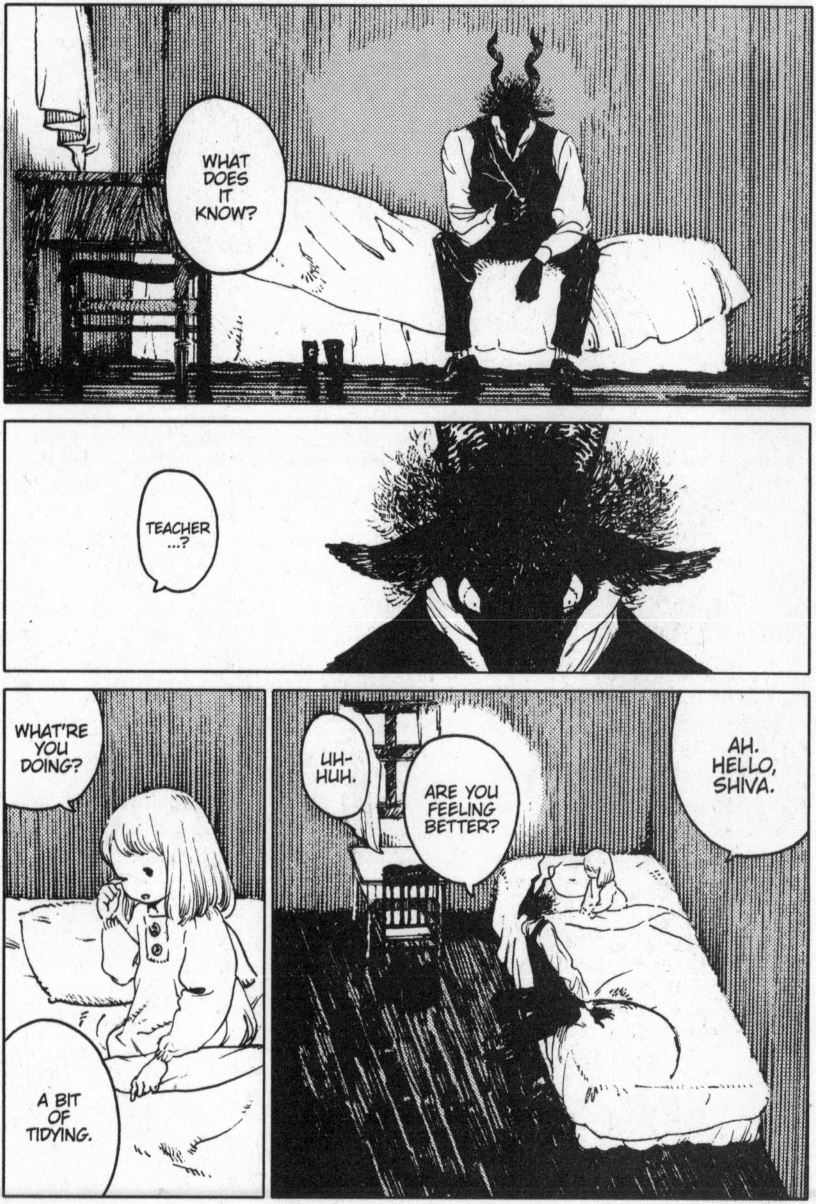
WHAT DOES IT KNOW?
TEACHER ...?
AH. HELLO, SHIVA.
ARE YOU FEELING BETTER?
UH-HUH.
WHAT'RE YOU DOING?
A BIT OF TIDYING.

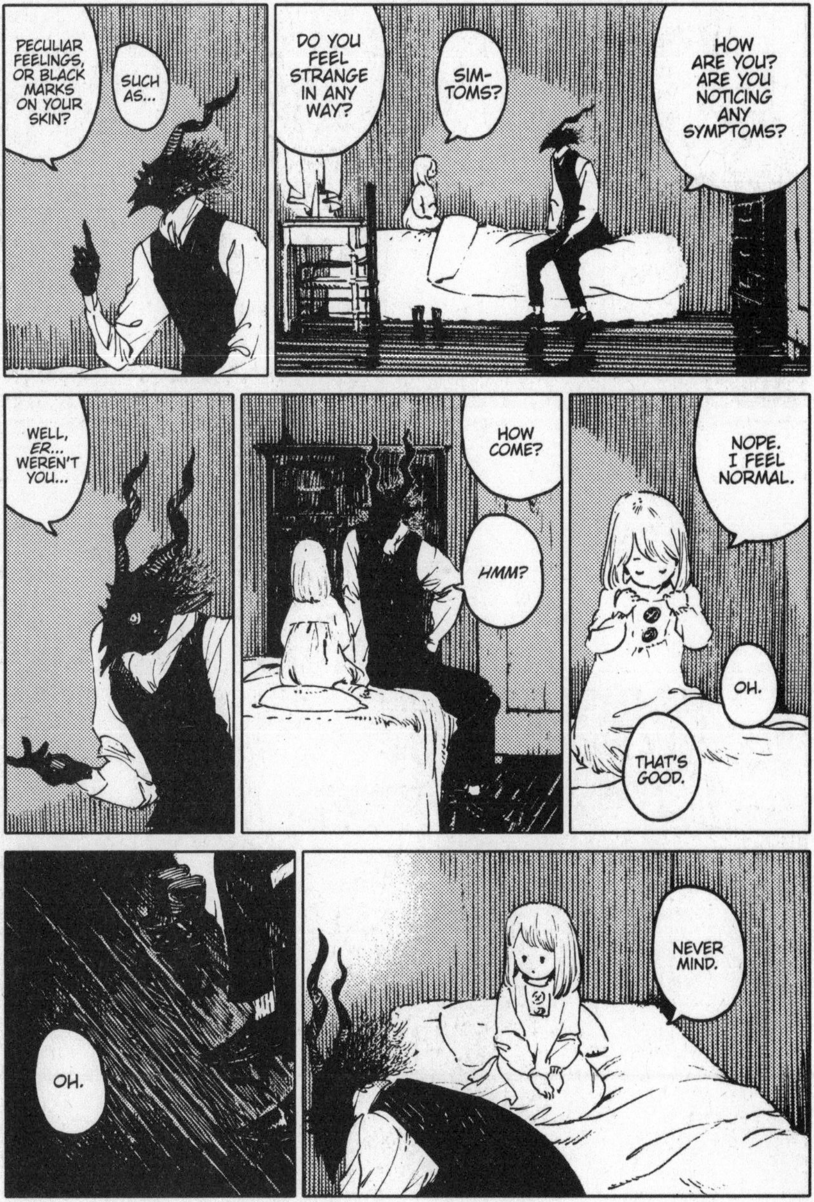
HOW ARE YOU? ARE YOU NOTICING ANY SYMPTOMS?
SIM-TOMS?
DO YOU FEEL STRANGE IN ANY WAY?
SUCH AS...
PECULIAR FEELINGS, OR BLACK MARKS ON YOUR SKIN?
NOPE. I FEEL NORMAL.
OH.
THAT'S GOOD.
HMM?
HOW COME?
WELL, ER... WEREN'T YOU...
NEVER MIND.
OH.

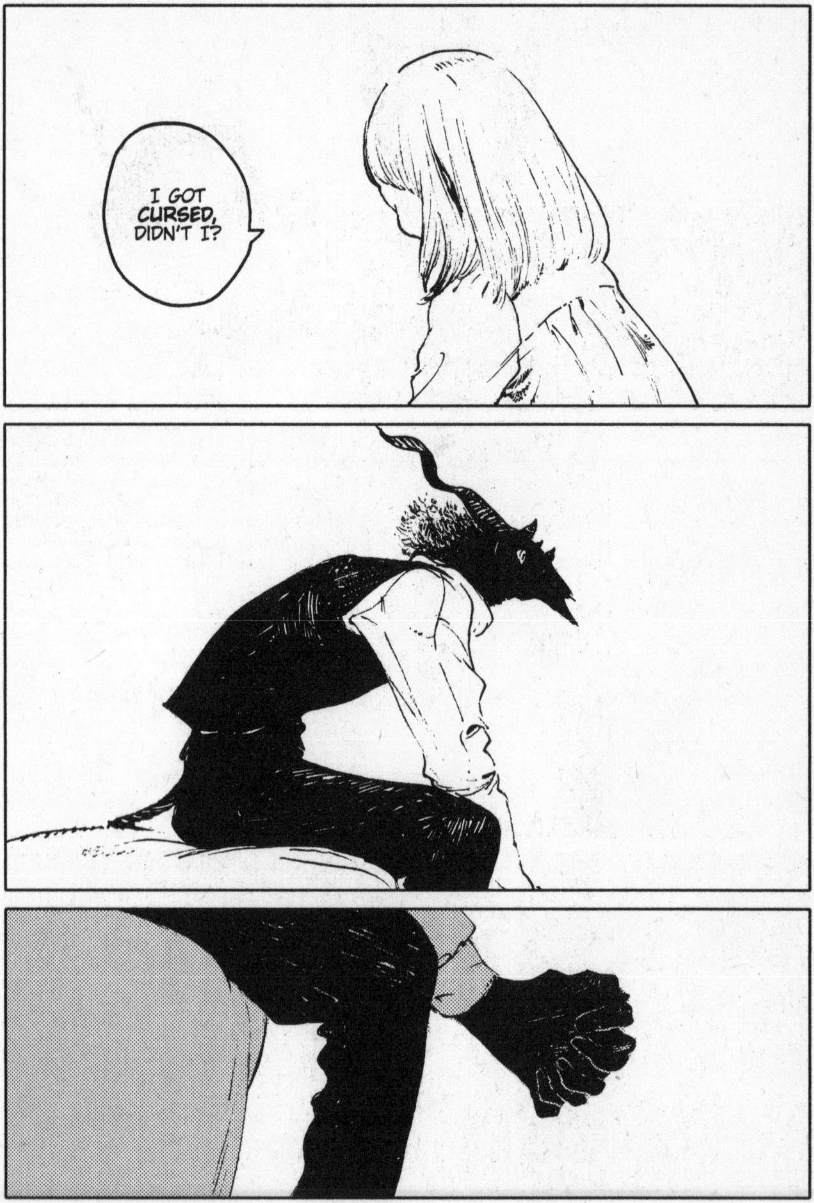
I GOT CURSED, DIDN'T I?

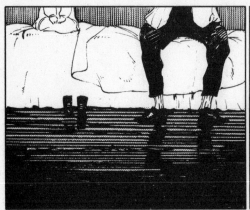

I'LL
...

GO GET
YOUR
BREAK-
FAST.

IT
SAID
THAT...

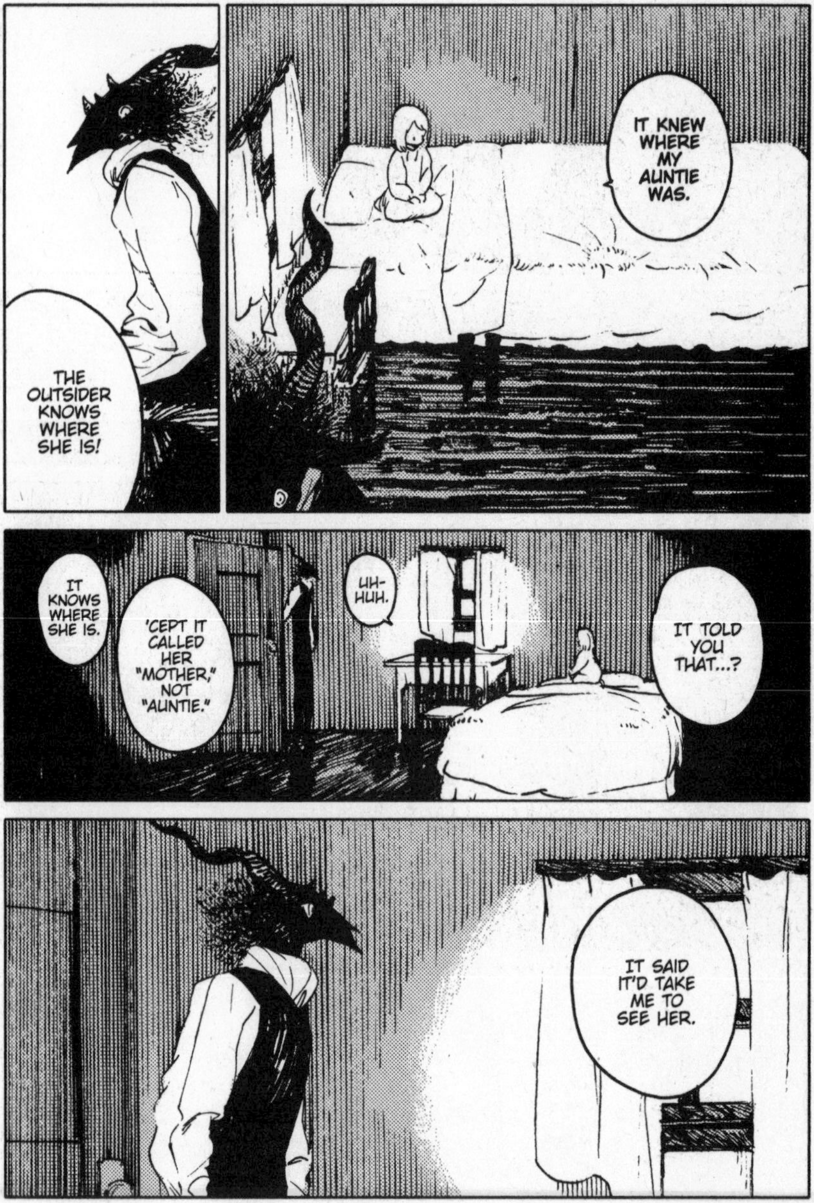
IT KNEW WHERE MY AUNTIE WAS.
THE OUTSIDER KNOWS WHERE SHE IS!
IT TOLD YOU THAT...?
UH-HUH.
IT KNOWS WHERE SHE IS.
'CEPT IT CALLED HER "MOTHER," NOT "AUNTIE."
IT SAID IT'D TAKE ME TO SEE HER.

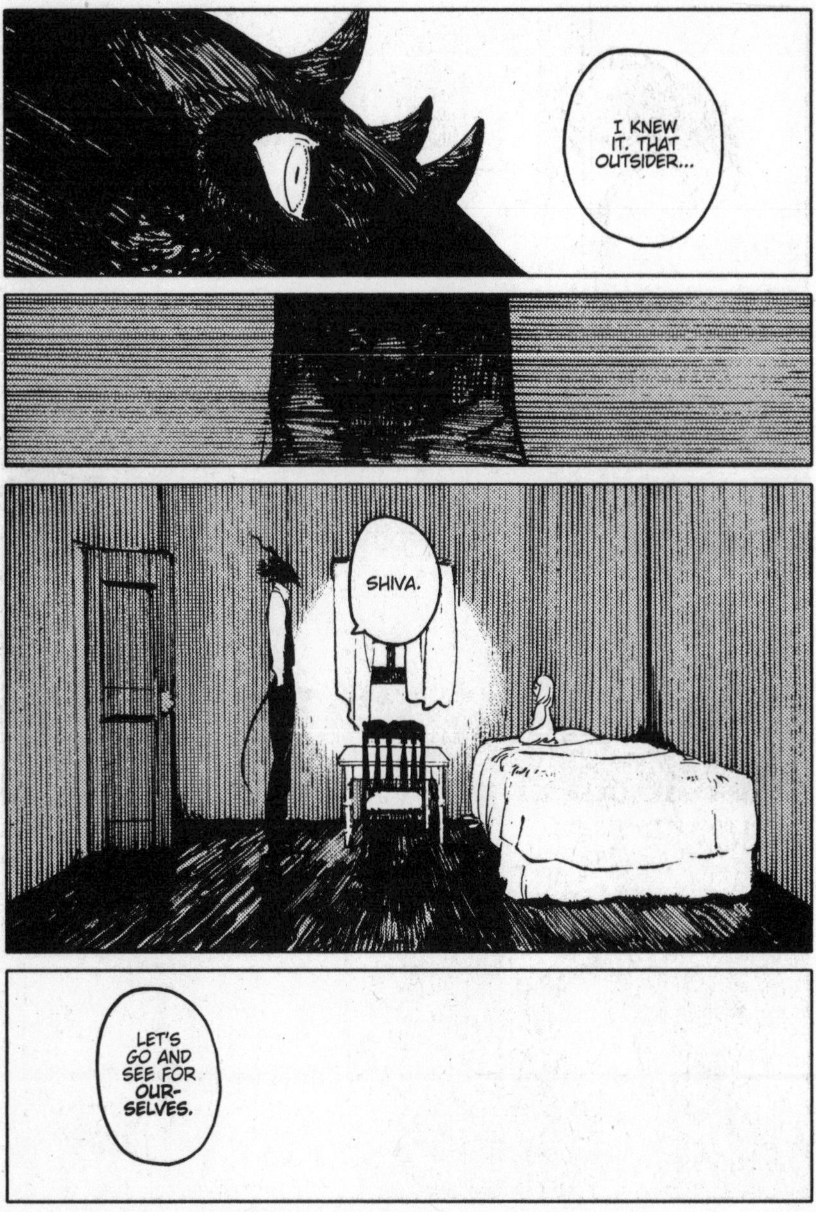
I KNEW IT. THAT OUTSIDER...
SHIVA.
LET'S GO AND SEE FOR OUR-SELVES.

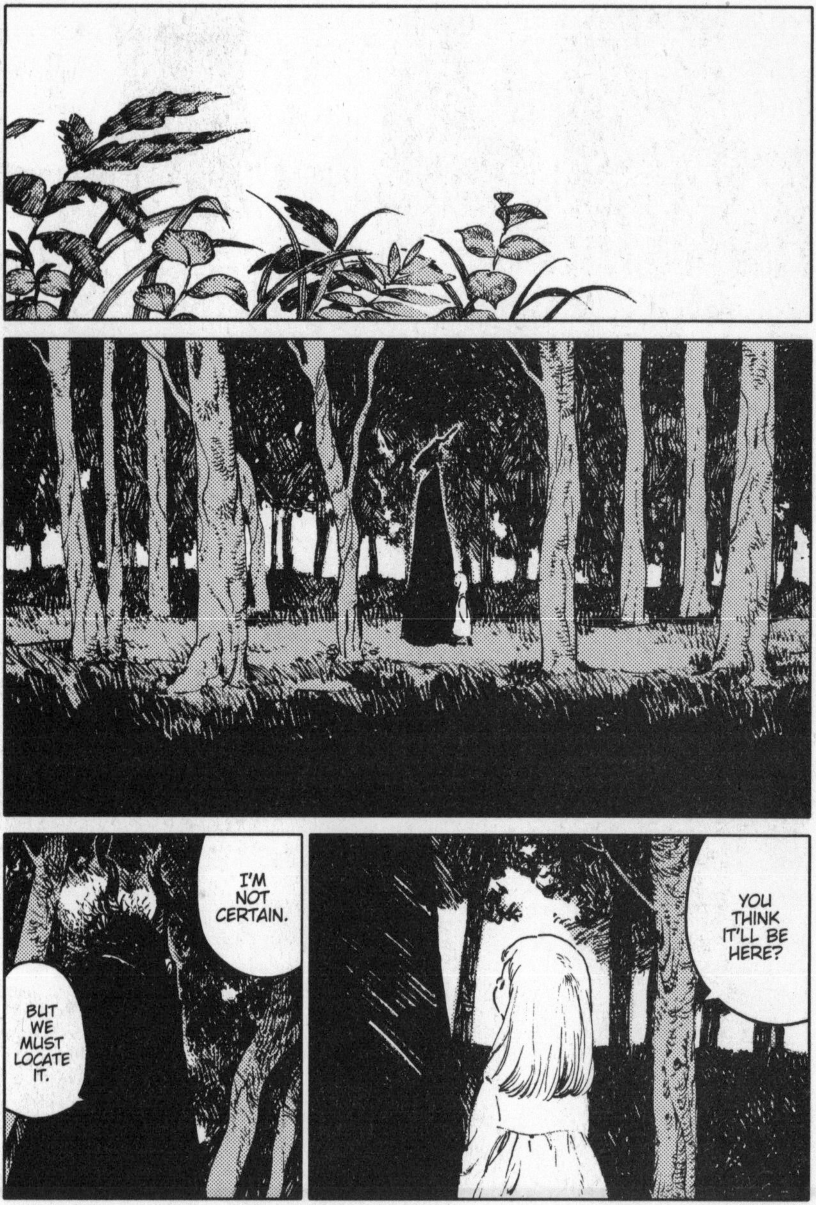
YOU THINK IT'LL BE HERE?
I'M NOT CERTAIN.
BUT WE MUST LOCATE IT.

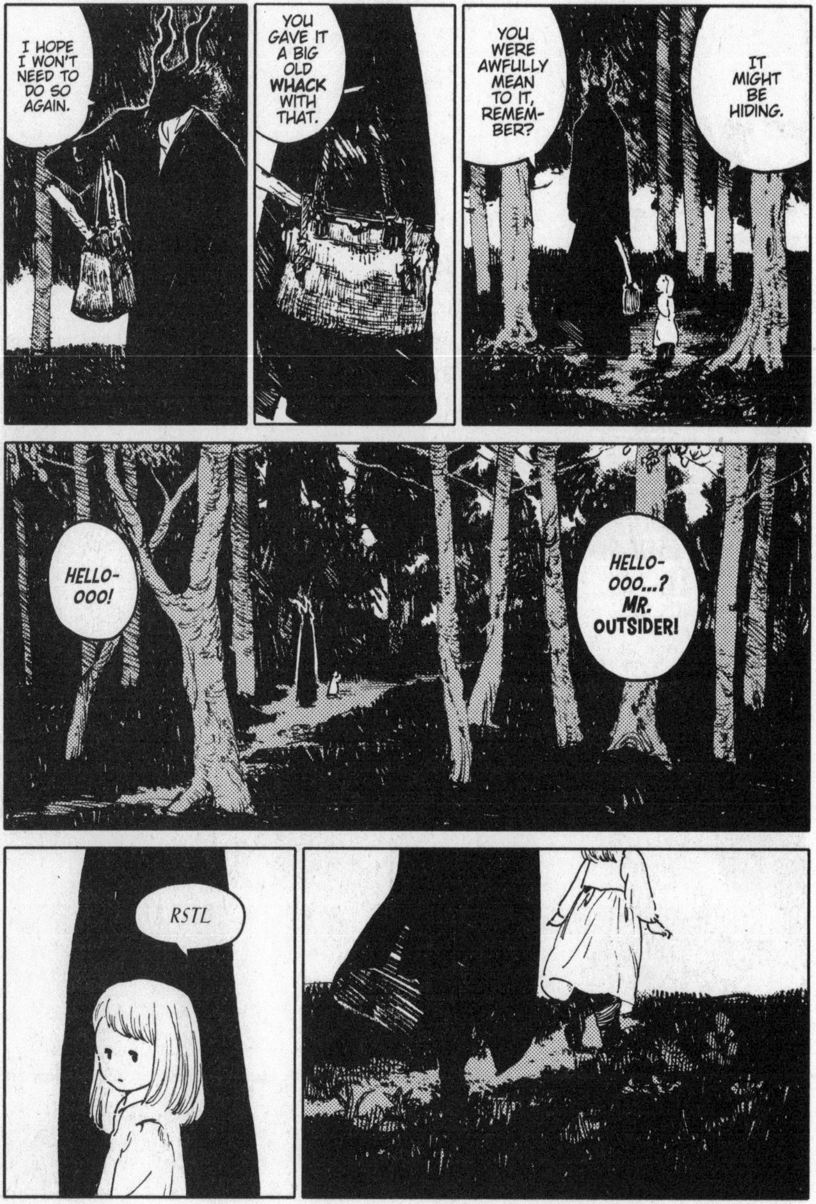
IT MIGHT BE HIDING.
YOU WERE AWFULLY MEAN TO IT, REMEMBER?
YOU GAVE IT A BIG OLD **WHACK** WITH THAT.
I HOPE I WON'T NEED TO DO SO AGAIN.
HELLO-OOO...? MR. OUTSIDER!
HELLO-OOO!
RSTL

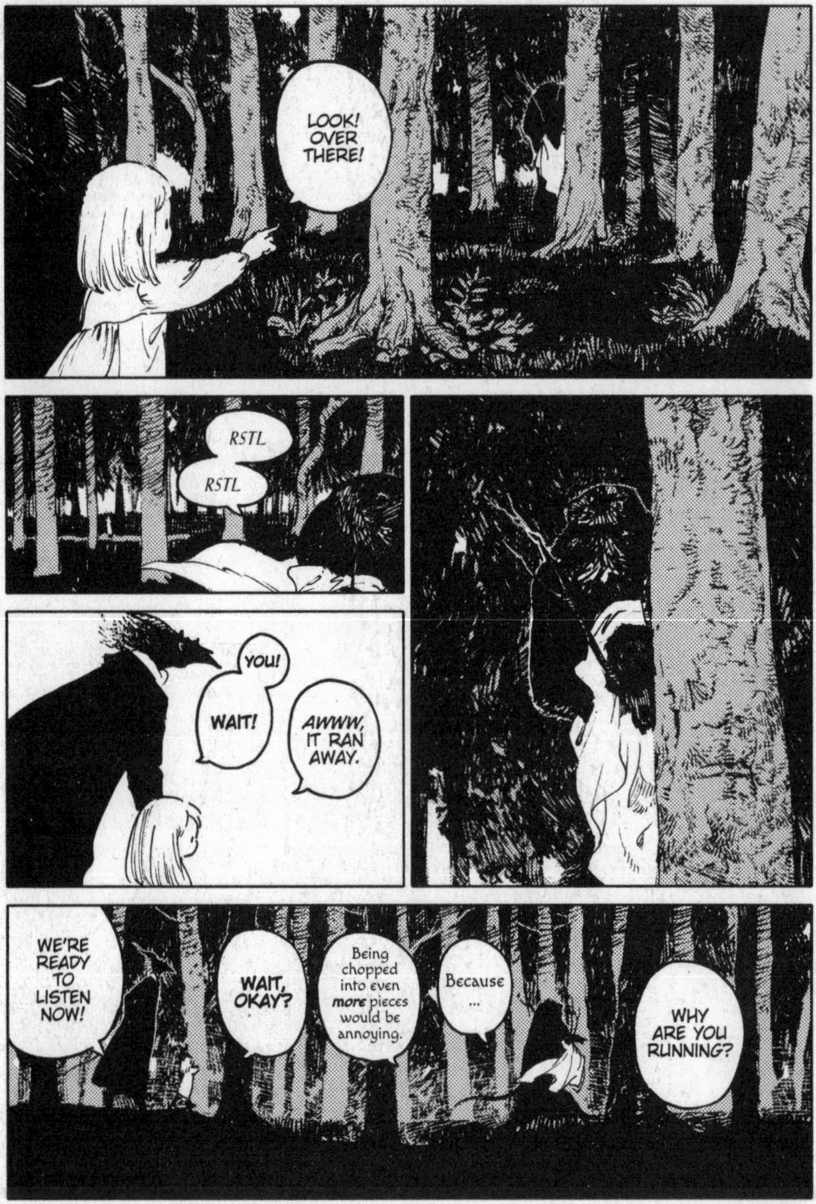
LOOK! OVER THERE!
RSTL
RSTL
AWWW, IT RAN AWAY.
YOU!
WAIT!
WHY ARE YOU RUNNING?
Because ...
Being chopped into even *more* pieces would be annoying.
WAIT, OKAY?
WE'RE READY TO LISTEN NOW!

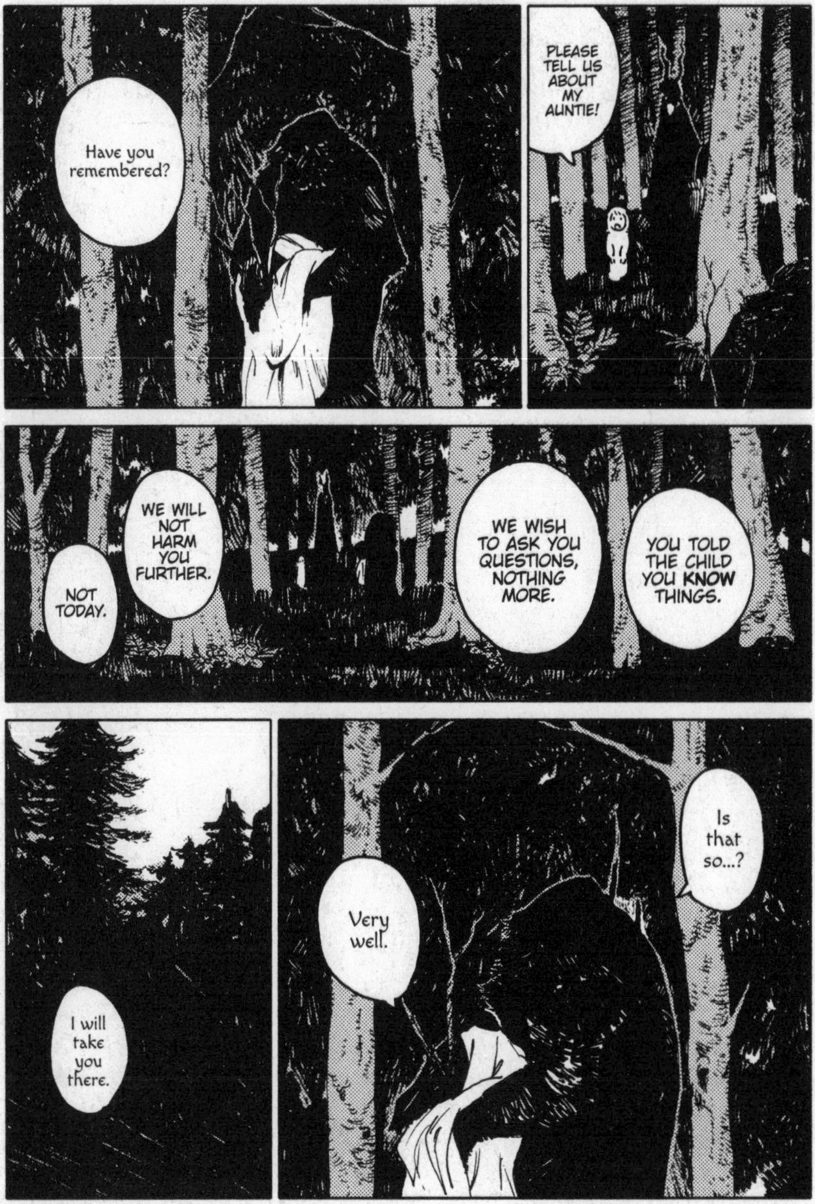
PLEASE TELL US ABOUT MY AUNTIE!
Have you remembered?
YOU TOLD THE CHILD YOU KNOW THINGS.
WE WISH TO ASK YOU QUESTIONS, NOTHING MORE.
WE WILL NOT HARM YOU FURTHER.
NOT TODAY.
Is that so...?
Very well.
I will take you there.

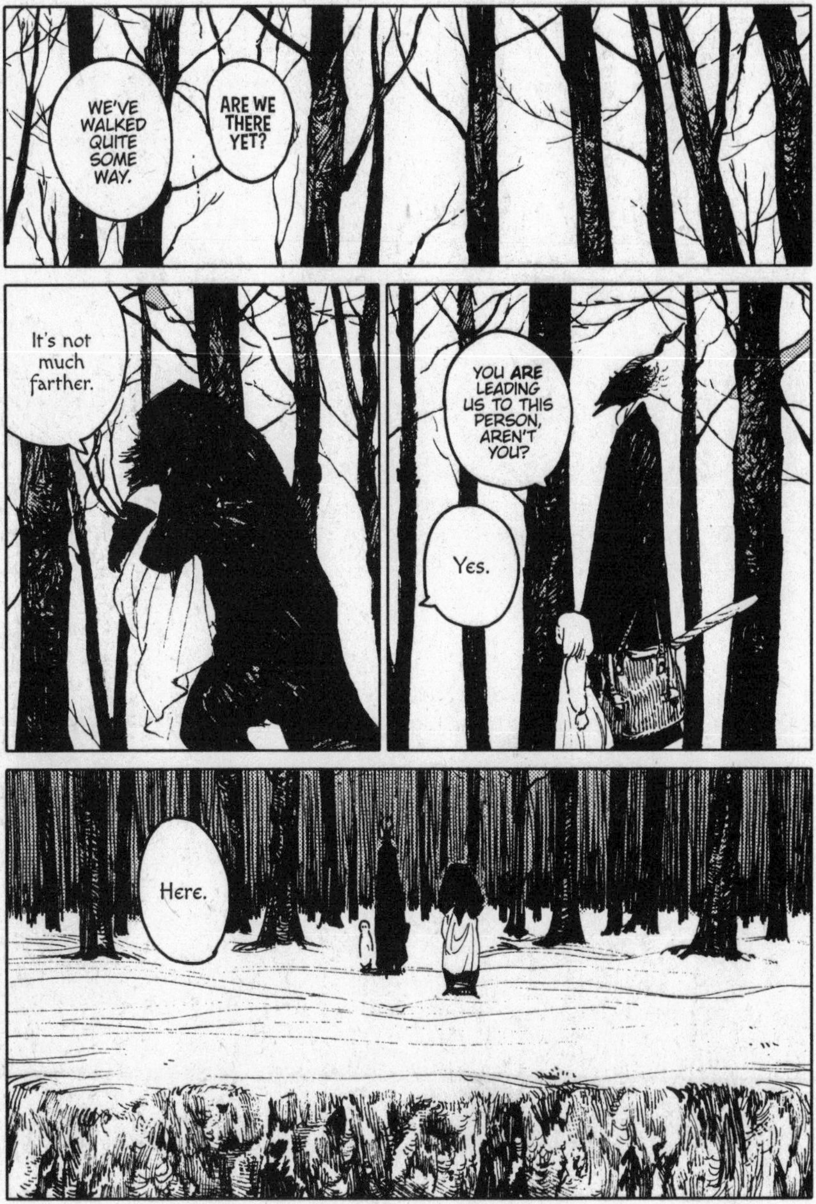
ARE WE THERE YET?
WE'VE WALKED QUITE SOME WAY.
YOU **ARE** LEADING US TO THIS PERSON, AREN'T YOU?
Yes.
It's not much farther.
Here.

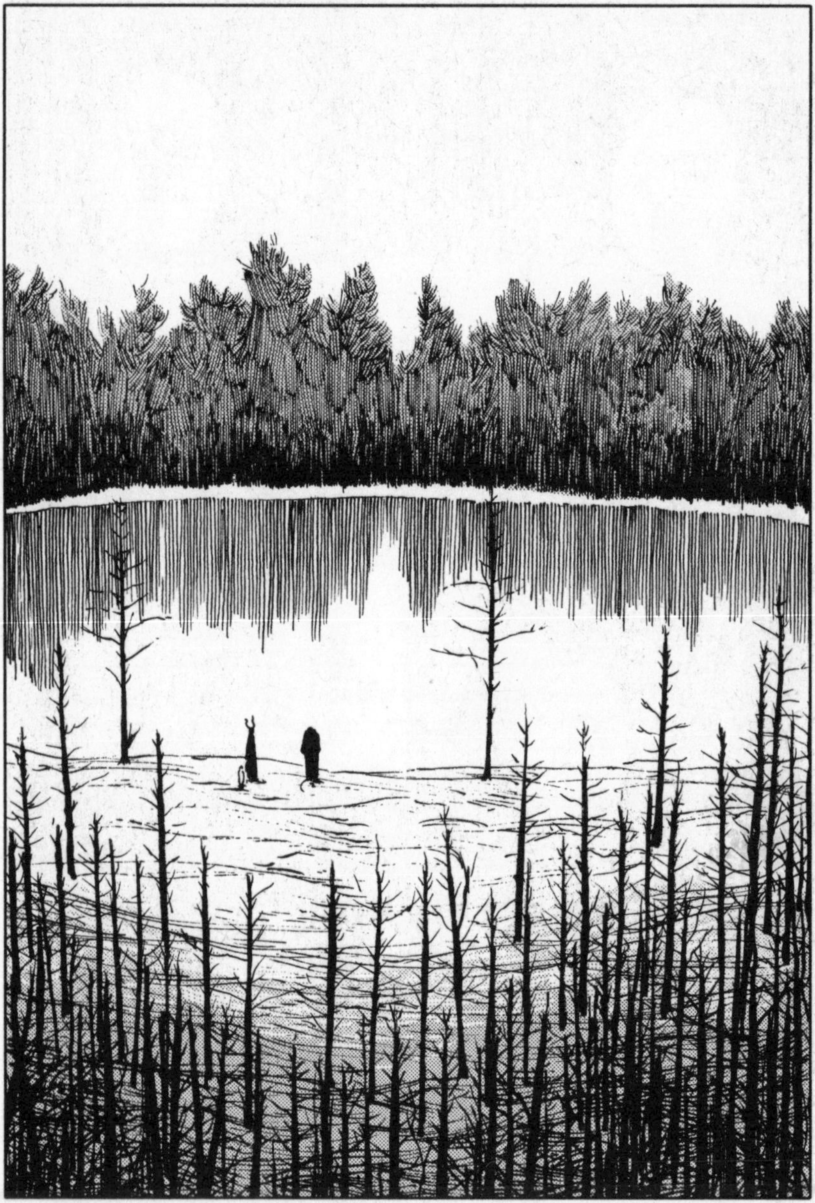

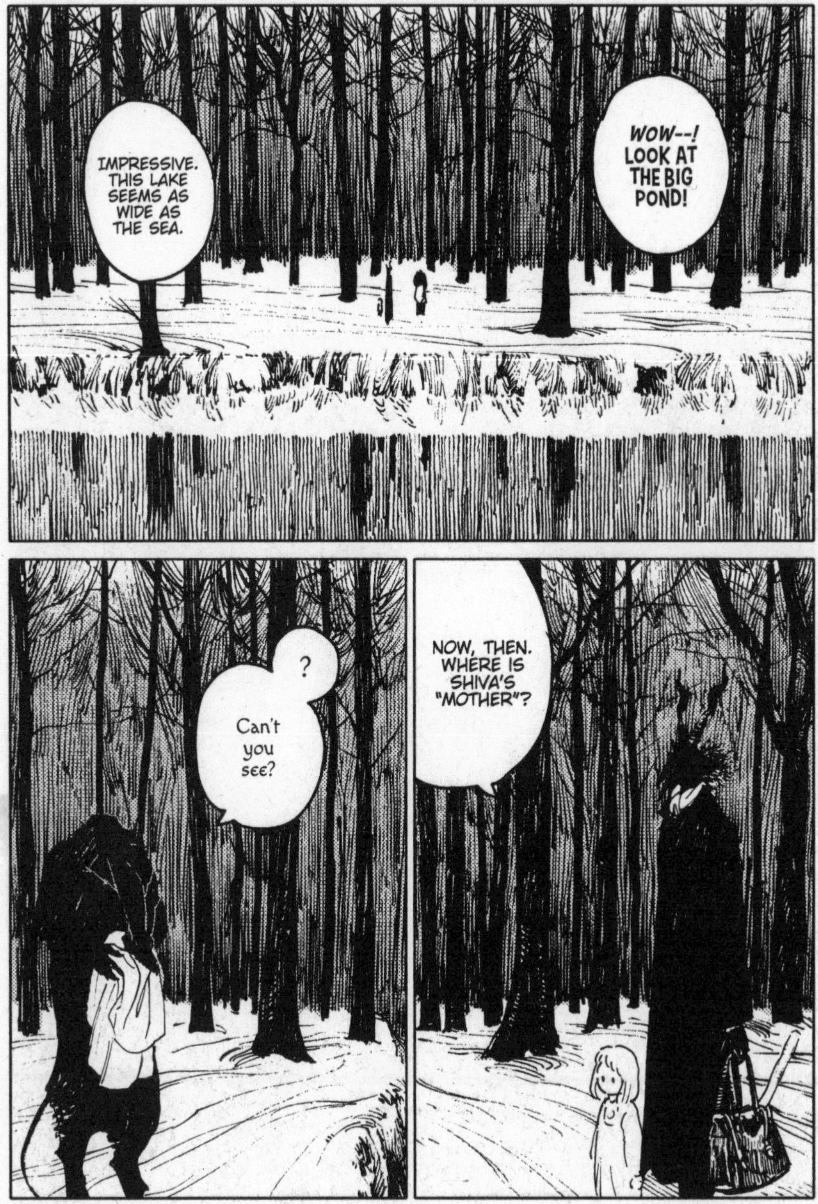
WOW--! LOOK AT THE BIG POND!
IMPRESSIVE. THIS LAKE SEEMS AS WIDE AS THE SEA.
NOW, THEN. WHERE IS SHIVA'S "MOTHER"?
?
Can't you see?

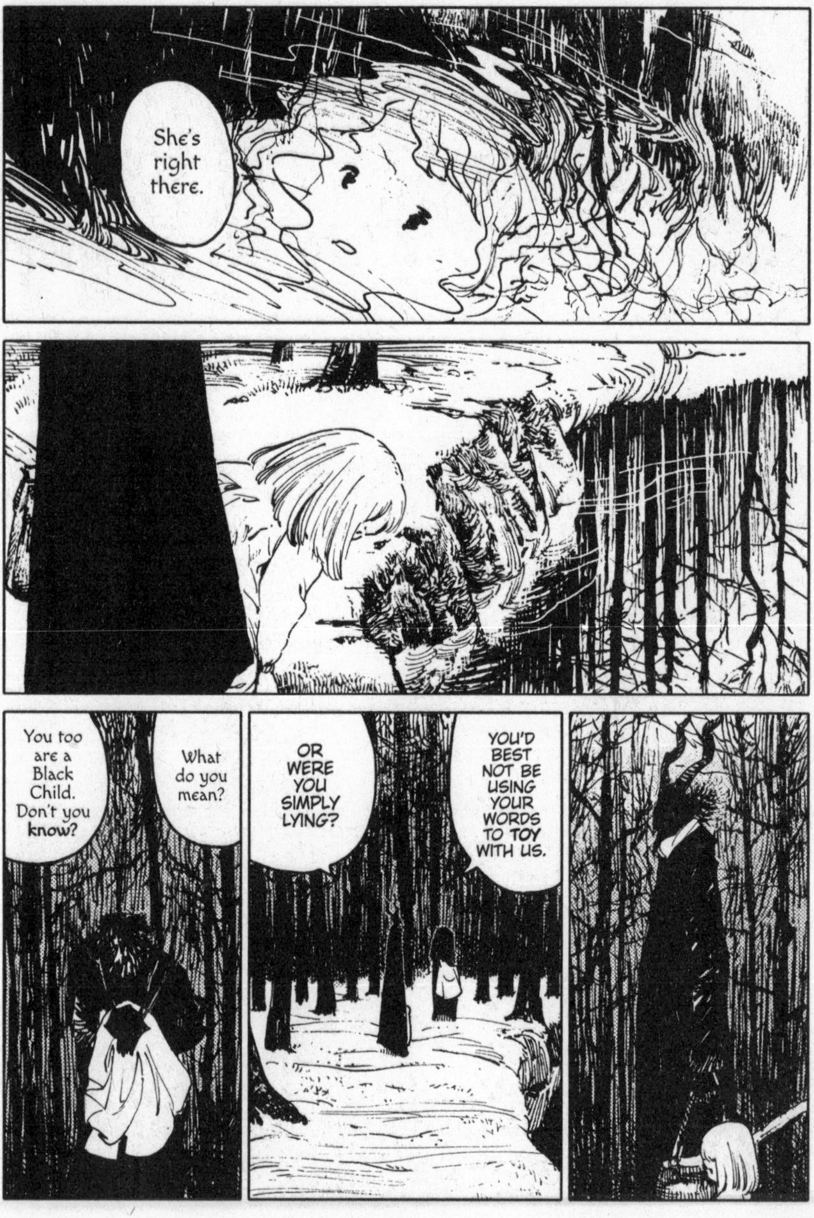
She's right there.
YOU'D BEST NOT BE USING YOUR WORDS TO **TOY** WITH US.
OR WERE YOU SIMPLY LYING?
What do you mean?
You too are a Black Child. Don't you **know**?

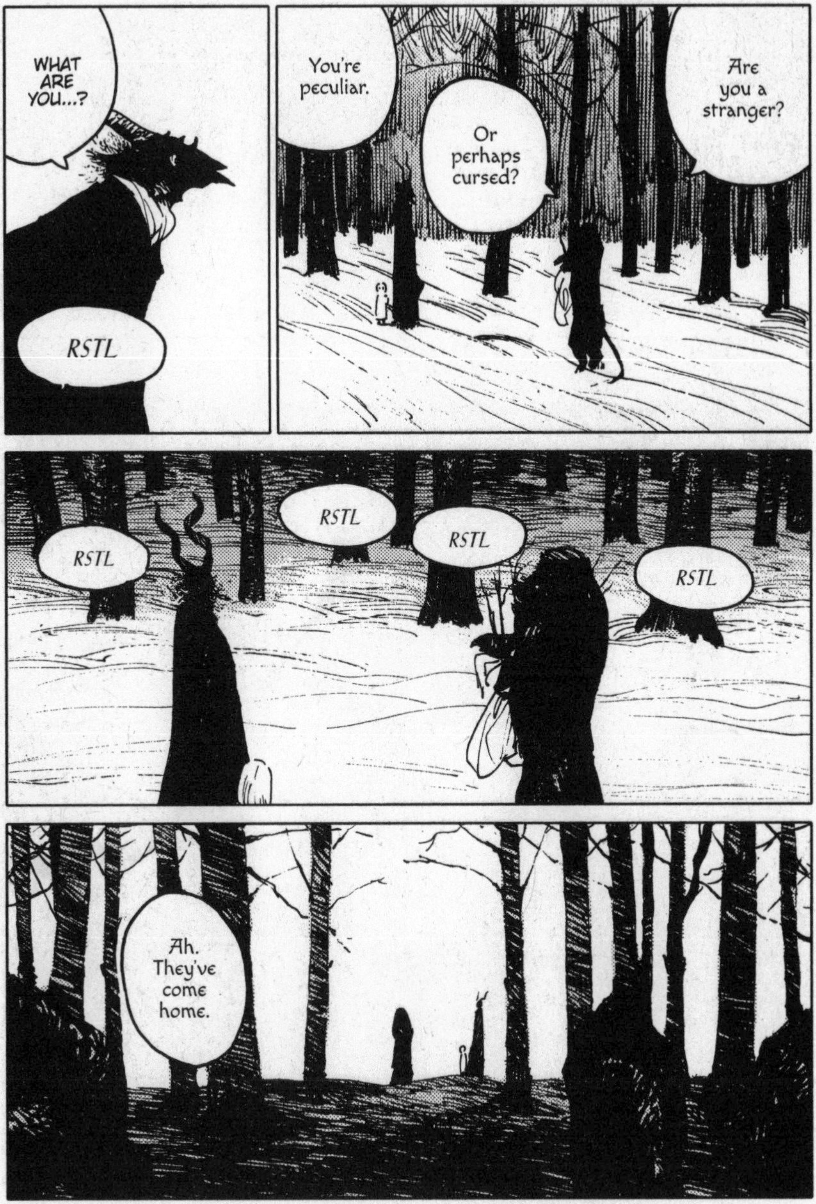
Are you a stranger?
Or perhaps cursed?
You're peculiar.
WHAT ARE YOU...?
RSTL
RSTL
RSTL
RSTL
RSTL
Ah. They've come home.

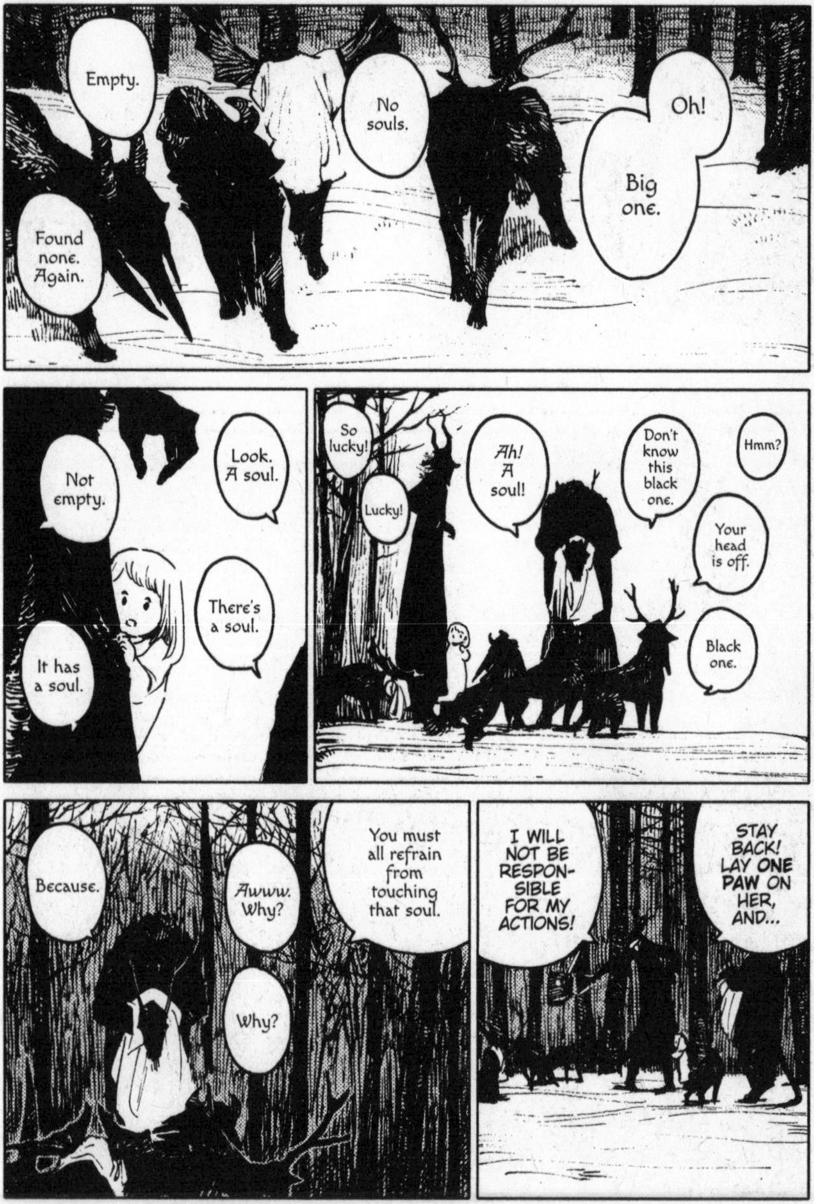
Oh!
Big one.
No souls.
Empty.
Found none. Again.
Hmm?
Don't know this black one.
Your head is off.
Black one.
Ah! A soul!
So lucky!
Lucky!
Look. A soul.
Not empty.
There's a soul.
It has a soul.
STAY BACK! LAY ONE PAW ON HER, AND...
I WILL NOT BE RESPONSIBLE FOR MY ACTIONS!
You must all refrain from touching that soul.
Awww. Why?
Because.
Why?

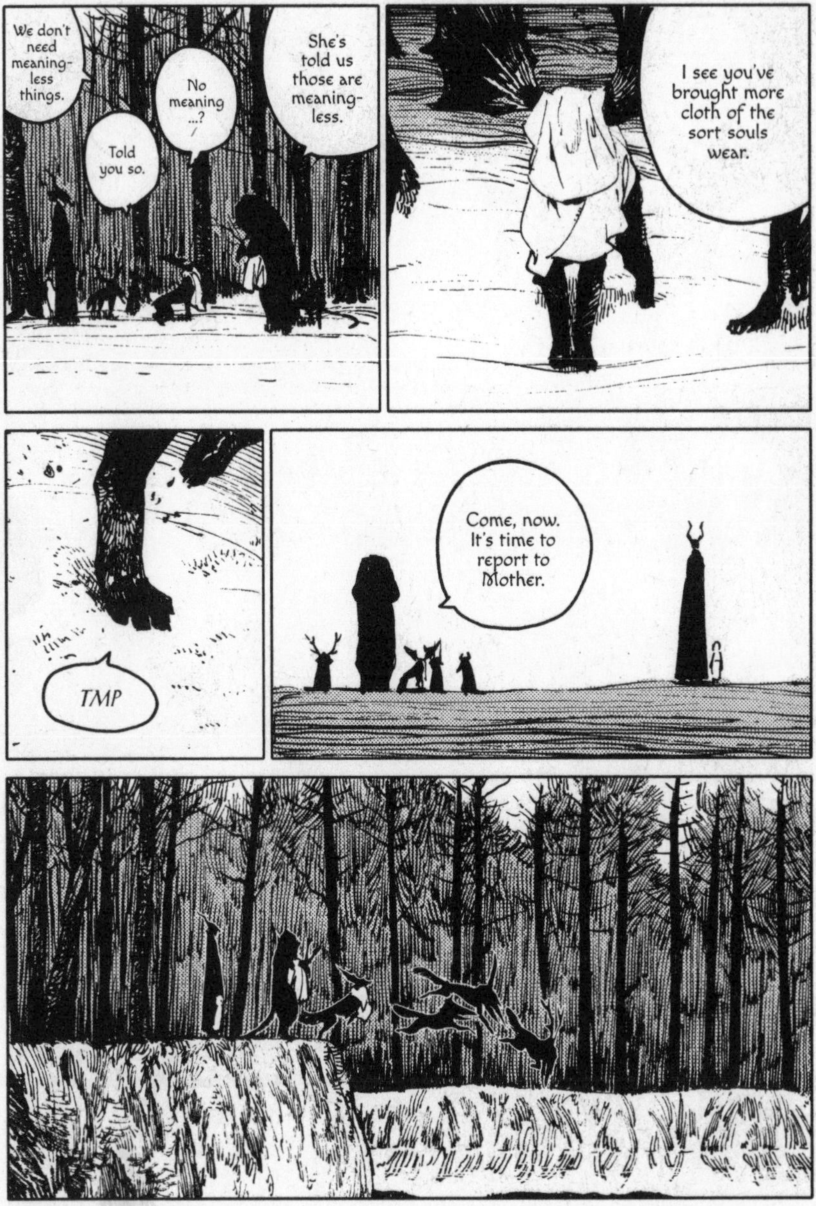
I see you've brought more cloth of the sort souls wear.
She's told us those are meaningless.
No meaning ...?
We don't need meaningless things.
Told you so.
Come, now. It's time to report to Mother.
TMP

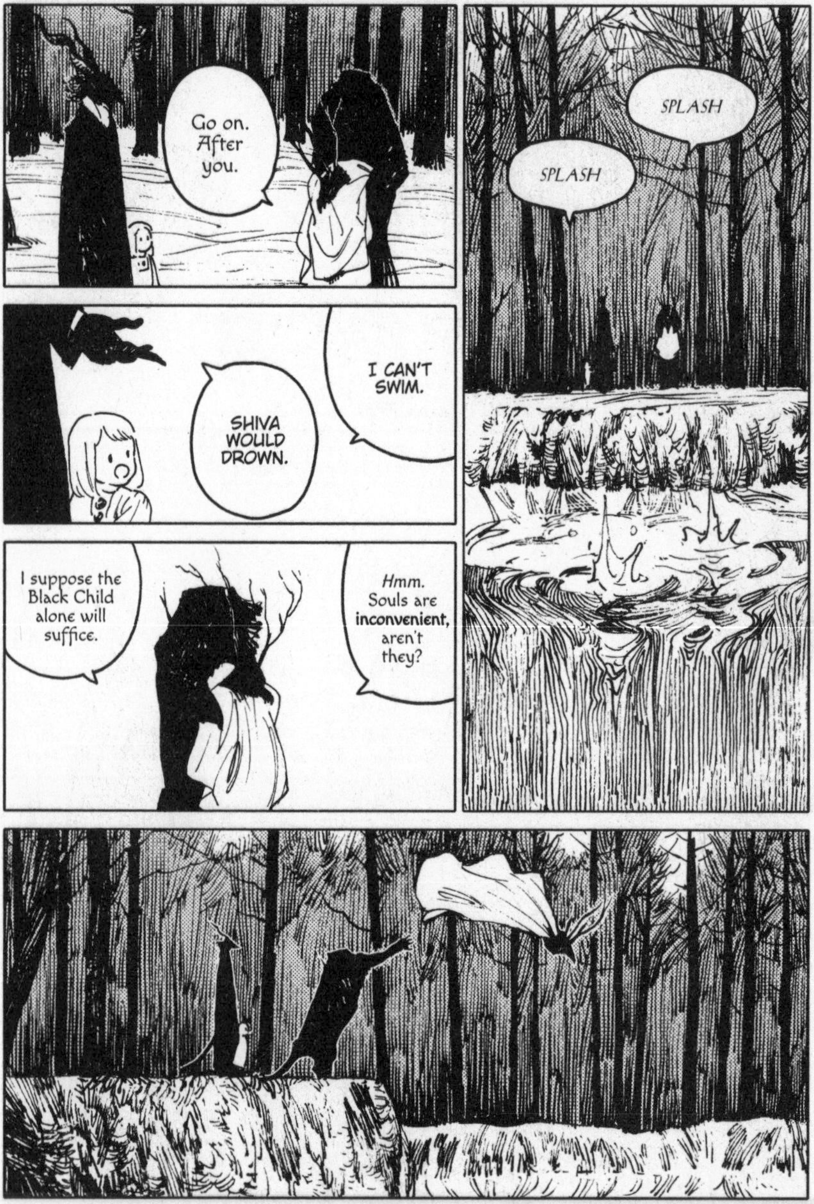
SPLASH
SPLASH
Go on. After you.
I CAN'T SWIM.
SHIVA WOULD DROWN.
Hmm. Souls are **inconvenient,** aren't they?
I suppose the Black Child alone will suffice.

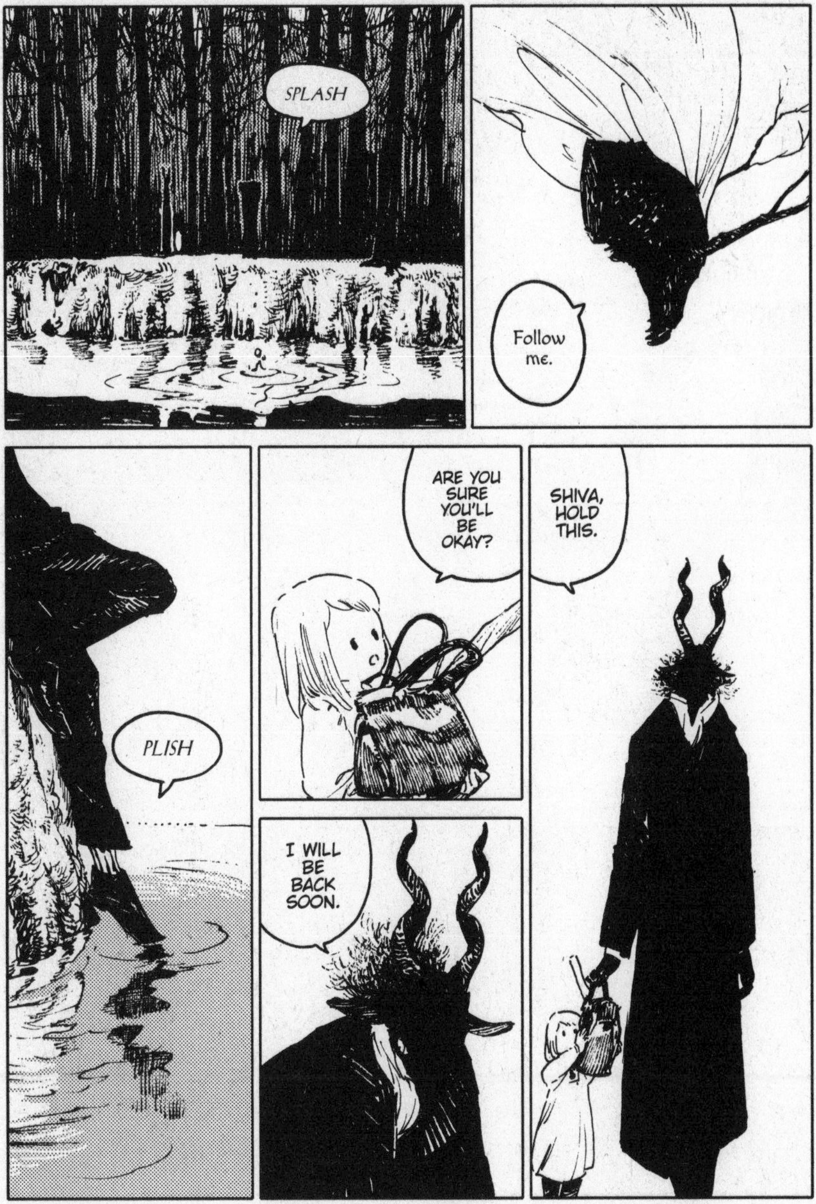
Follow me.
SPLASH
SHIVA, HOLD THIS.
ARE YOU SURE YOU'LL BE OKAY?
I WILL BE BACK SOON.
PLISH

PLOSH

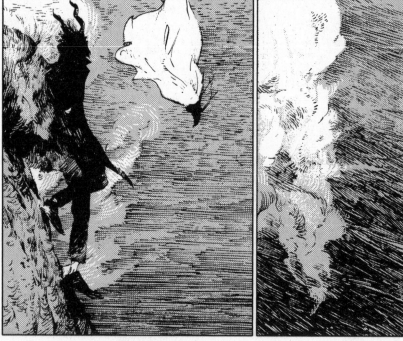

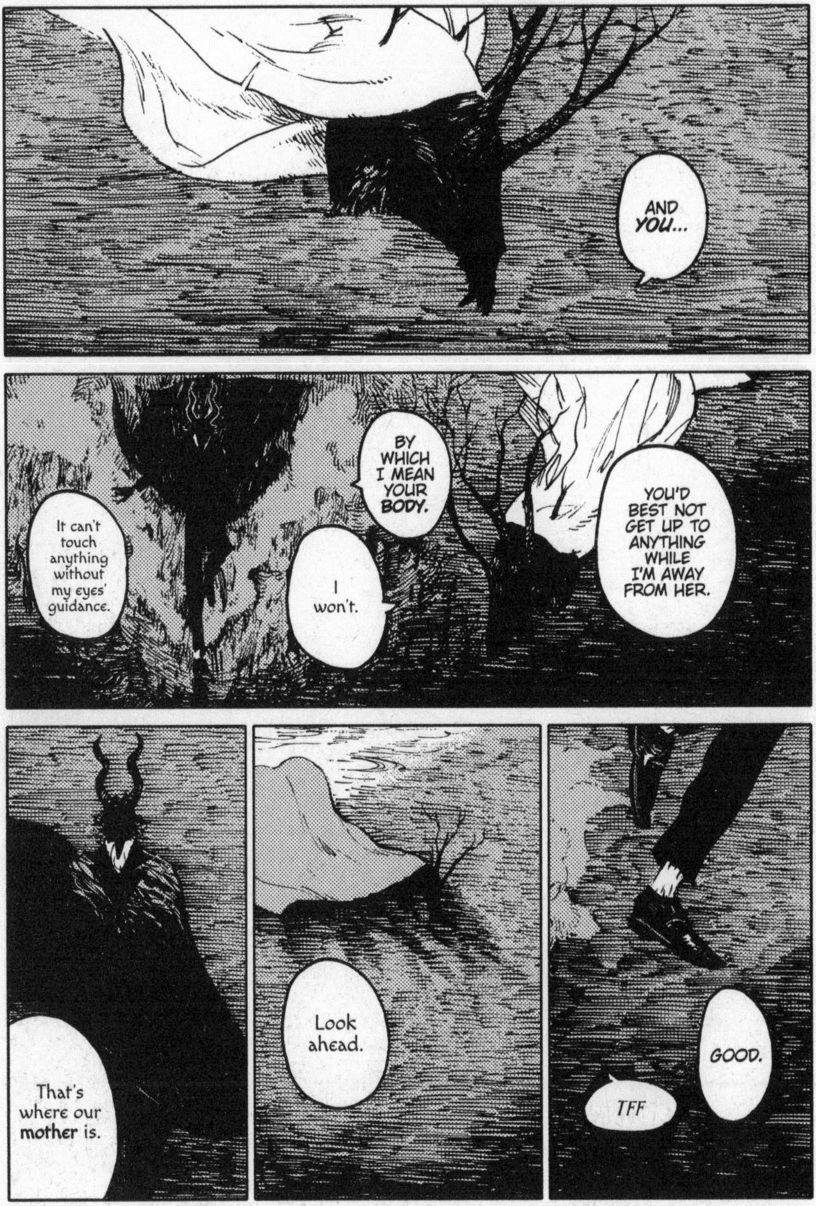
AND YOU...
YOU'D BEST NOT GET UP TO ANYTHING WHILE I'M AWAY FROM HER.
BY WHICH I MEAN YOUR BODY.
I won't.
It can't touch anything without my eyes' guidance.
GOOD.
TFF
Look ahead.
That's where our mother is.

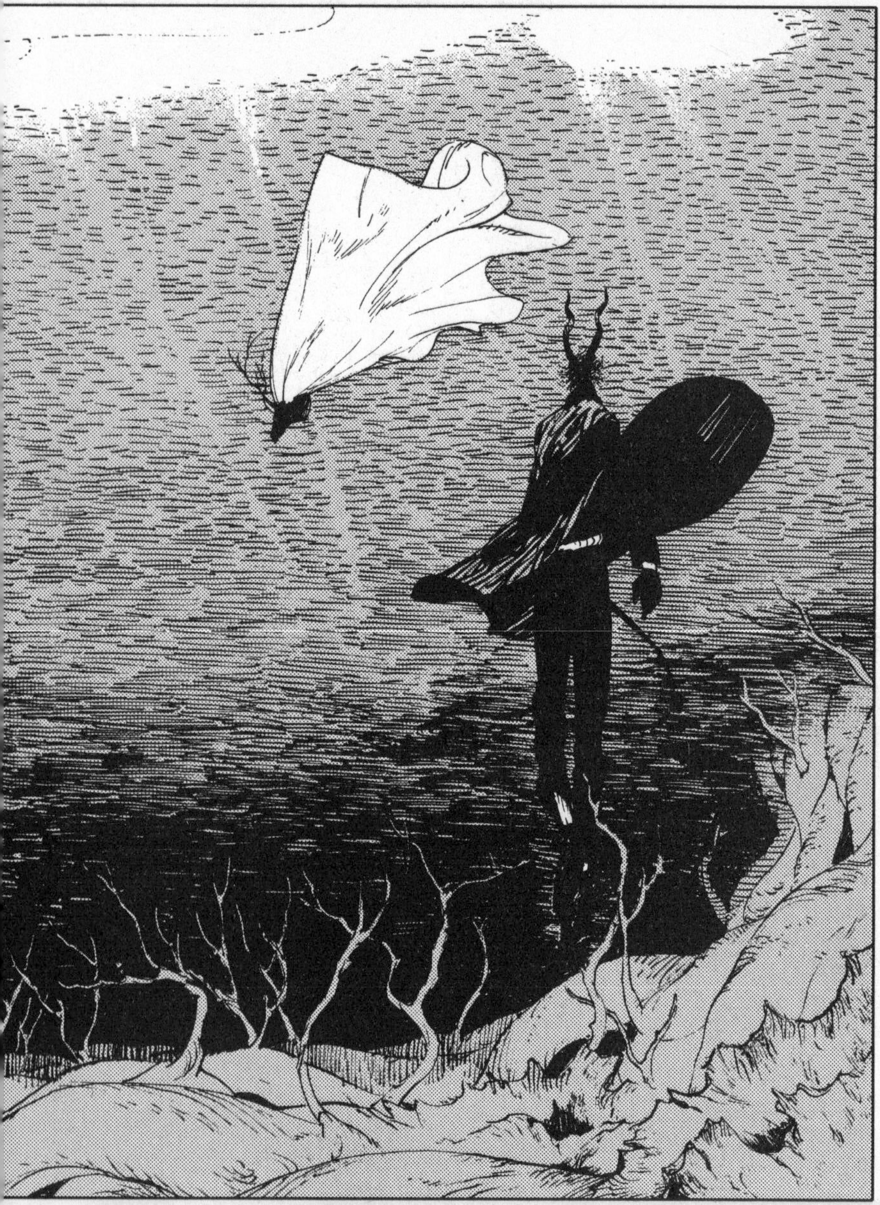

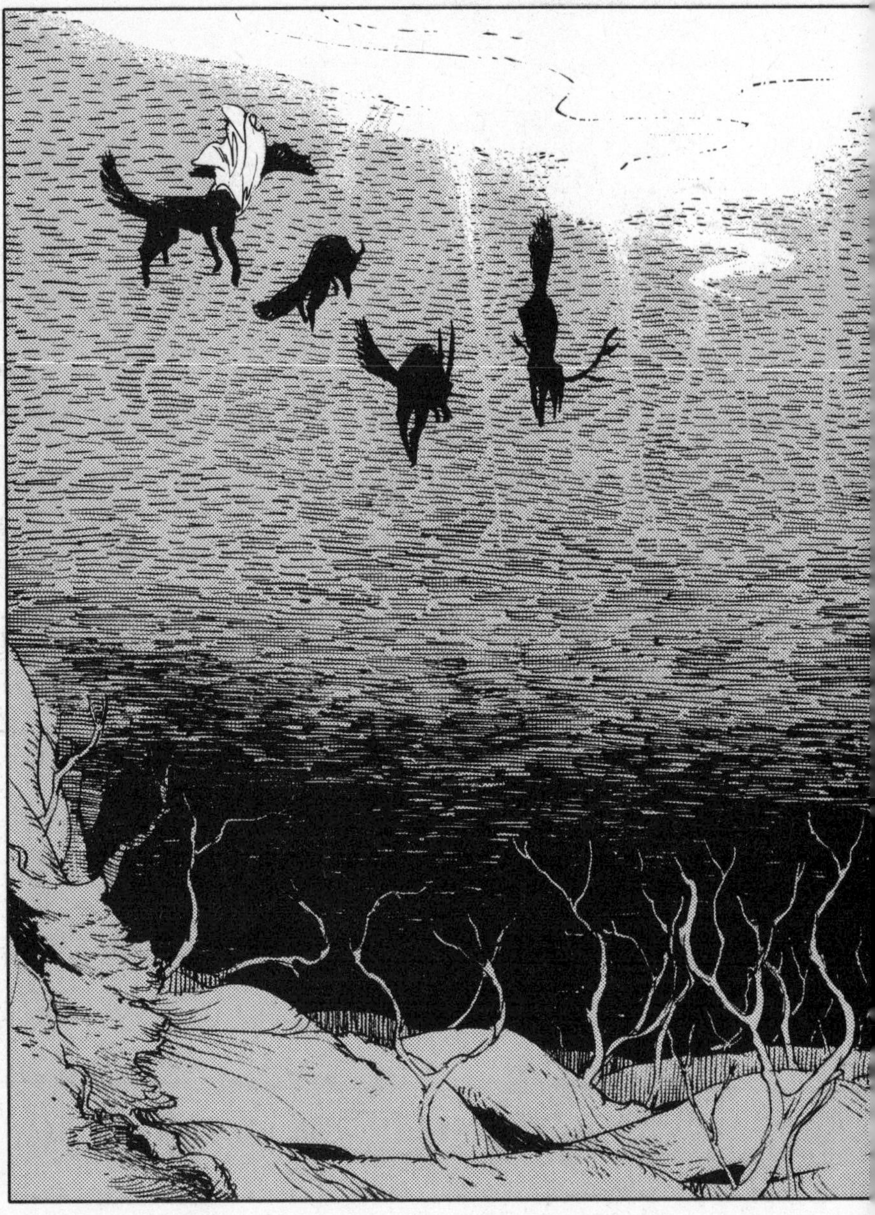

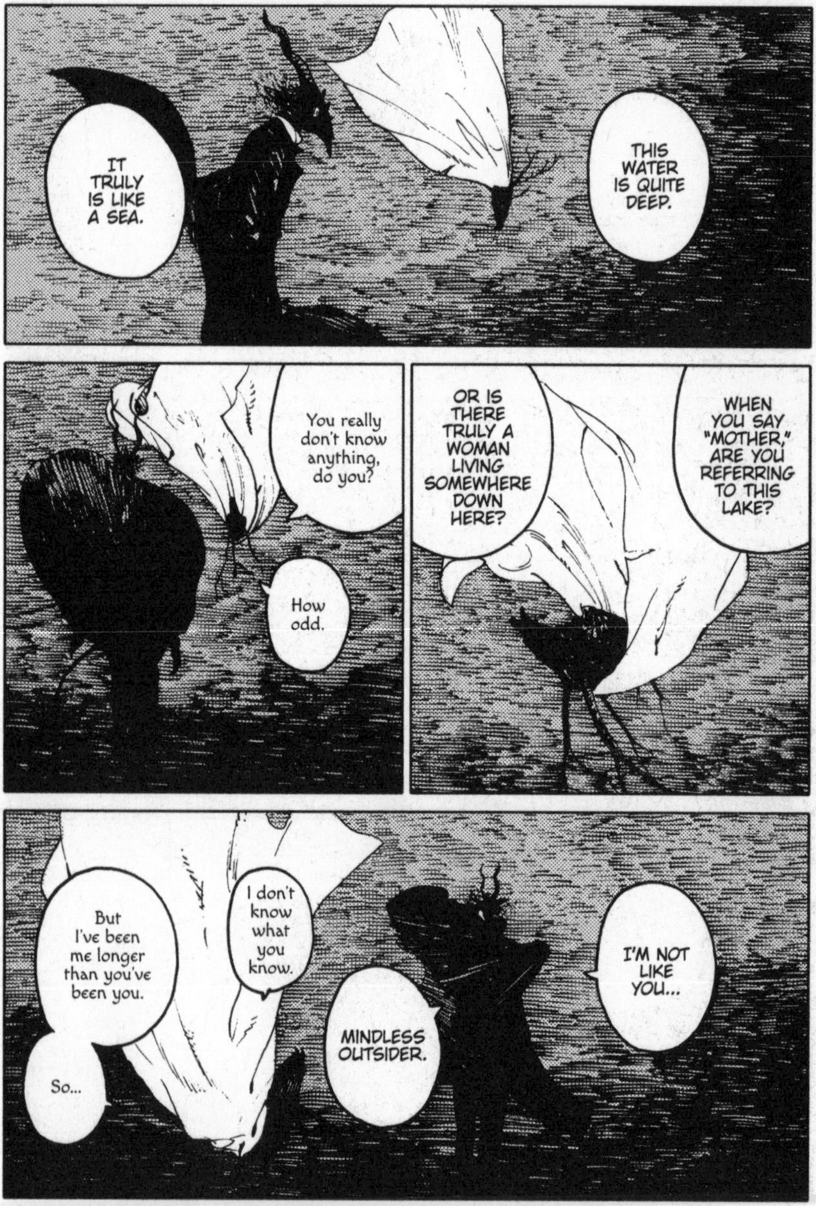
THIS WATER IS QUITE DEEP.
IT TRULY IS LIKE A SEA.
WHEN YOU SAY "MOTHER," ARE YOU REFERRING TO THIS LAKE?
OR IS THERE TRULY A WOMAN LIVING SOMEWHERE DOWN HERE?
You really don't know anything, do you?
How odd.
I'M NOT LIKE YOU...
MINDLESS OUTSIDER.
I don't know what you know.
But I've been me longer than you've been you.
So...

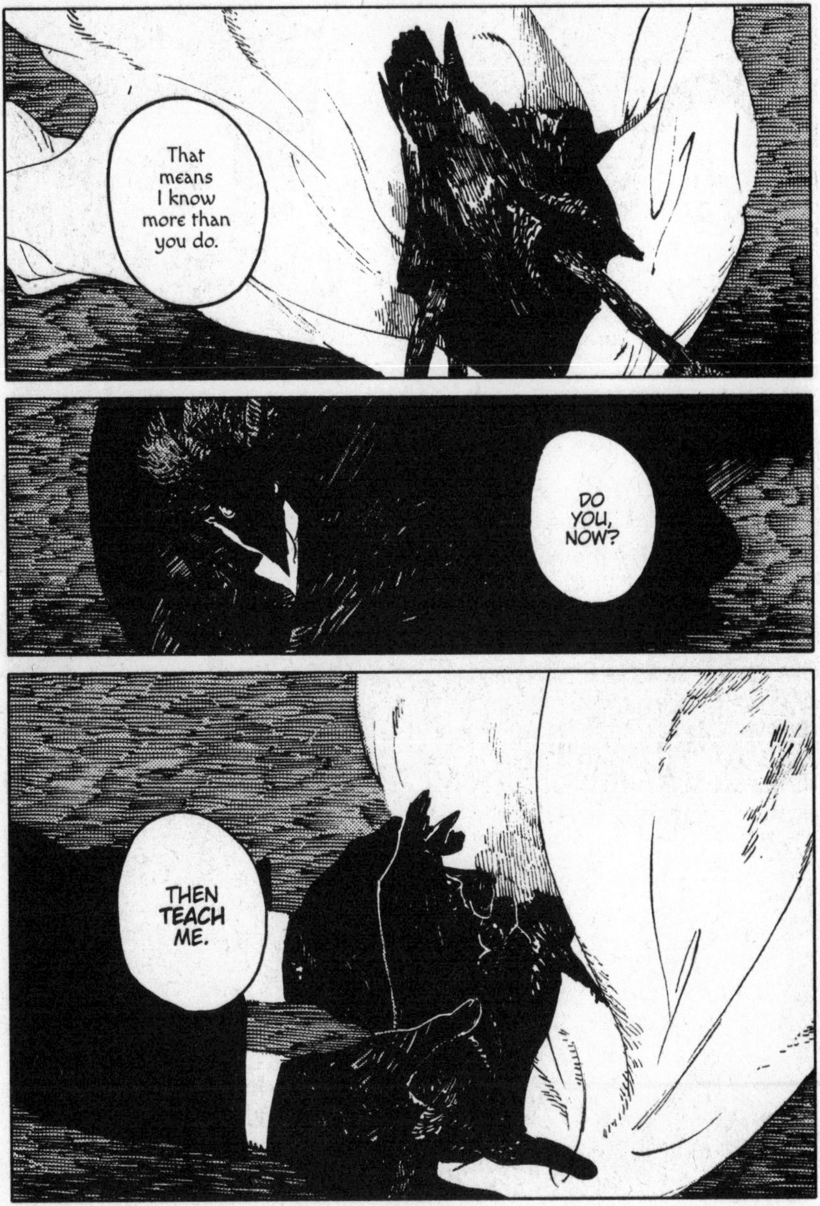
That means I know more than you do.
DO YOU, NOW?
THEN TEACH ME.

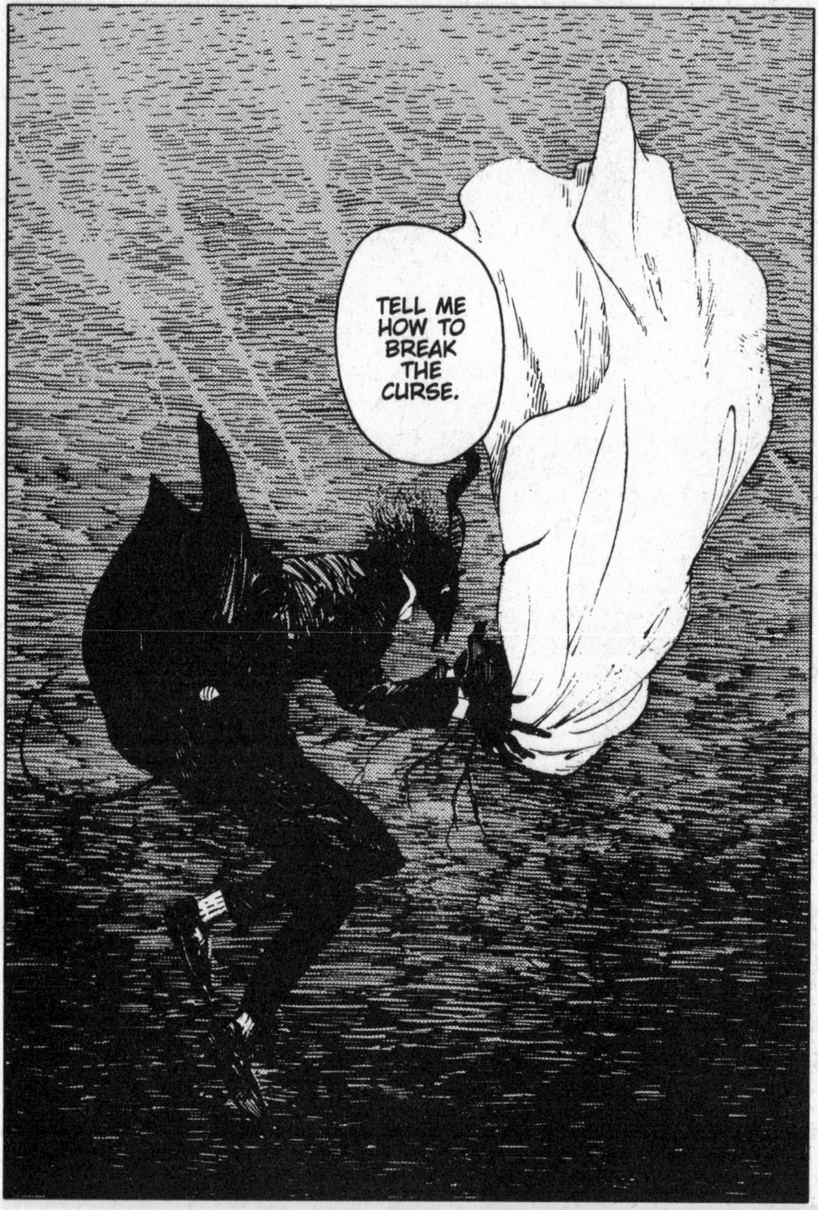
TELL ME HOW TO BREAK THE CURSE.

Siúil, a Rún

The Girl from the Other Side

Siúil, a Rún
The Girl from the Other Side

Chapter 8

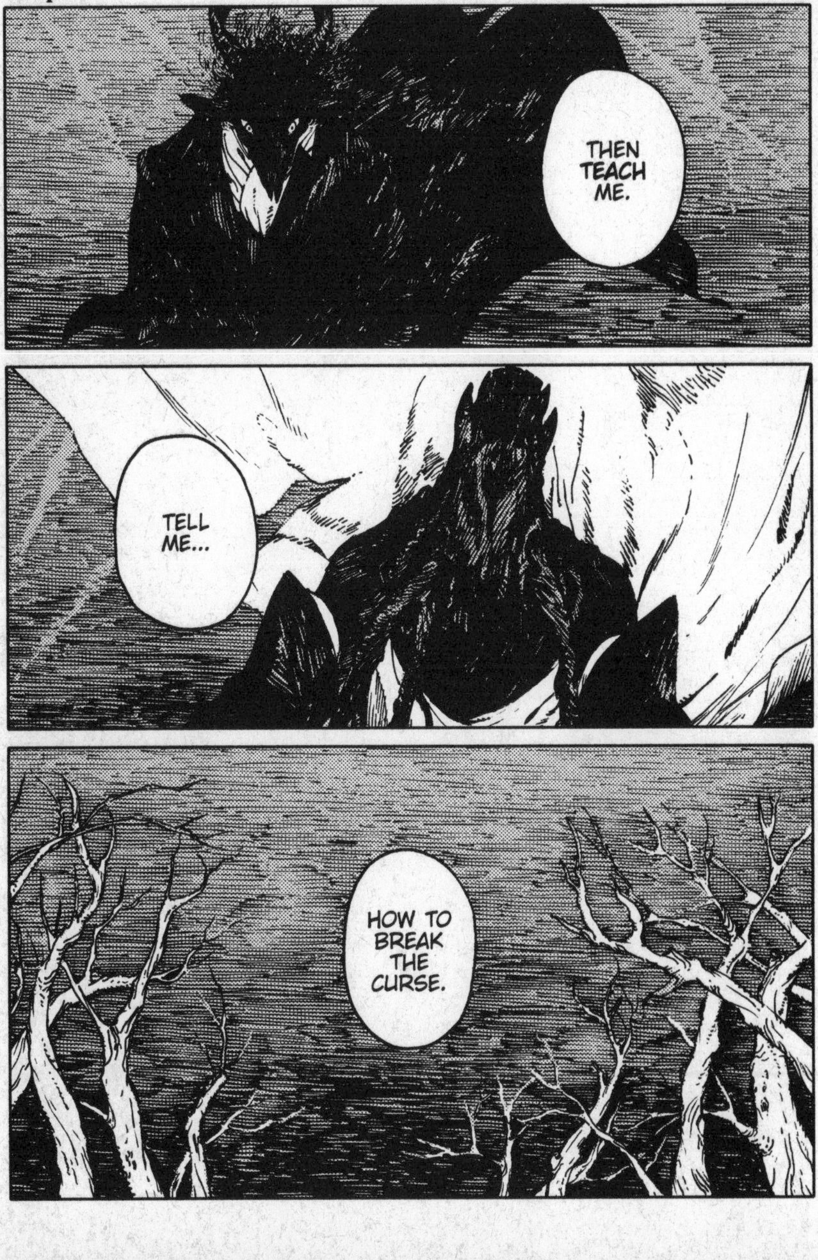
THEN TEACH ME.
TELL ME...
HOW TO BREAK THE CURSE.

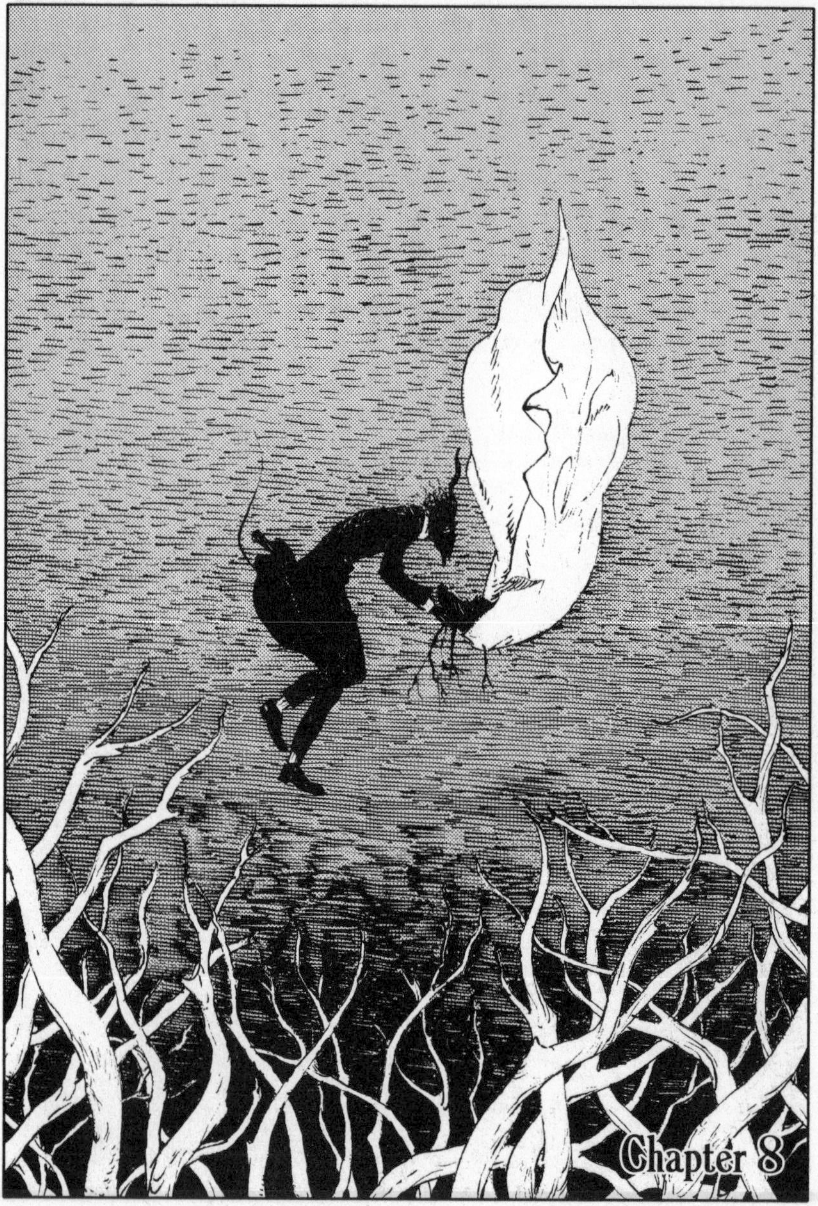
Chapter 8

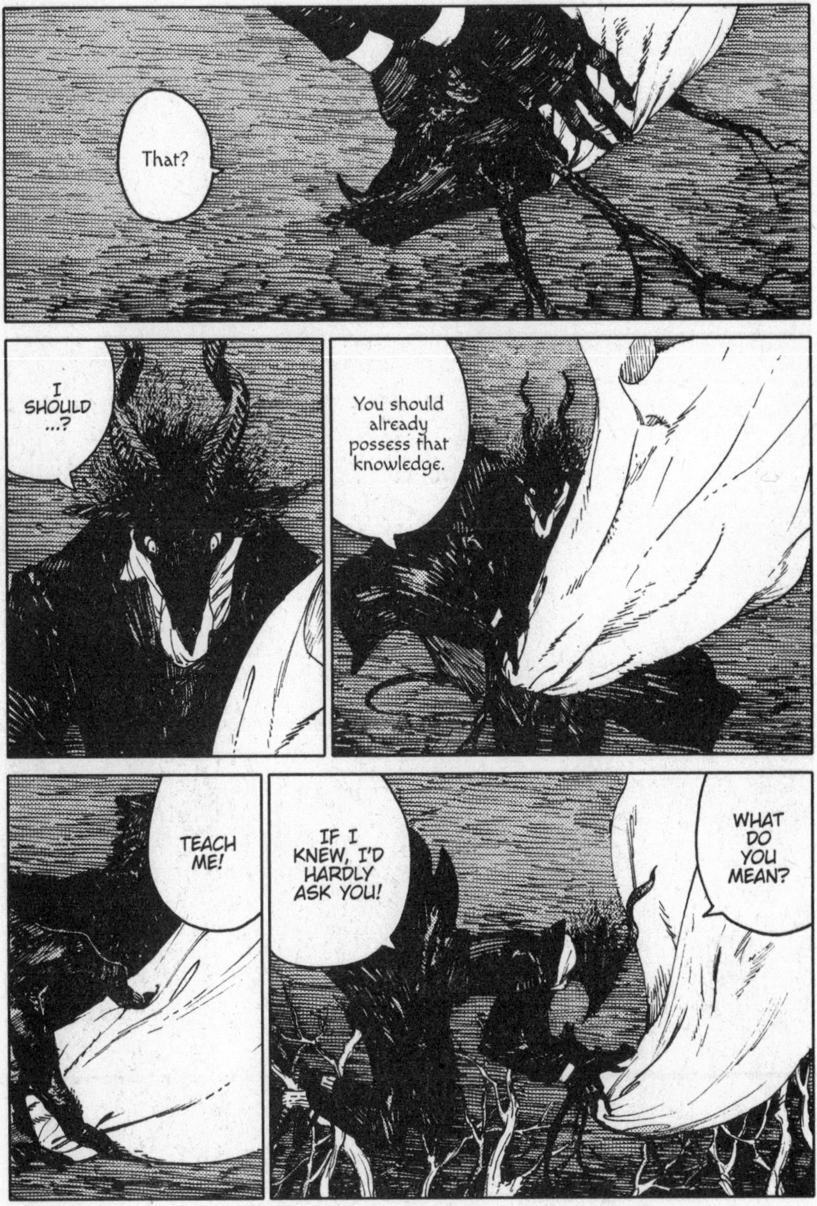
That?
You should already possess that knowledge.
I SHOULD ...?
WHAT DO YOU MEAN?
IF I KNEW, I'D HARDLY ASK YOU!
TEACH ME!

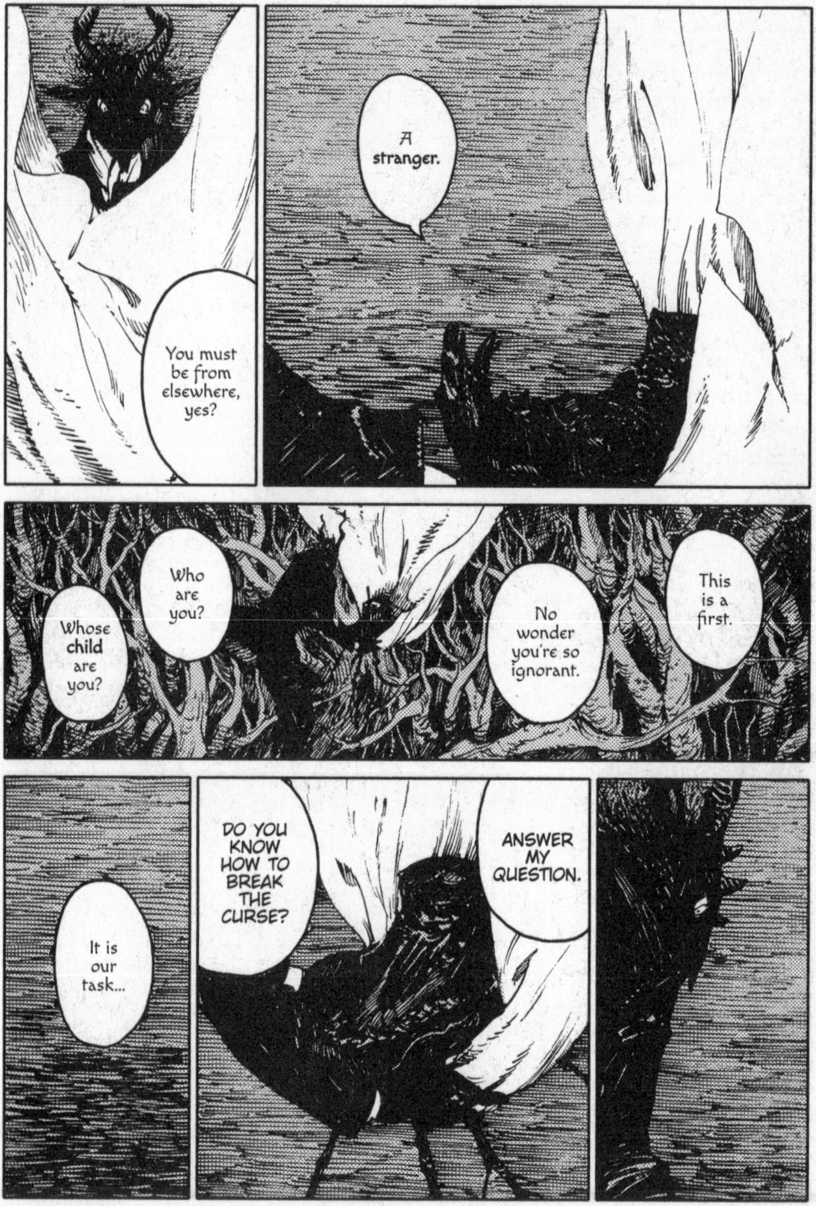
A stranger.
You must be from elsewhere, yes?
This is a first.
No wonder you're so ignorant.
Who are you?
Whose child are you?
ANSWER MY QUESTION.
DO YOU KNOW HOW TO BREAK THE CURSE?
It is our task...

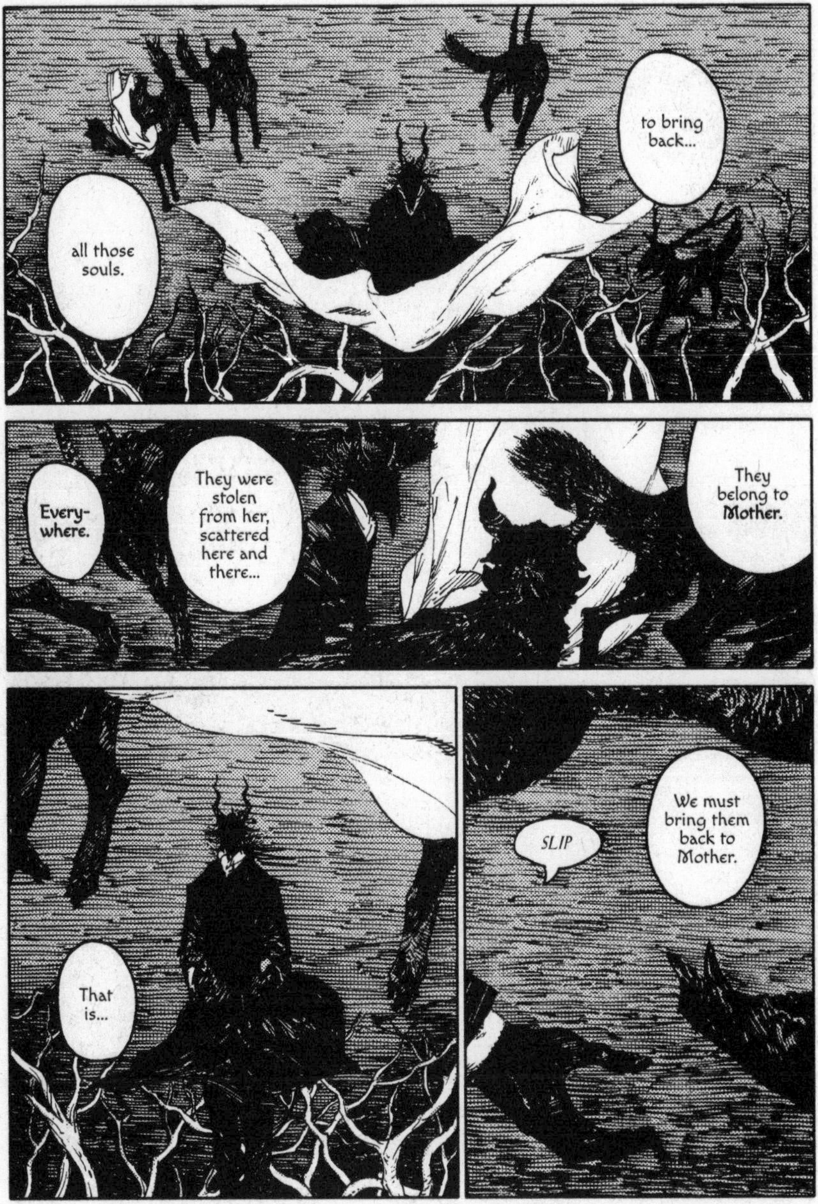
to bring back...
all those souls.
They belong to Mother.
They were stolen from her, scattered here and there...
Every-where.
We must bring them back to Mother.
SLIP
That is...

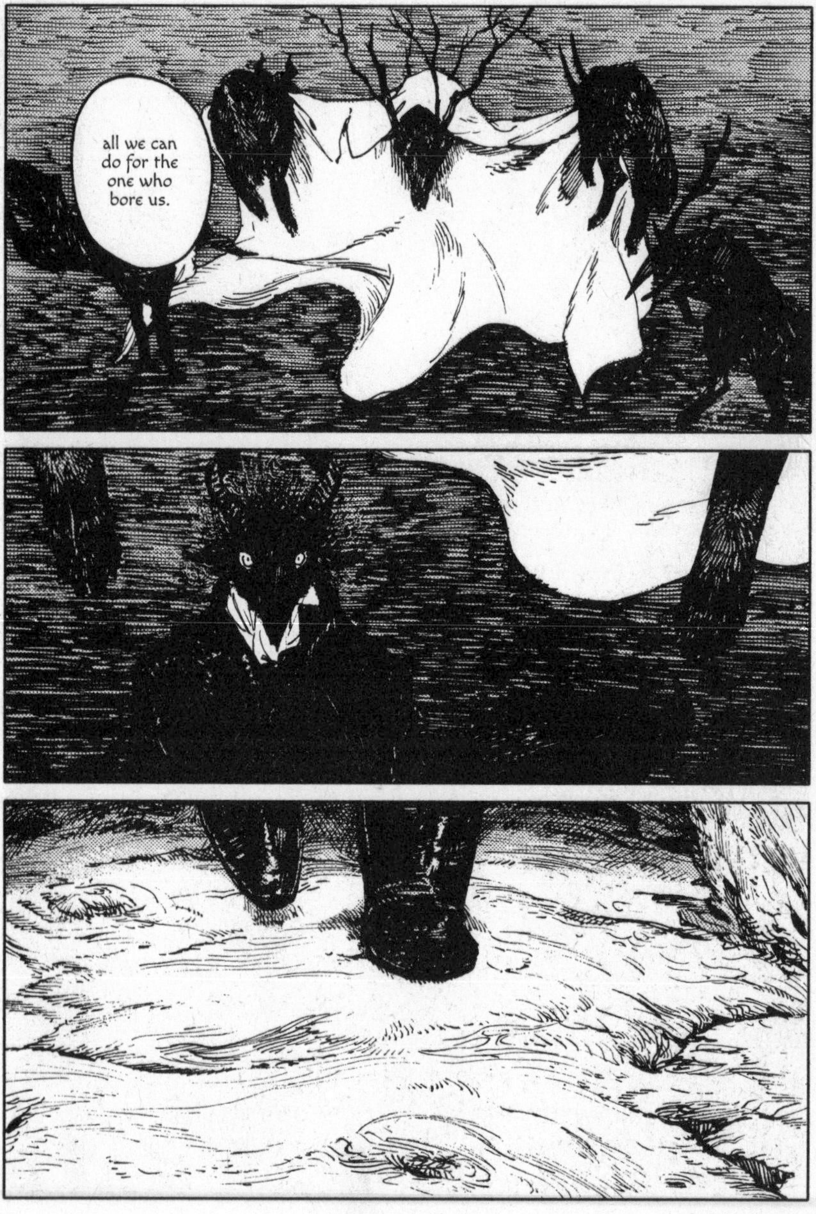
all we can do for the one who bore us.

Come closer.

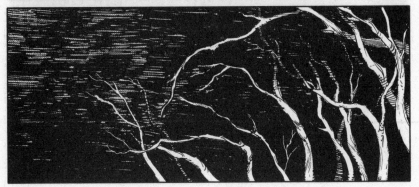

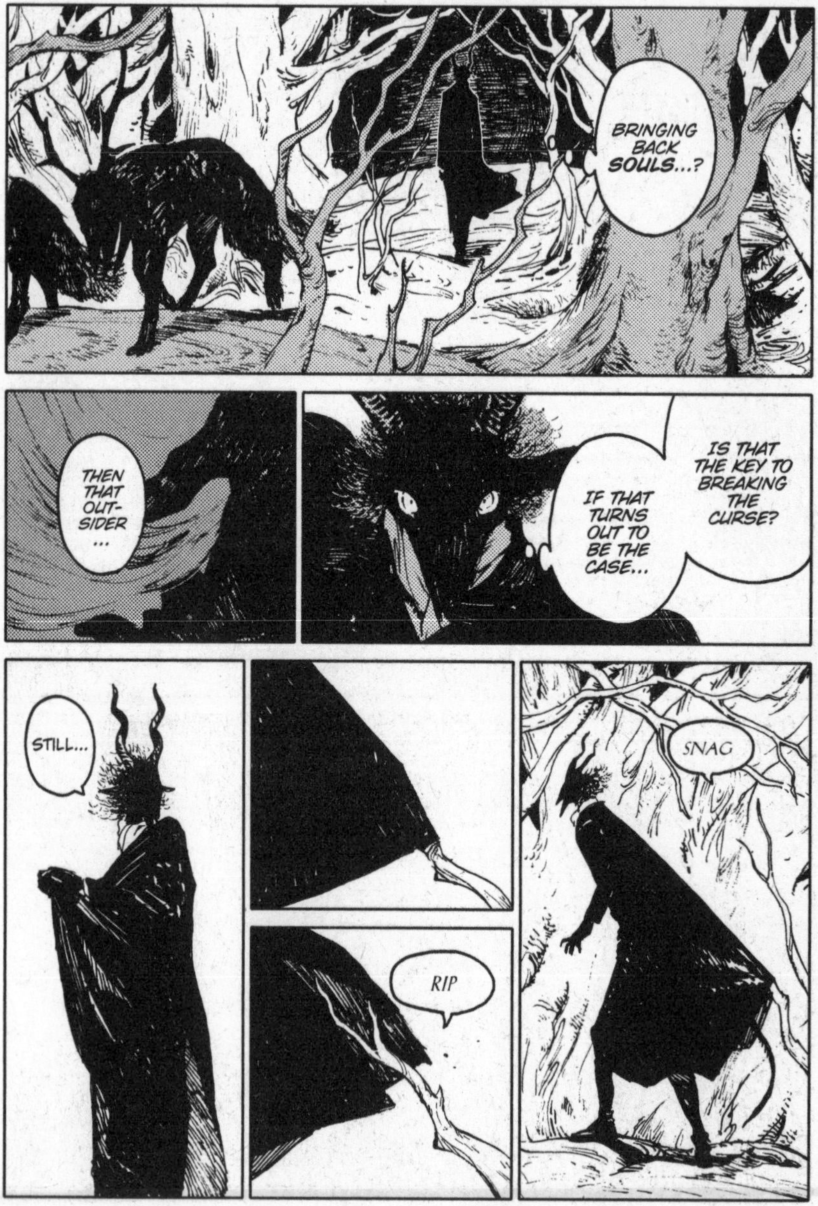
BRINGING BACK SOULS...?
IS THAT THE KEY TO BREAKING THE CURSE?
IF THAT TURNS OUT TO BE THE CASE...
THEN THAT OUT-SIDER ...
SNAG
RIP
STILL...

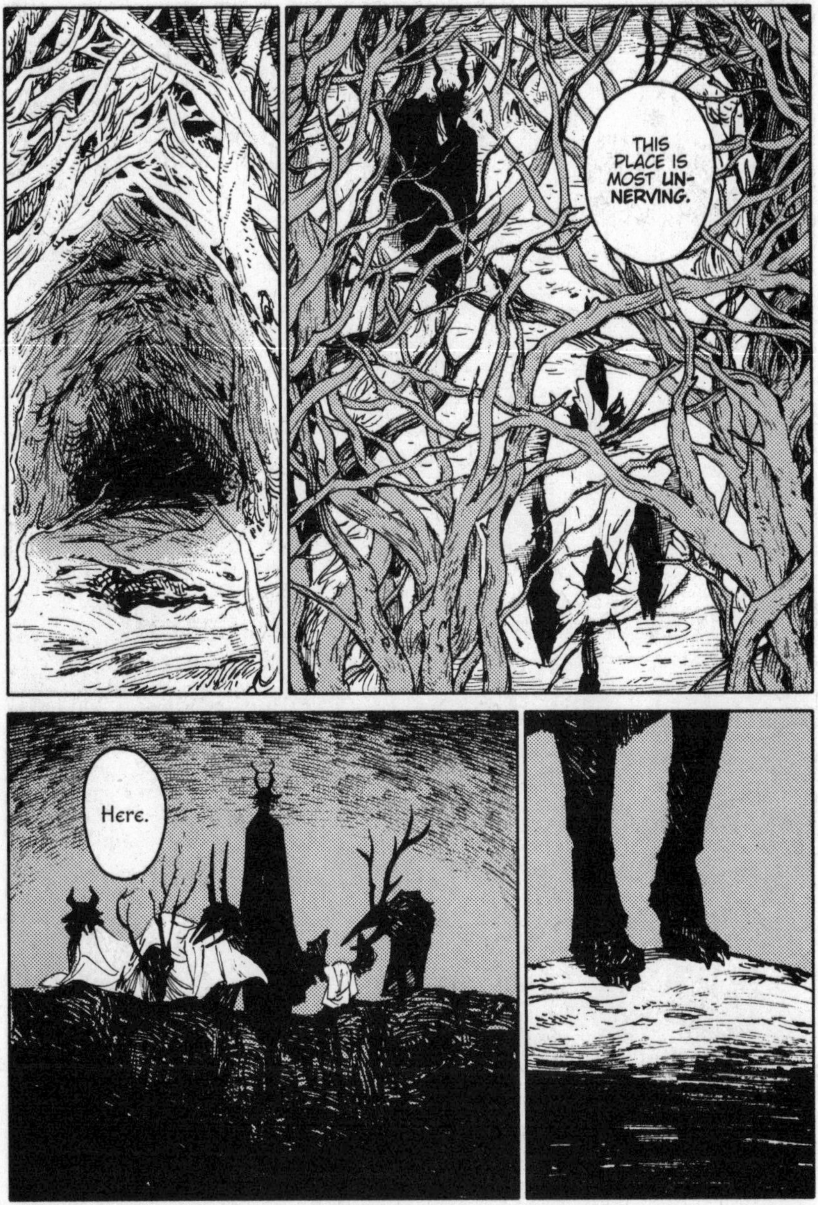
THIS PLACE IS MOST UN-NERVING.
Here.

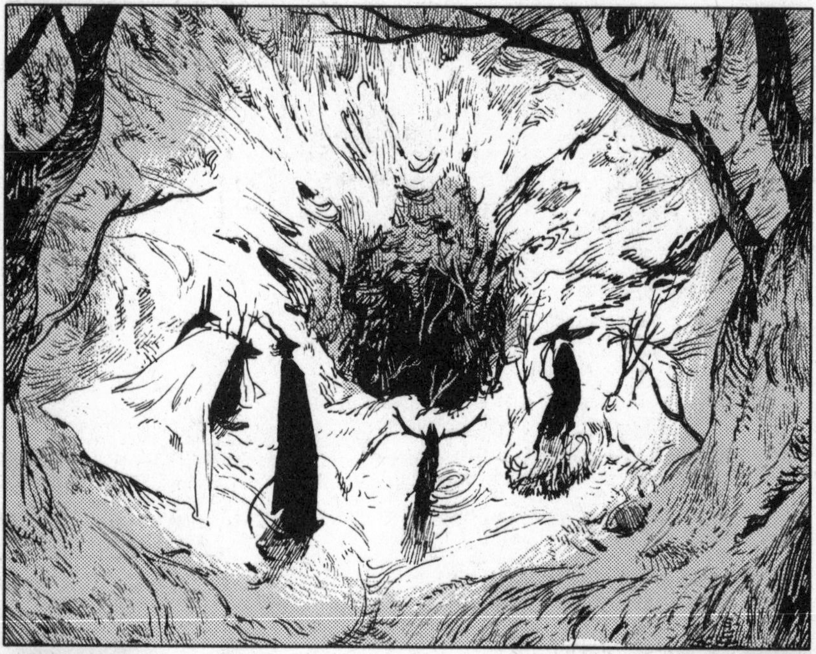

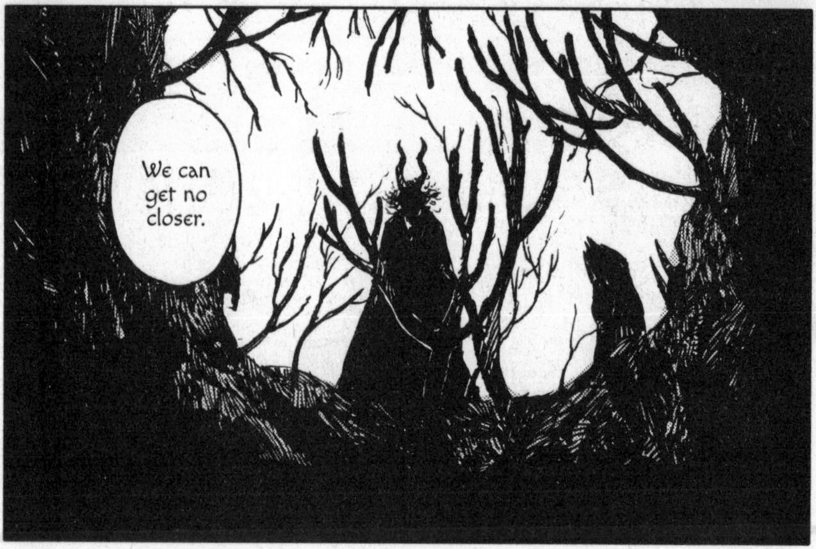
We can get no closer.

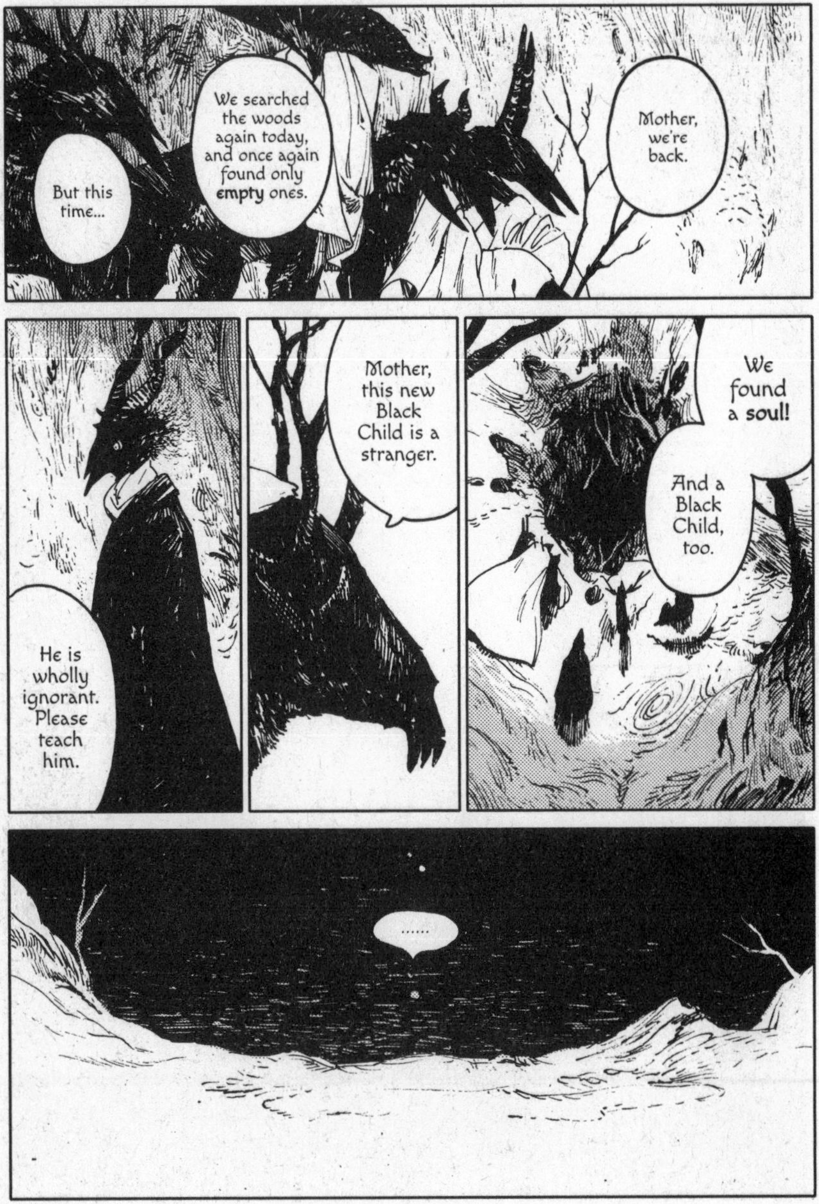
Mother, we're back.
We searched the woods again today, and once again found only **empty** ones.
But this time...
We found a **soul**!
And a Black Child, too.
Mother, this new Black Child is a stranger.
He is wholly ignorant. Please teach him.
......

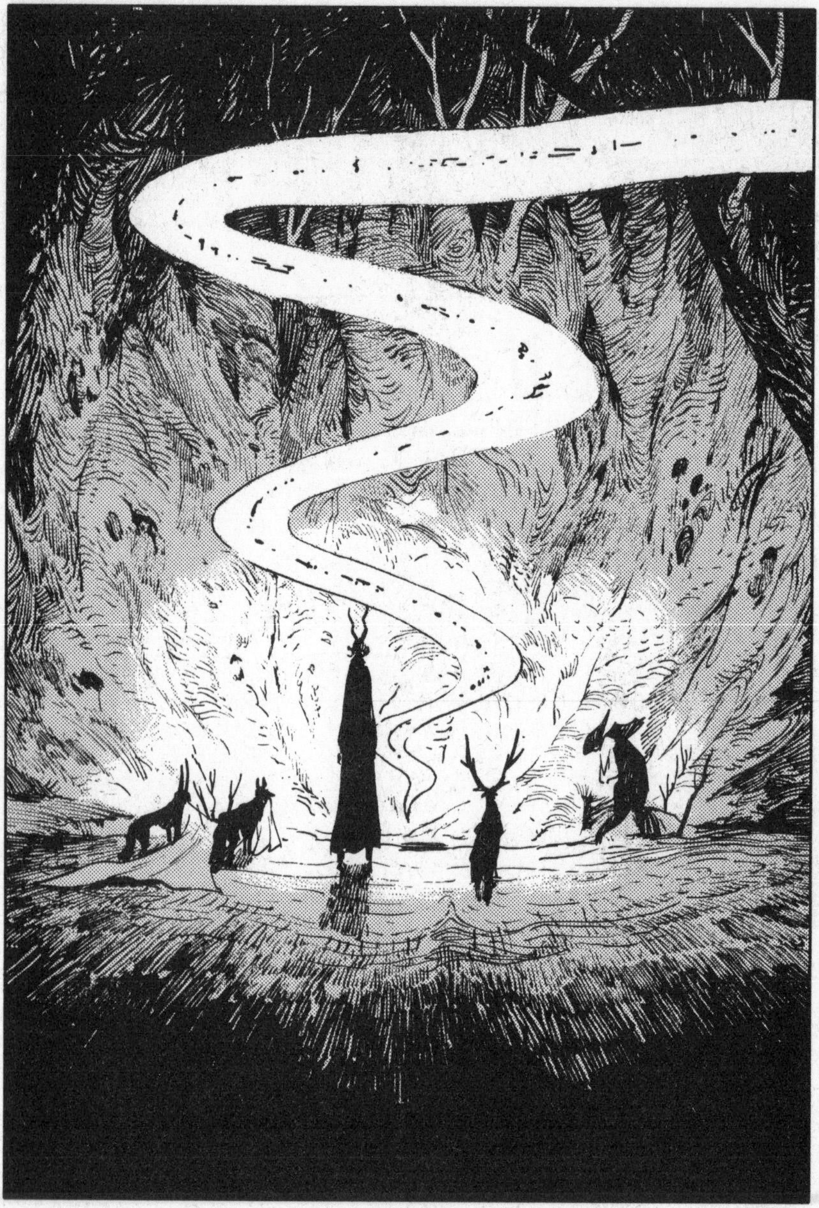

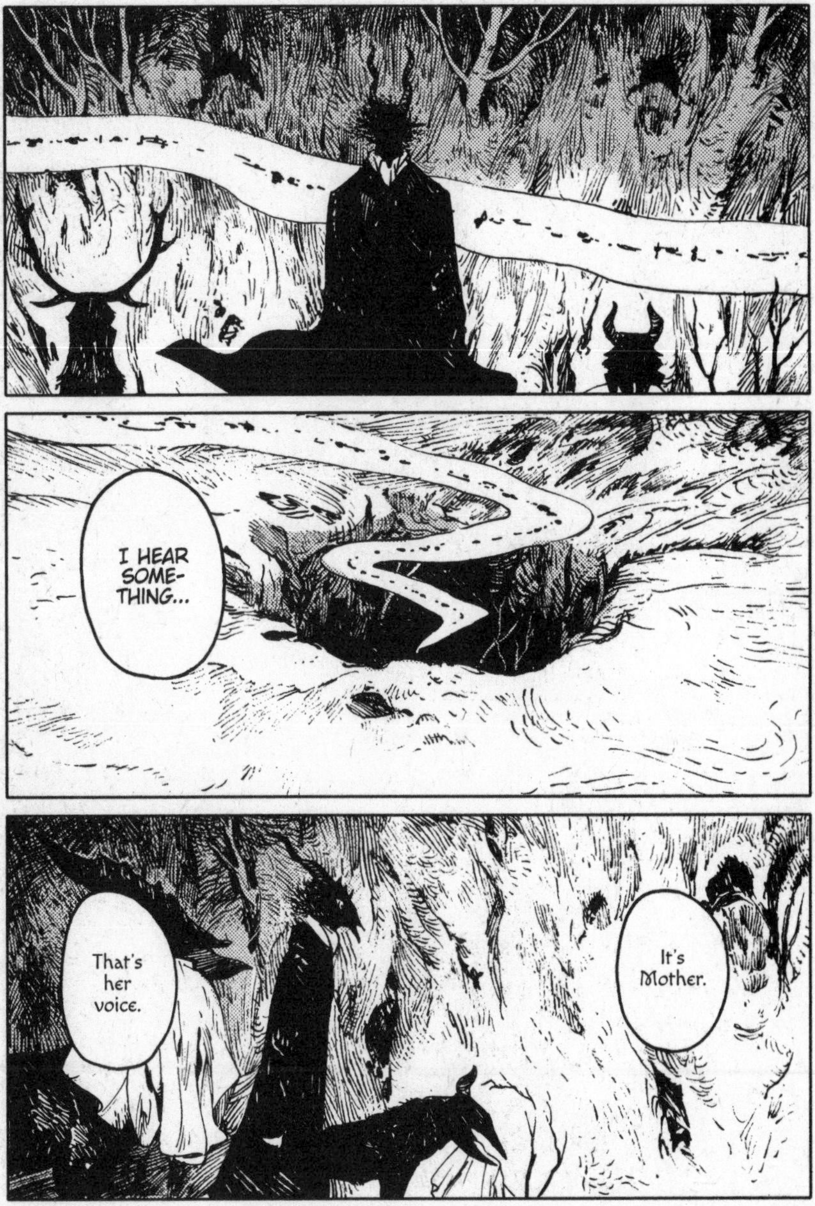
I HEAR SOME-THING...
It's Mother.
That's her voice.

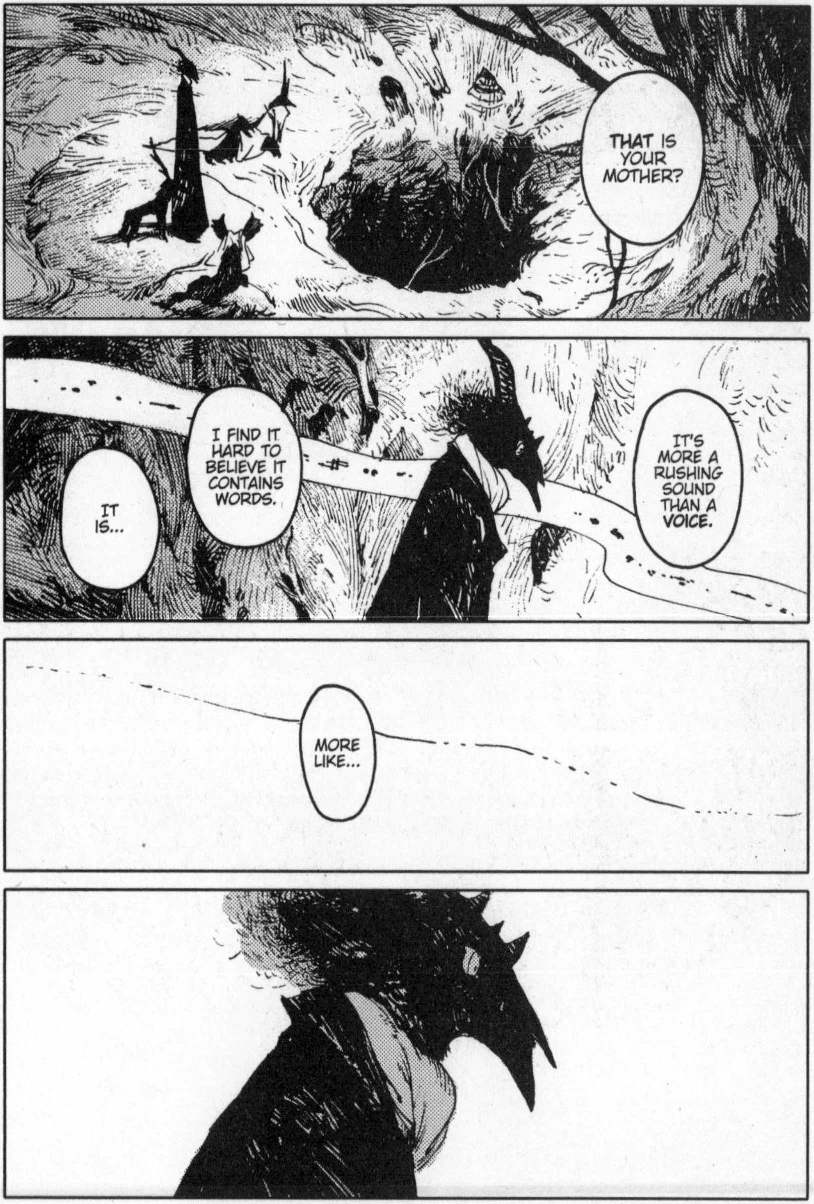
THAT IS YOUR MOTHER?
IT'S MORE A RUSHING SOUND THAN A VOICE.
I FIND IT HARD TO BELIEVE IT CONTAINS WORDS.
IT IS...
MORE LIKE...

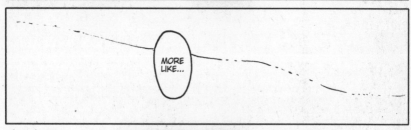

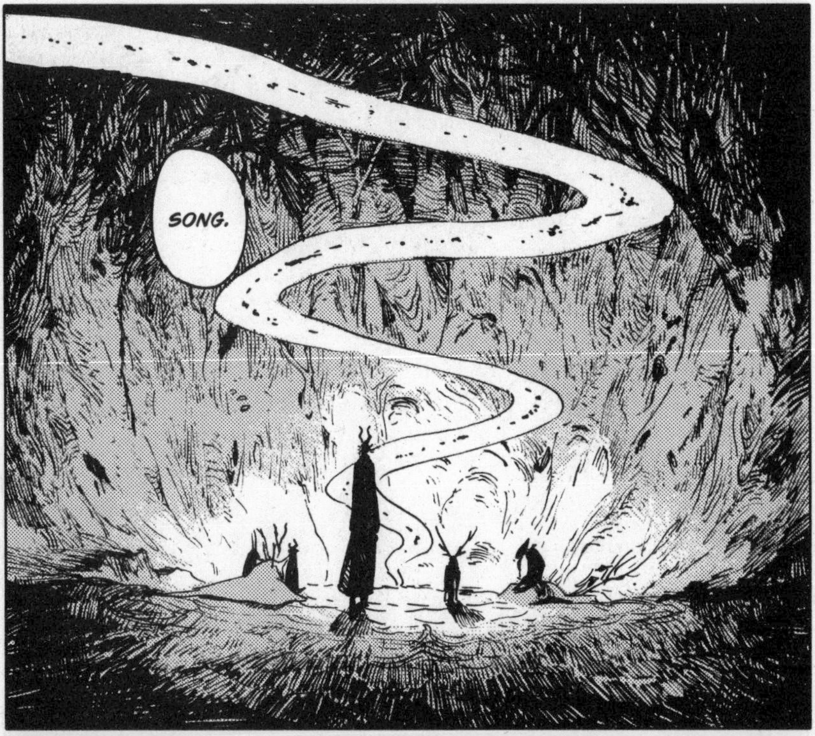
SONG.
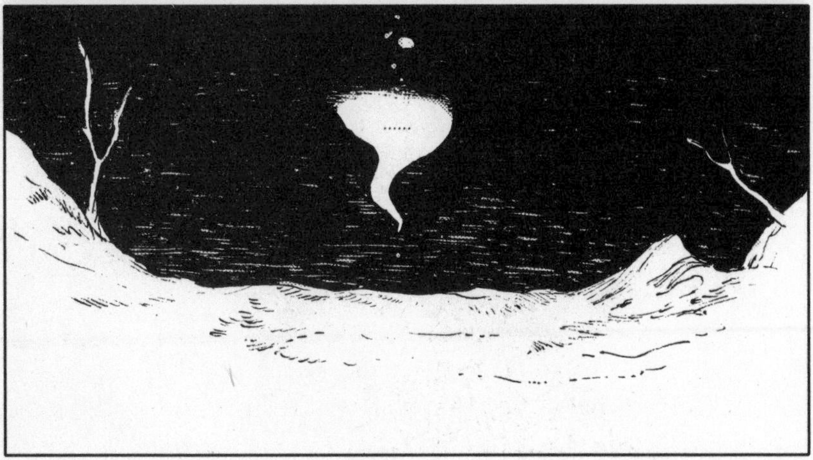
......

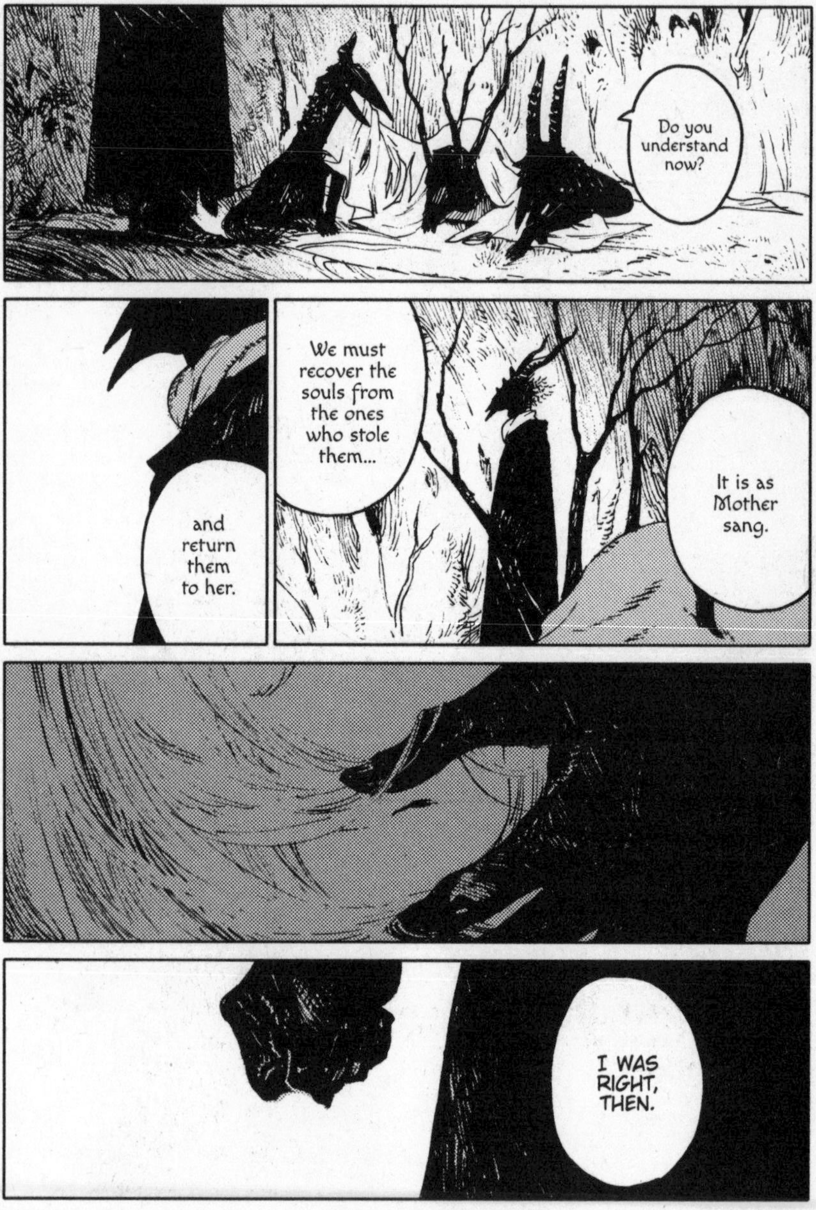
Do you understand now?
It is as Mother sang.
We must recover the souls from the ones who stole them...
and return them to her.
I WAS RIGHT, THEN.

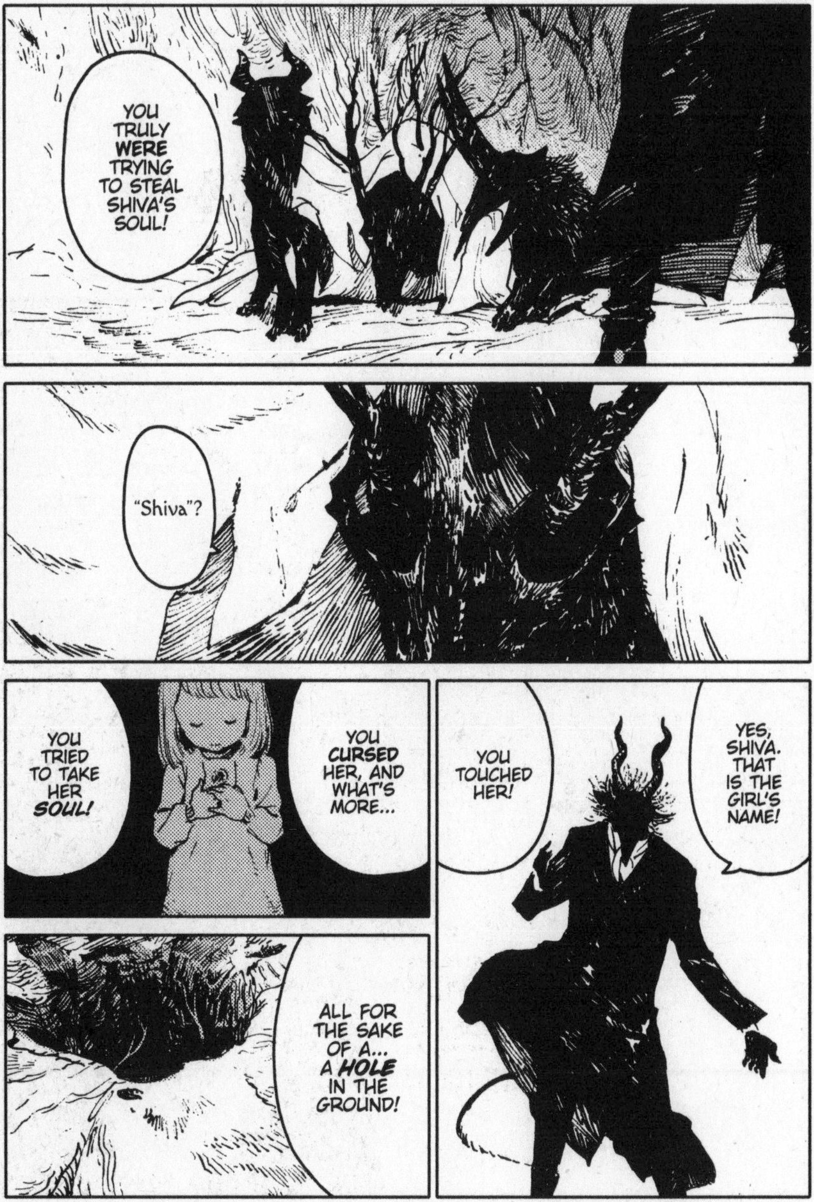
YOU TRULY WERE TRYING TO STEAL SHIVA'S SOUL!
"Shiva"?
YES, SHIVA. THAT IS THE GIRL'S NAME!
YOU TOUCHED HER!
YOU CURSED HER, AND WHAT'S MORE...
YOU TRIED TO TAKE HER SOUL!
ALL FOR THE SAKE OF A... A HOLE IN THE GROUND!

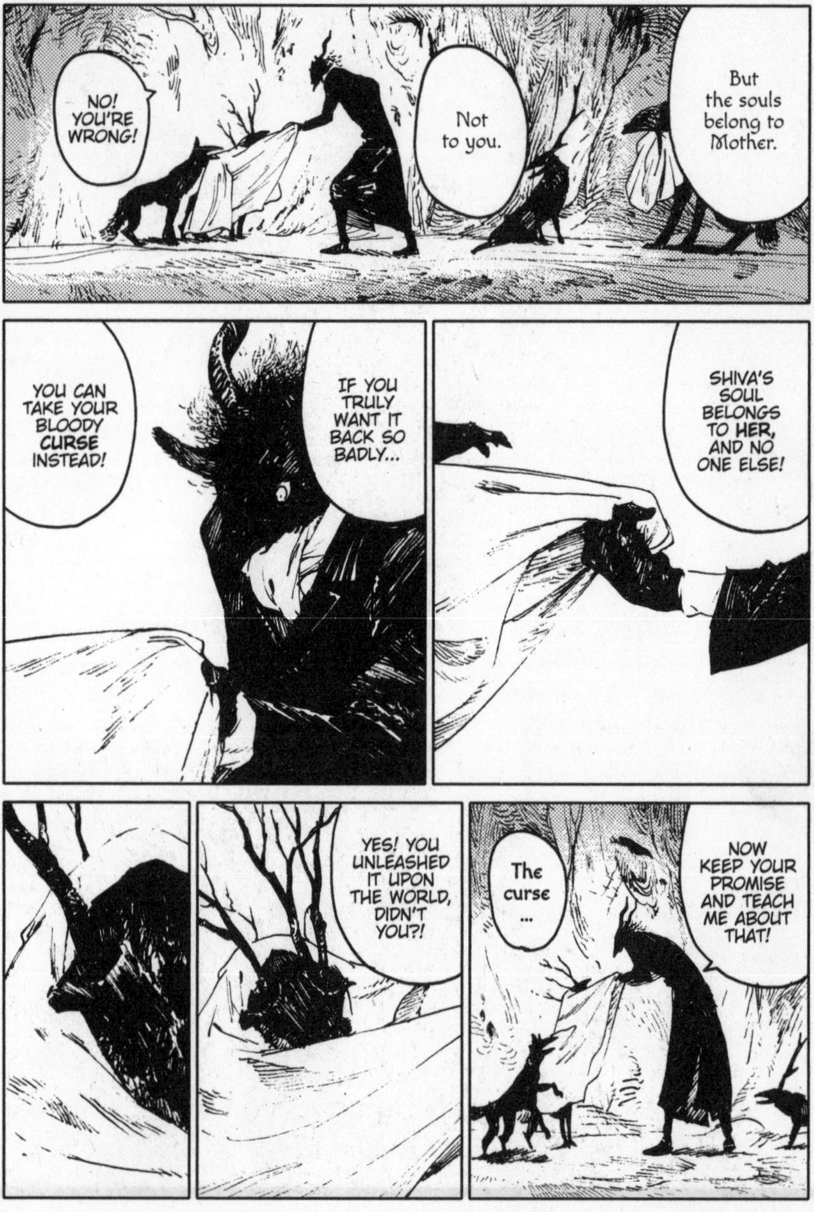
But the souls belong to Mother.
Not to you.
NO! YOU'RE WRONG!
SHIVA'S SOUL BELONGS TO **HER**, AND NO ONE ELSE!
IF YOU TRULY WANT IT BACK SO BADLY...
YOU CAN TAKE YOUR BLOODY **CURSE** INSTEAD!
NOW KEEP YOUR PROMISE AND TEACH ME ABOUT THAT!
The curse ...
YES! YOU UNLEASHED IT UPON THE WORLD, DIDN'T YOU?!

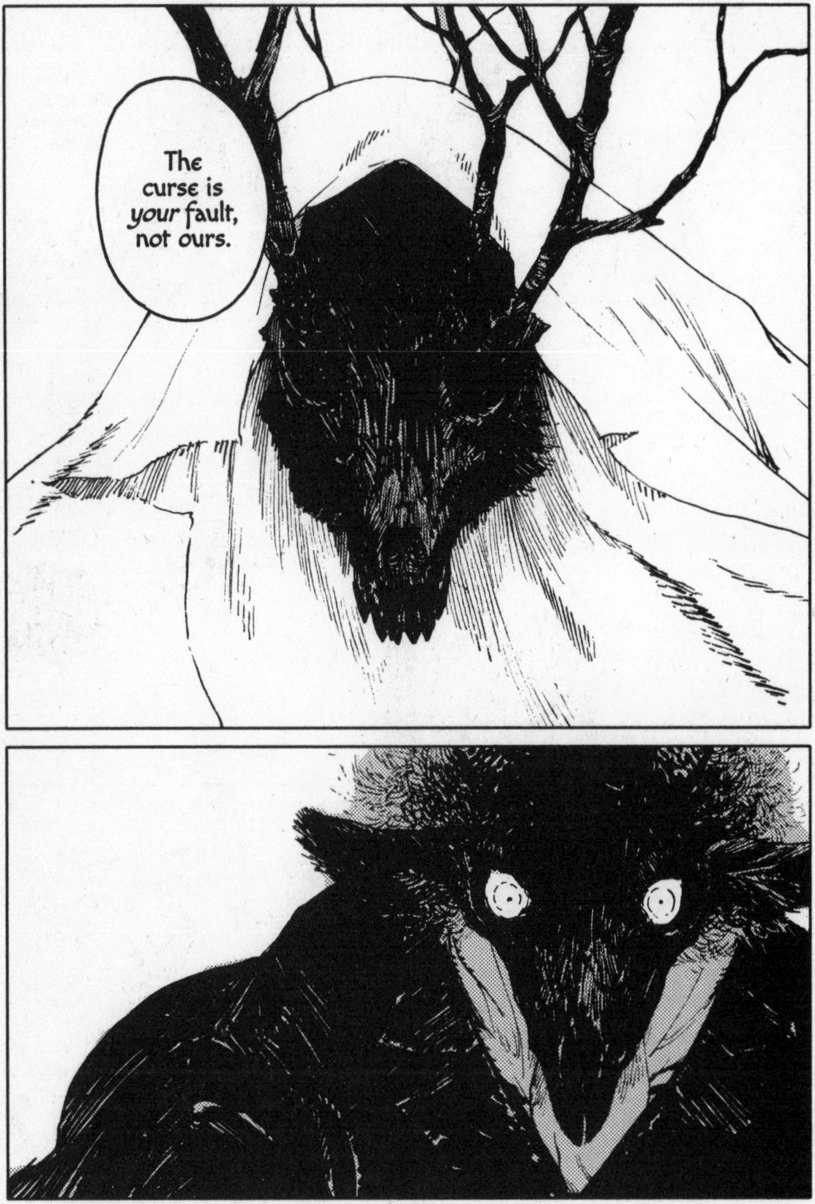
The curse is *your* fault, not ours.

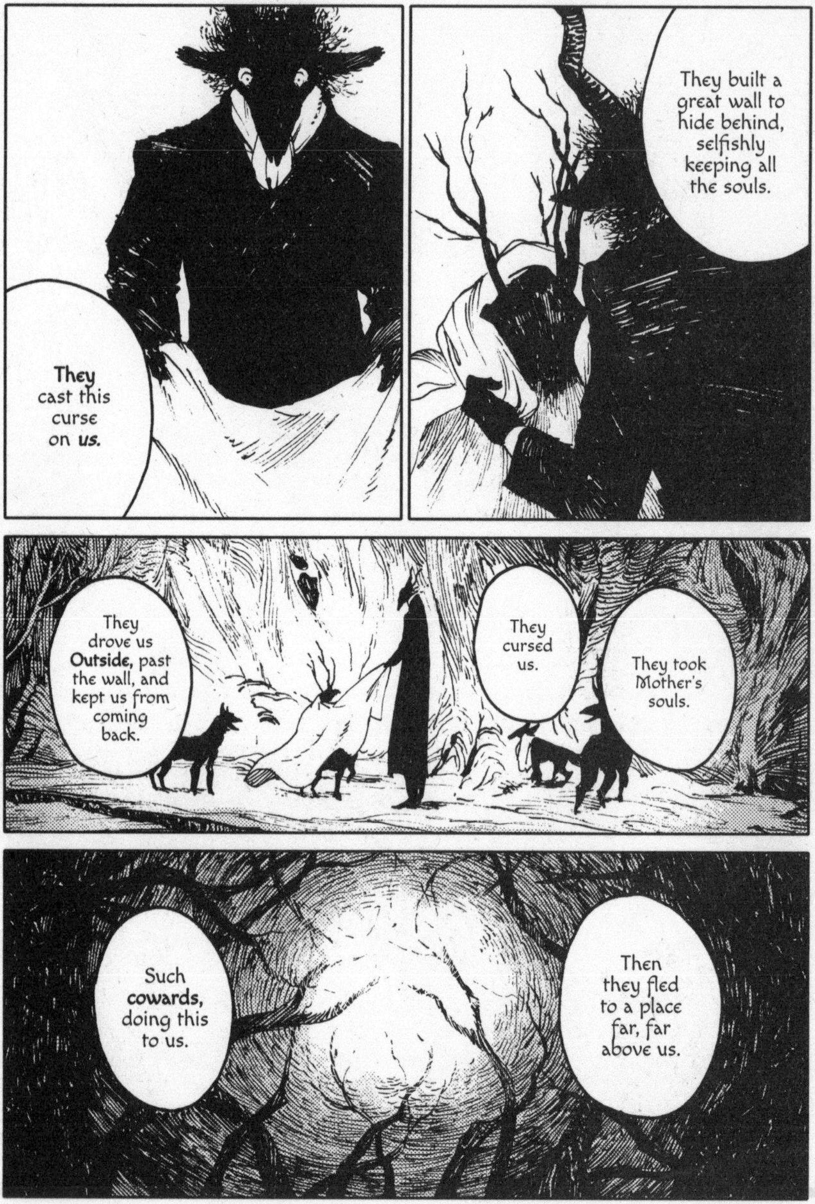
They built a great wall to hide behind, selfishly keeping all the souls.
They cast this curse on ***us.***
They took Mother's souls.
They cursed us.
They drove us **Outside,** past the wall, and kept us from coming back.
Then they fled to a place far, far above us.
Such **cowards,** doing this to us.

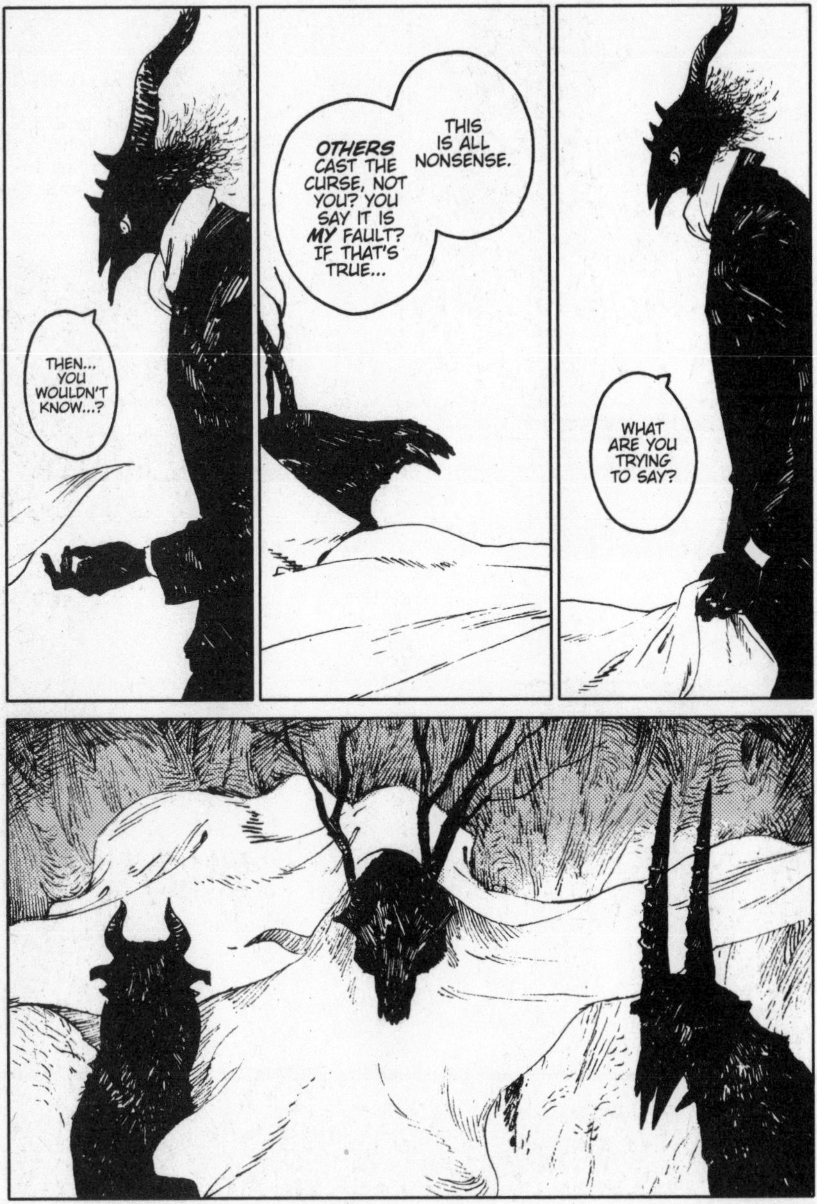
WHAT ARE YOU TRYING TO SAY?
THIS IS ALL NONSENSE.
OTHERS CAST THE CURSE, NOT YOU? YOU SAY IT IS ***MY*** FAULT? IF THAT'S TRUE...
THEN... YOU WOULDN'T KNOW...?

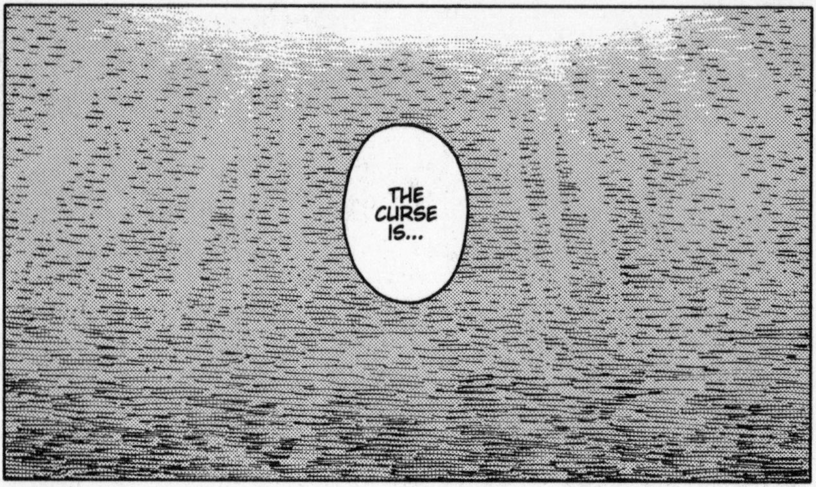
THE CURSE IS...

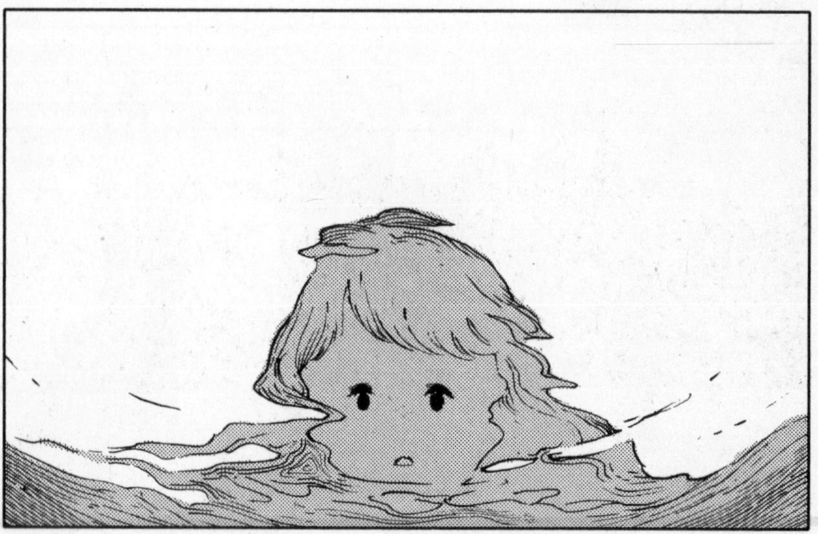

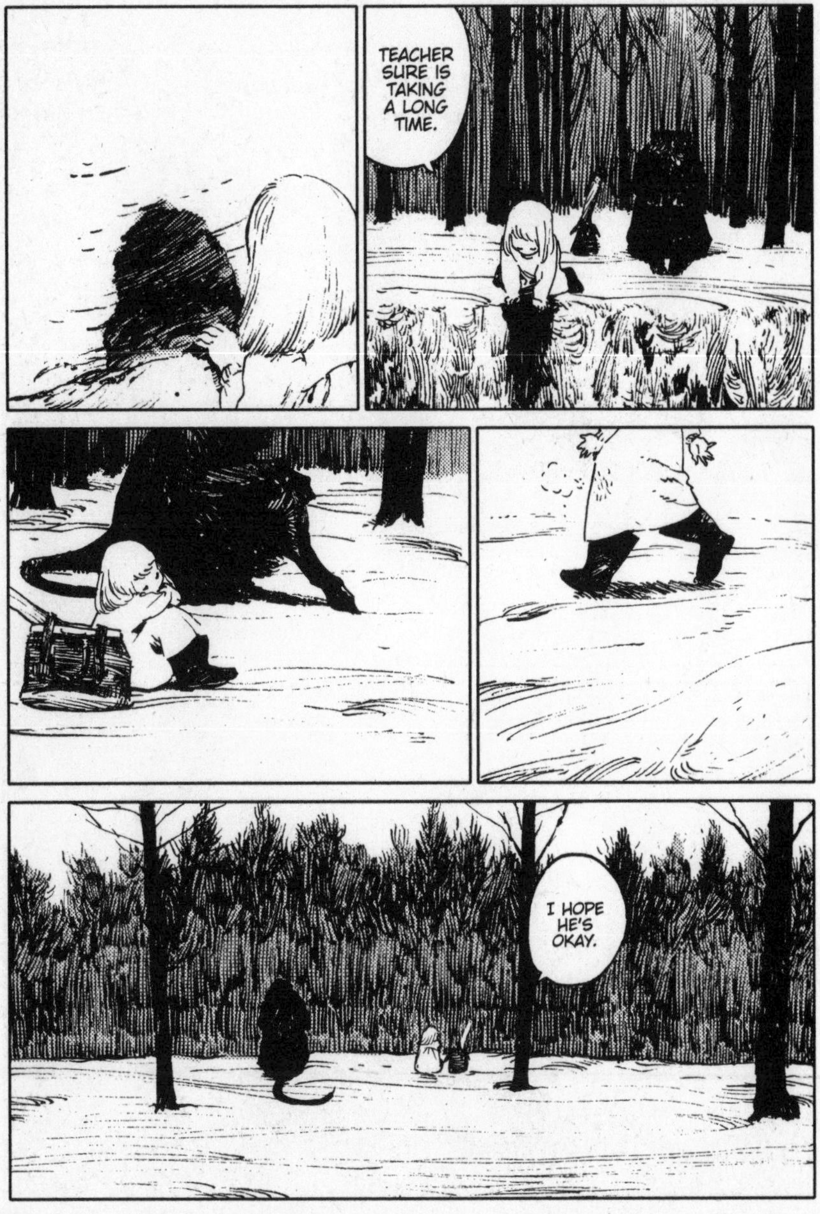
TEACHER SURE IS TAKING A LONG TIME.
I HOPE HE'S OKAY.

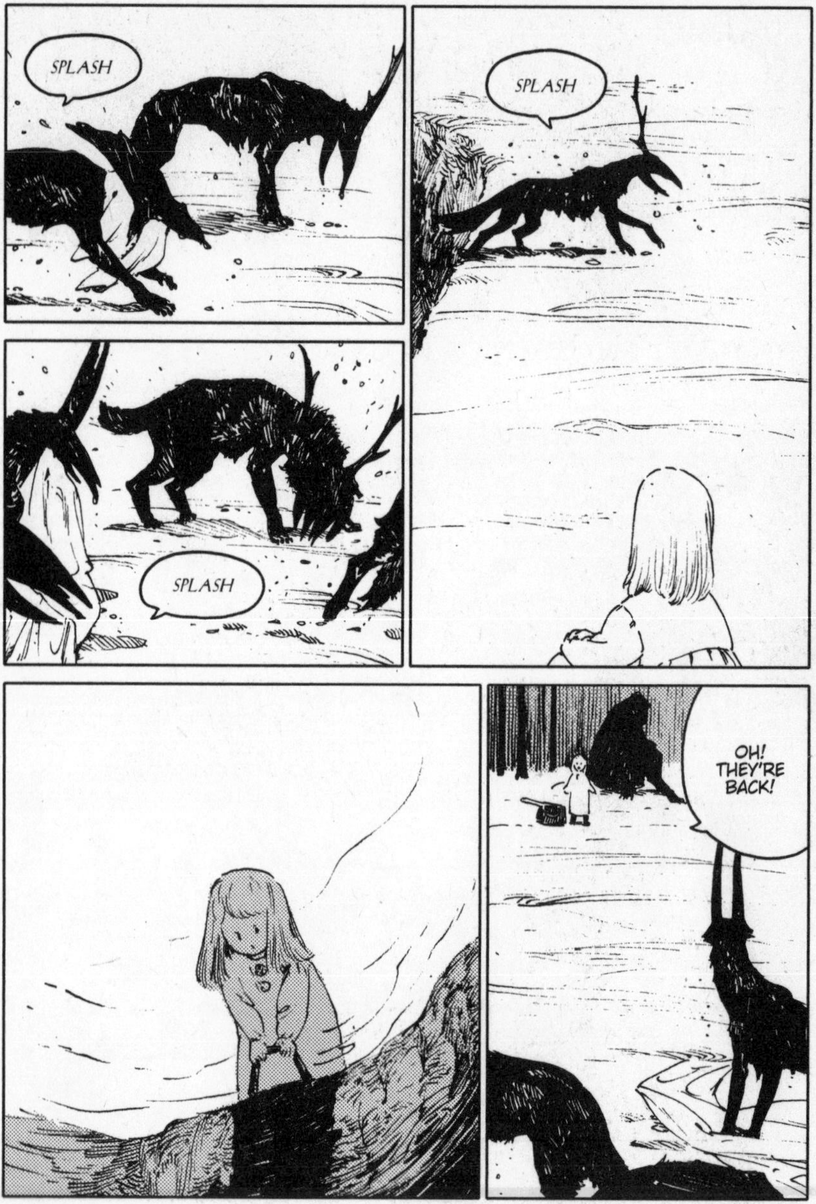
SPLASH
SPLASH
SPLASH
OH! THEY'RE BACK!

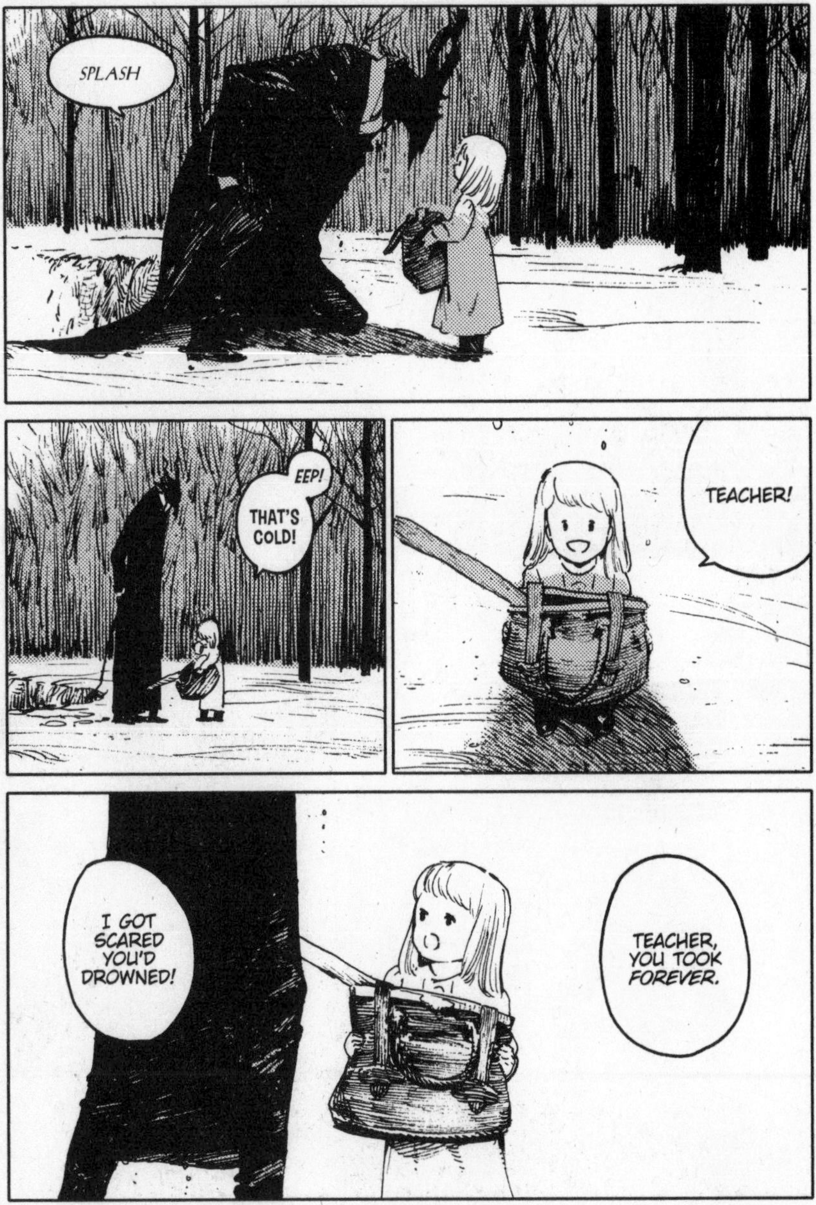
SPLASH
TEACHER!
EEP!
THAT'S COLD!
TEACHER, YOU TOOK FOREVER.
I GOT SCARED YOU'D DROWNED!

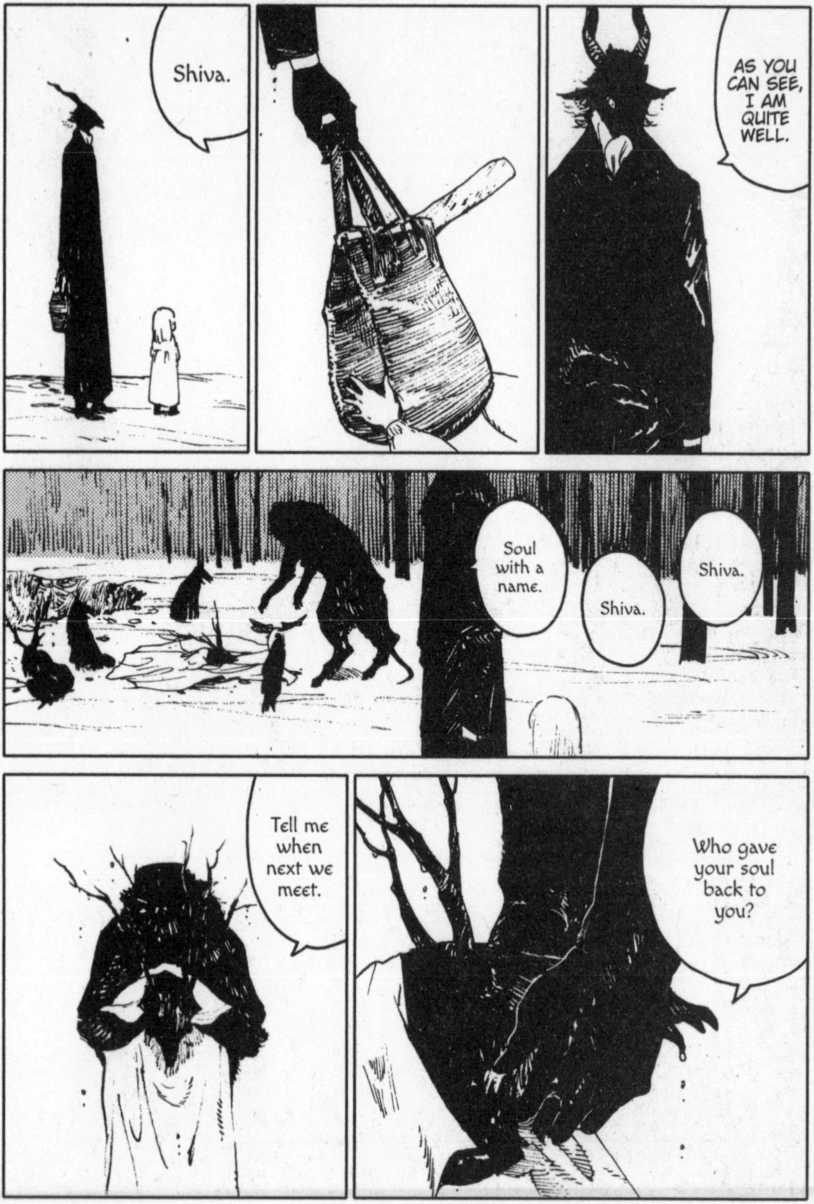
AS YOU CAN SEE, I AM QUITE WELL.
Shiva.
Shiva.
Shiva.
Soul with a name.
Who gave your soul back to you?
Tell me when next we meet.

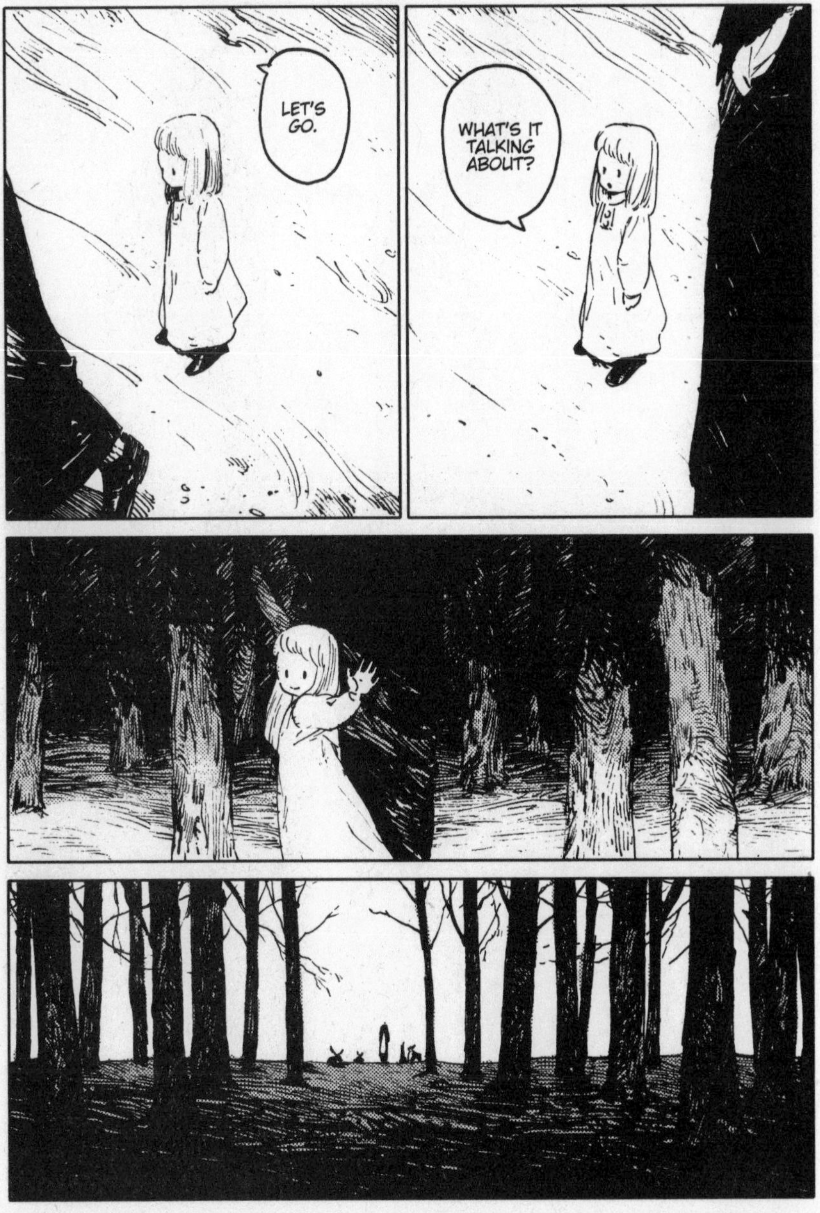
WHAT'S IT TALKING ABOUT?
LET'S GO.

TEACH-
ER?
YES?
WHAT'D YOU AND THE BIG BLACK ONE TALK ABOUT?
OH...
THIS AND THAT.
AHH.
DON'T WORRY, I DIDN'T FORGET.

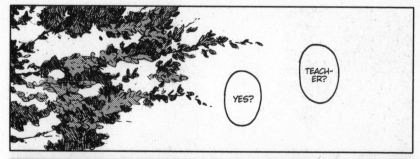

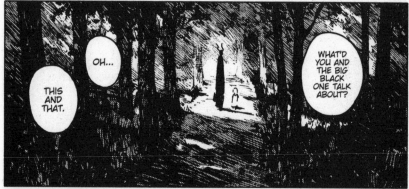

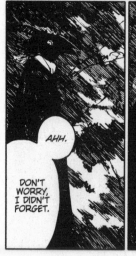

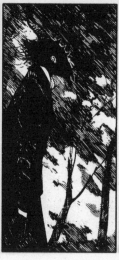

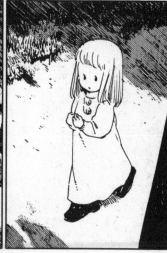

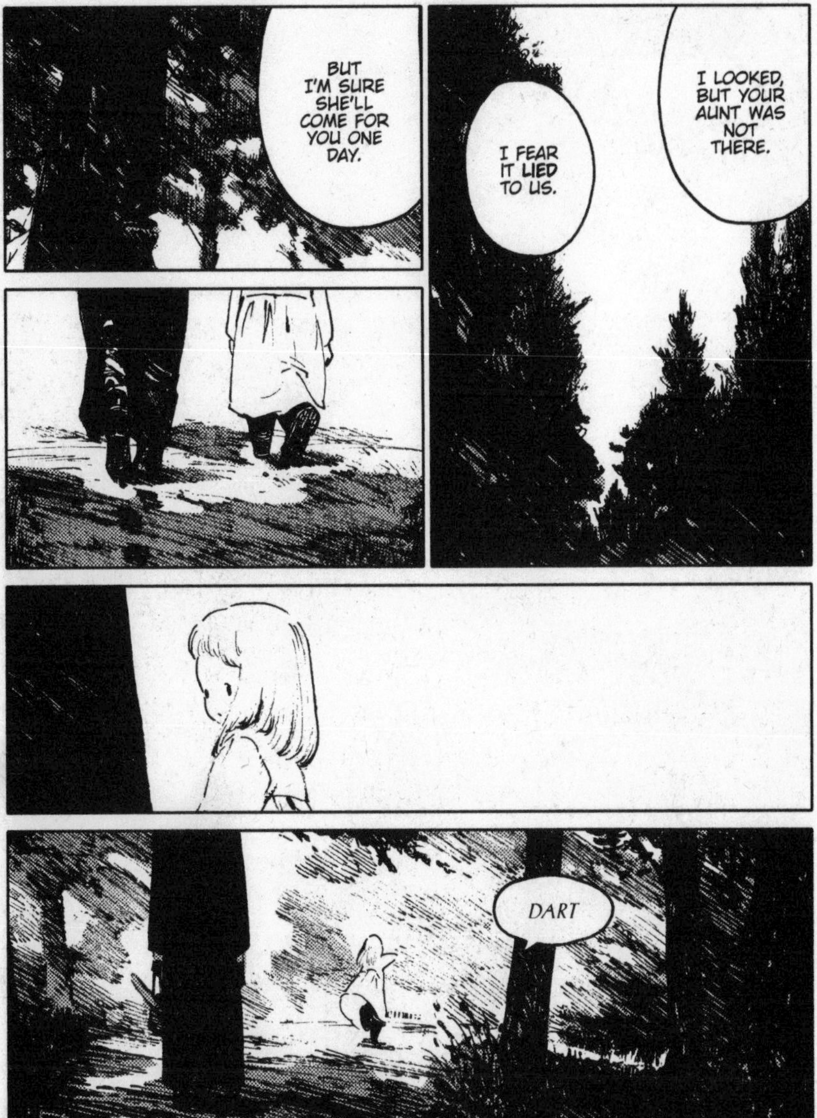
I LOOKED, BUT YOUR AUNT WAS NOT THERE.
I FEAR IT LIED TO US.
BUT I'M SURE SHE'LL COME FOR YOU ONE DAY.
DART

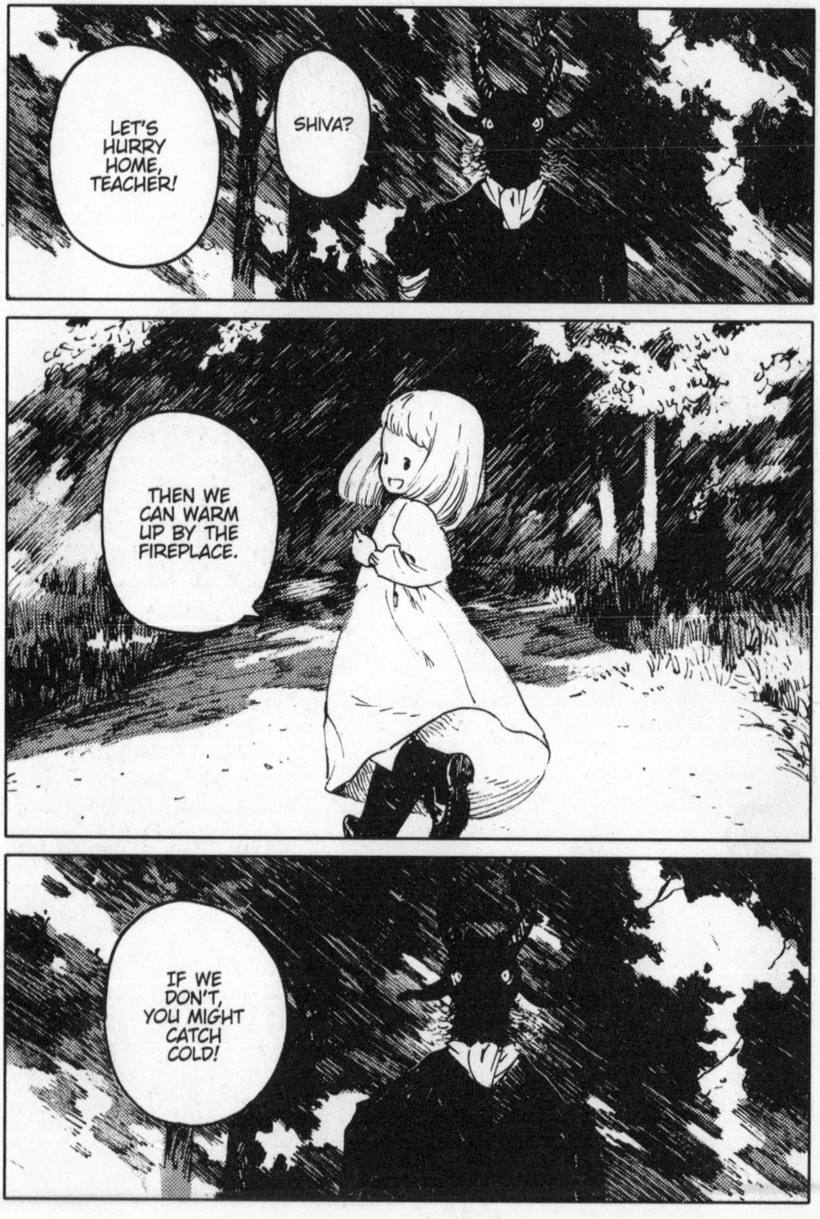
SHIVA?
LET'S HURRY HOME, TEACHER!
THEN WE CAN WARM UP BY THE FIREPLACE.
IF WE DON'T, YOU MIGHT CATCH COLD!

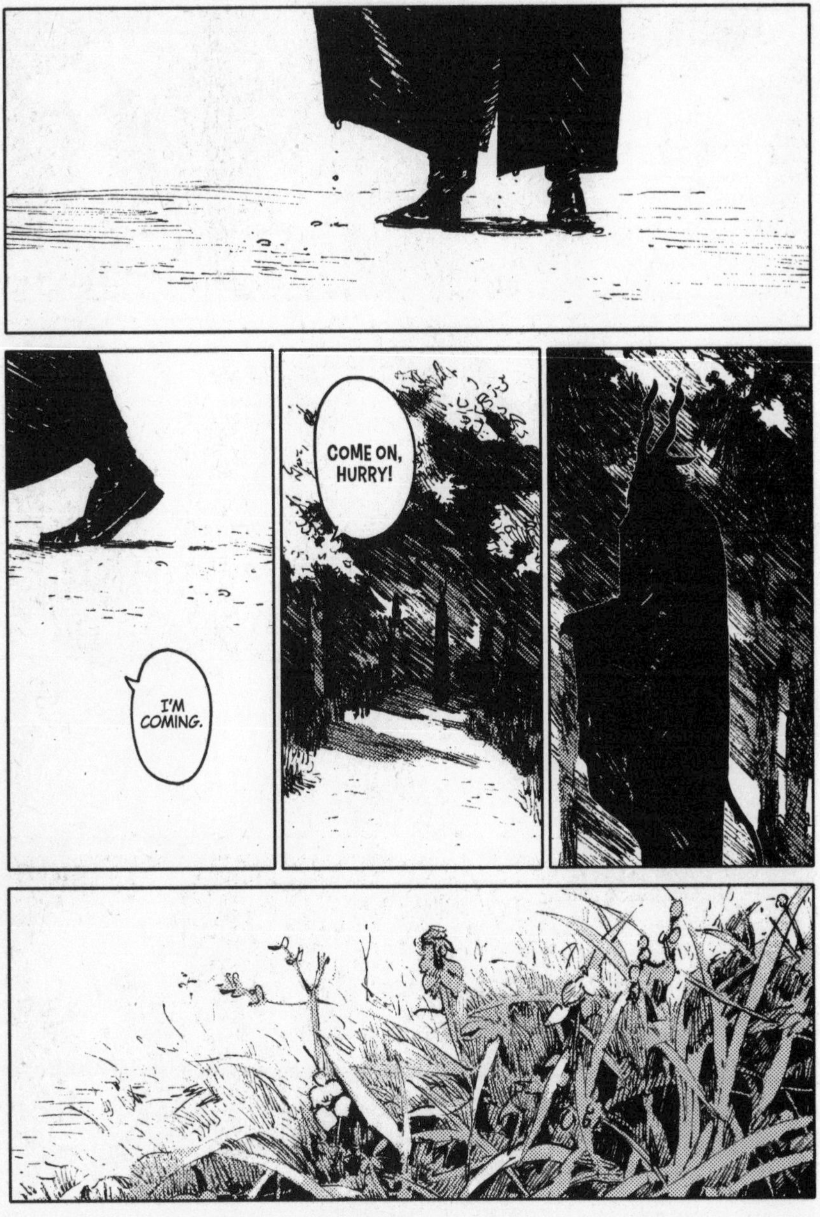
COME ON, HURRY!
I'M COMING.

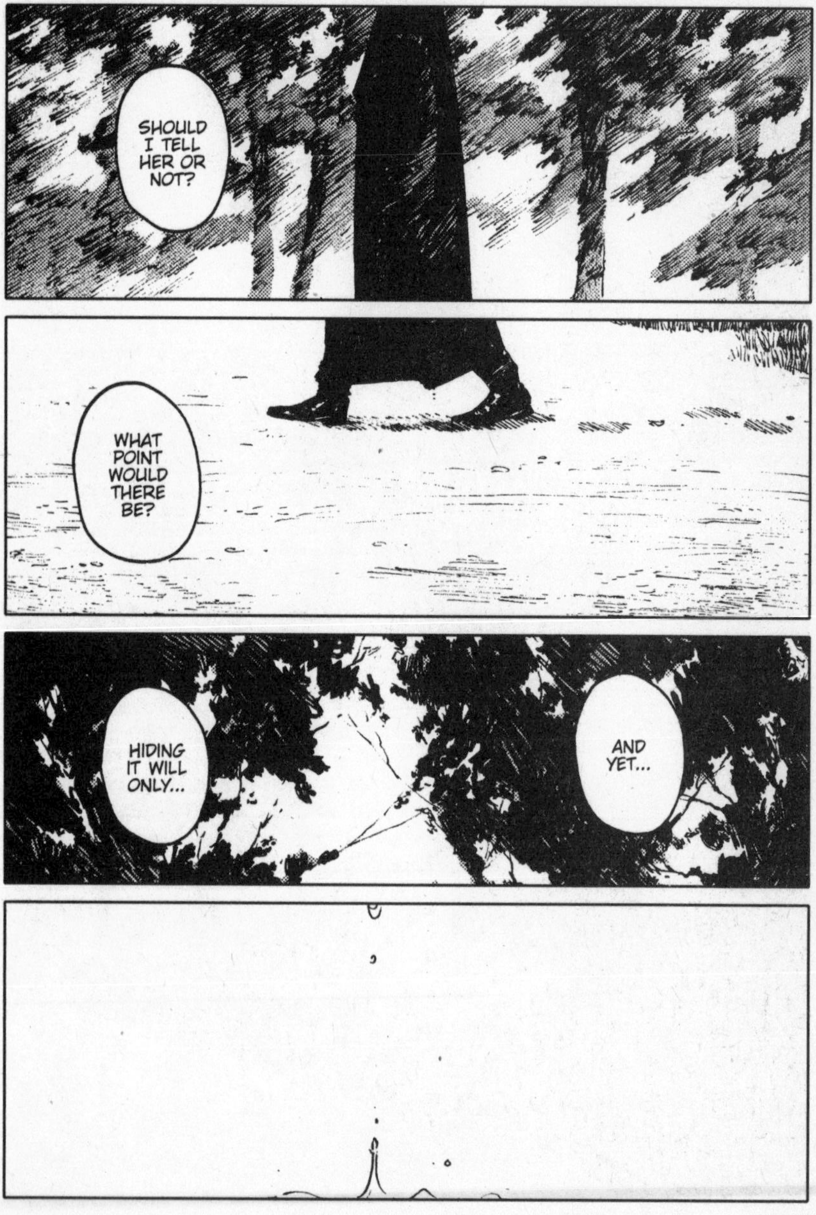
SHOULD I TELL HER OR NOT?
WHAT POINT WOULD THERE BE?
AND YET...
HIDING IT WILL ONLY...

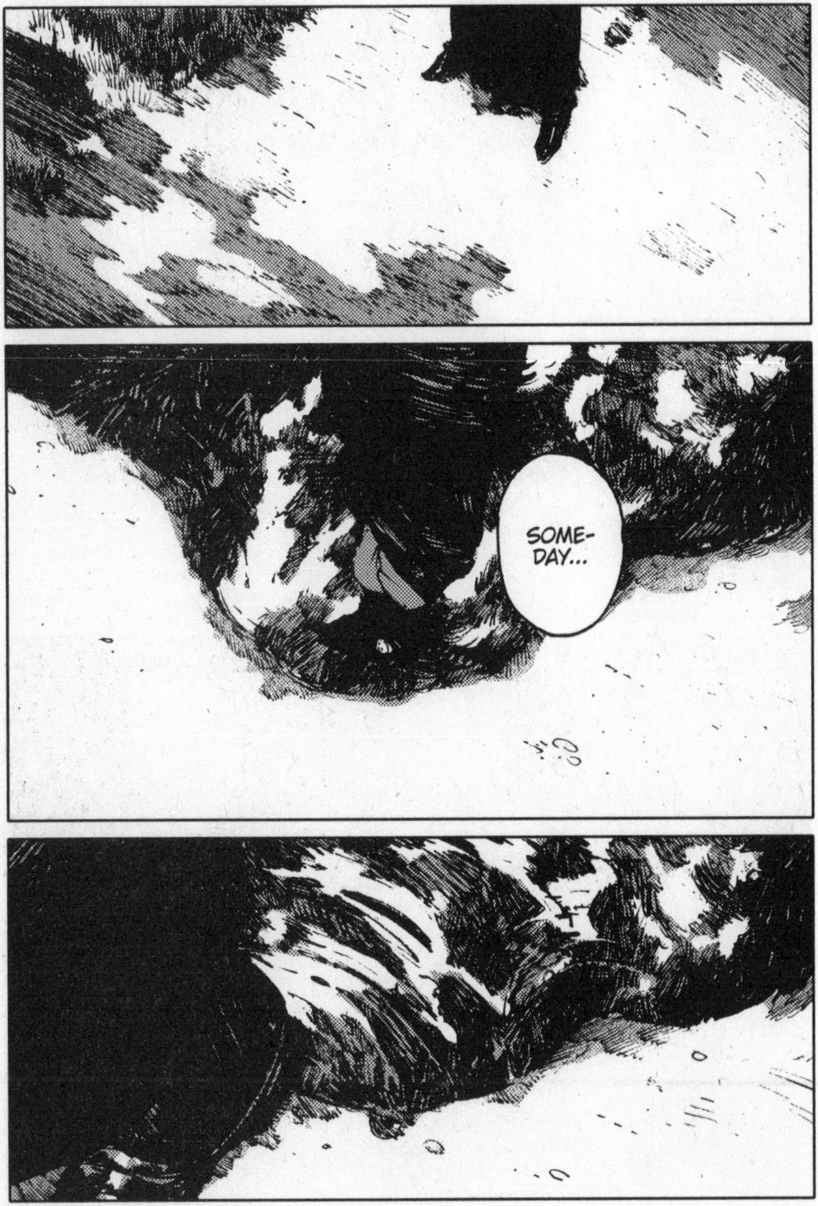
SOME-
DAY...

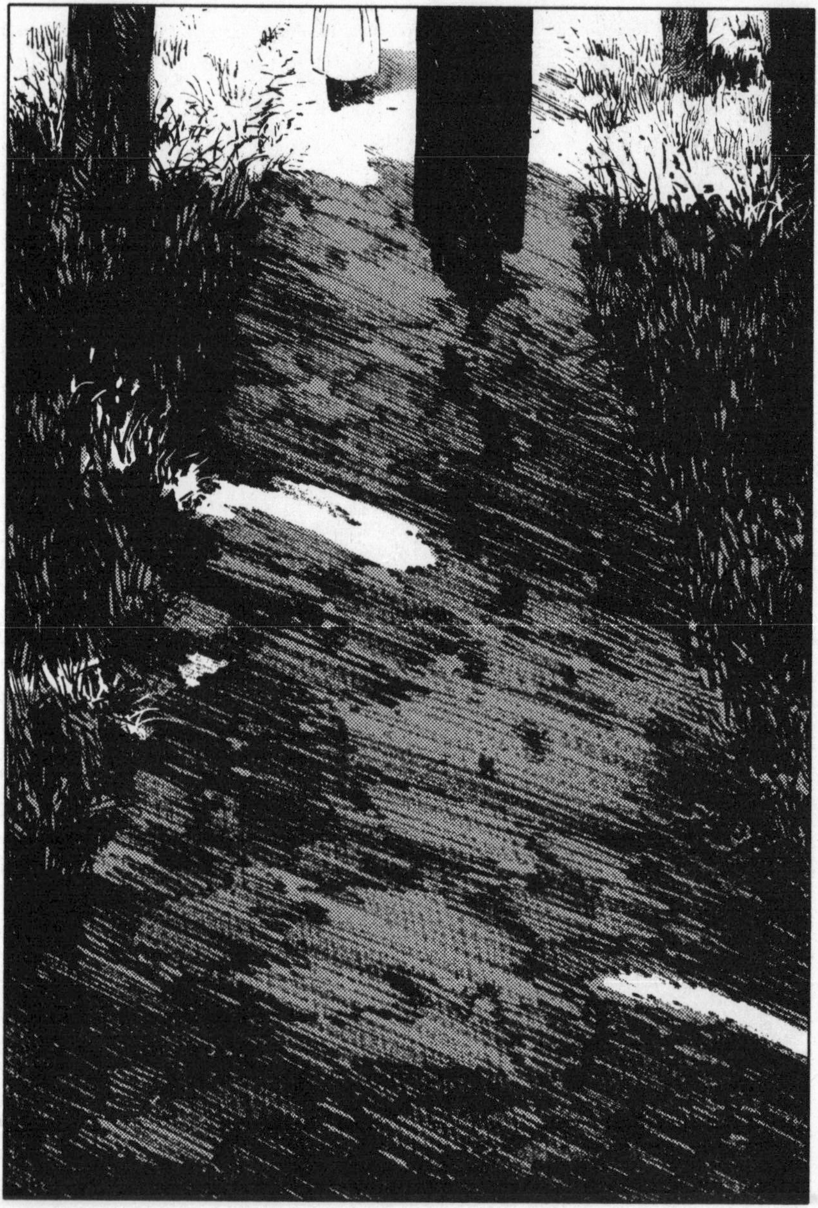

Chapter 9

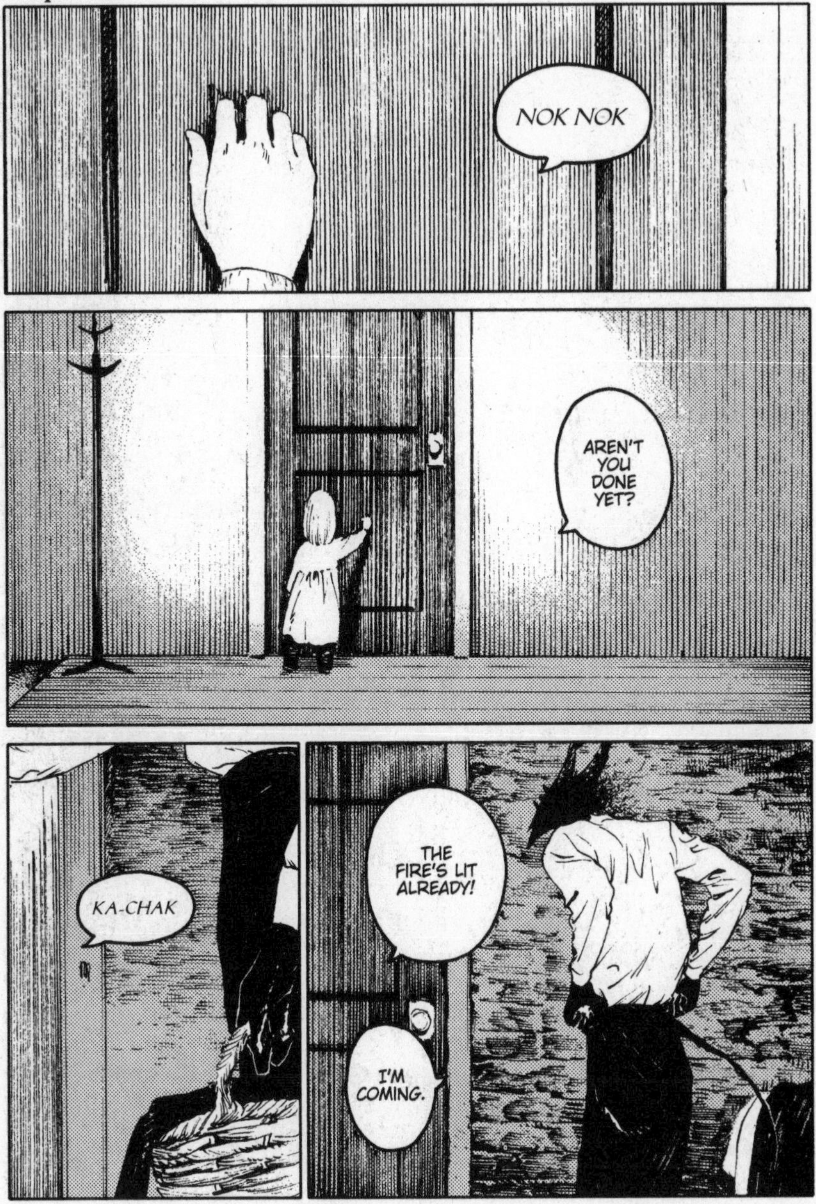
NOK NOK
AREN'T YOU DONE YET?
THE FIRE'S LIT ALREADY!
I'M COMING.
KA-CHAK

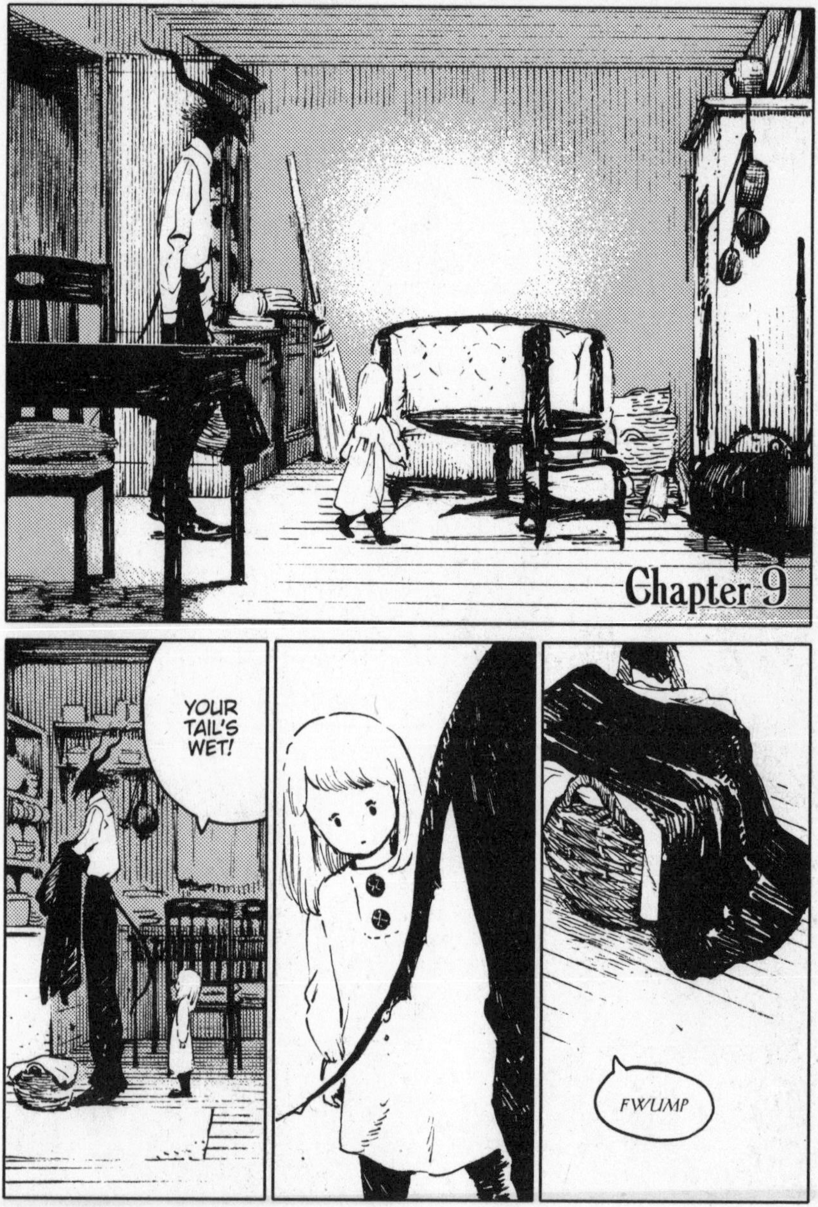
Chapter 9
FWUMP
YOUR TAIL'S WET!

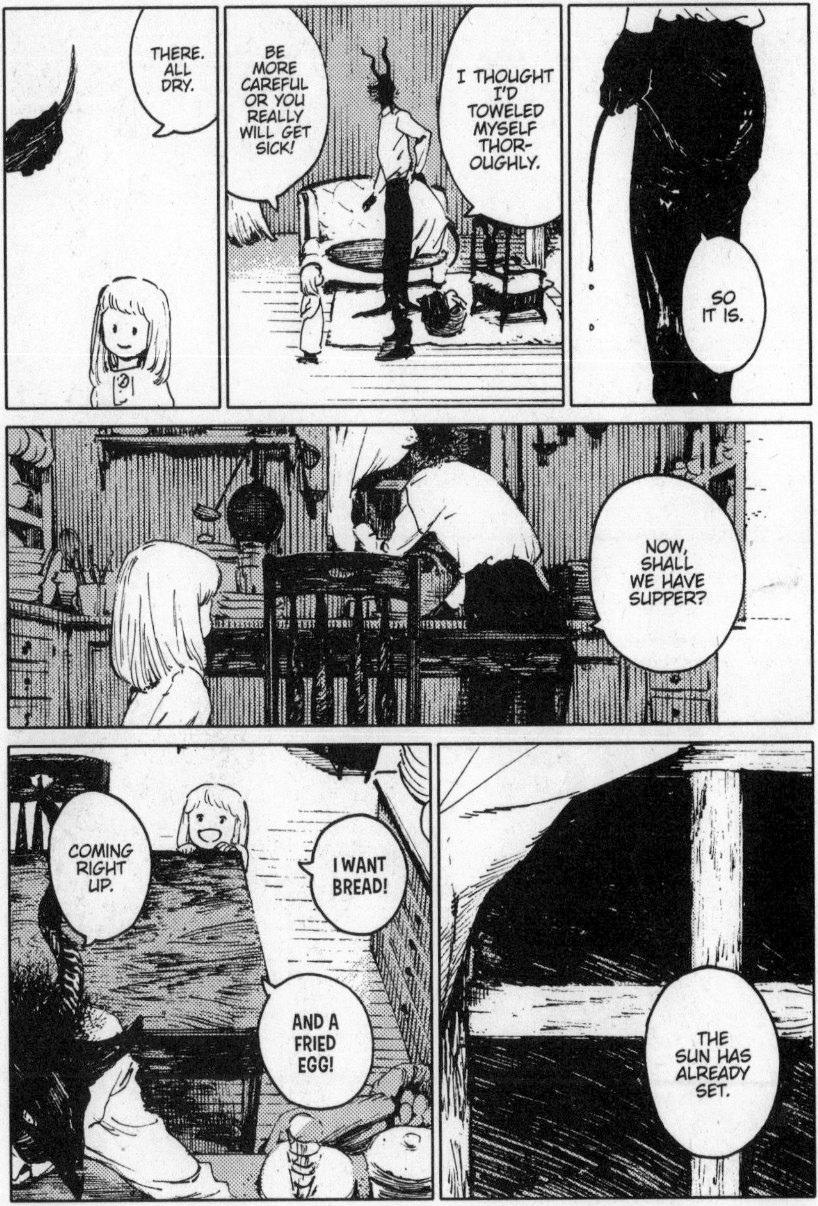
SO IT IS.
I THOUGHT I'D TOWELED MYSELF THOROUGHLY.
BE MORE CAREFUL OR YOU REALLY WILL GET SICK!
THERE. ALL DRY.
NOW, SHALL WE HAVE SUPPER?
THE SUN HAS ALREADY SET.
I WANT BREAD!
AND A FRIED EGG!
COMING RIGHT UP.

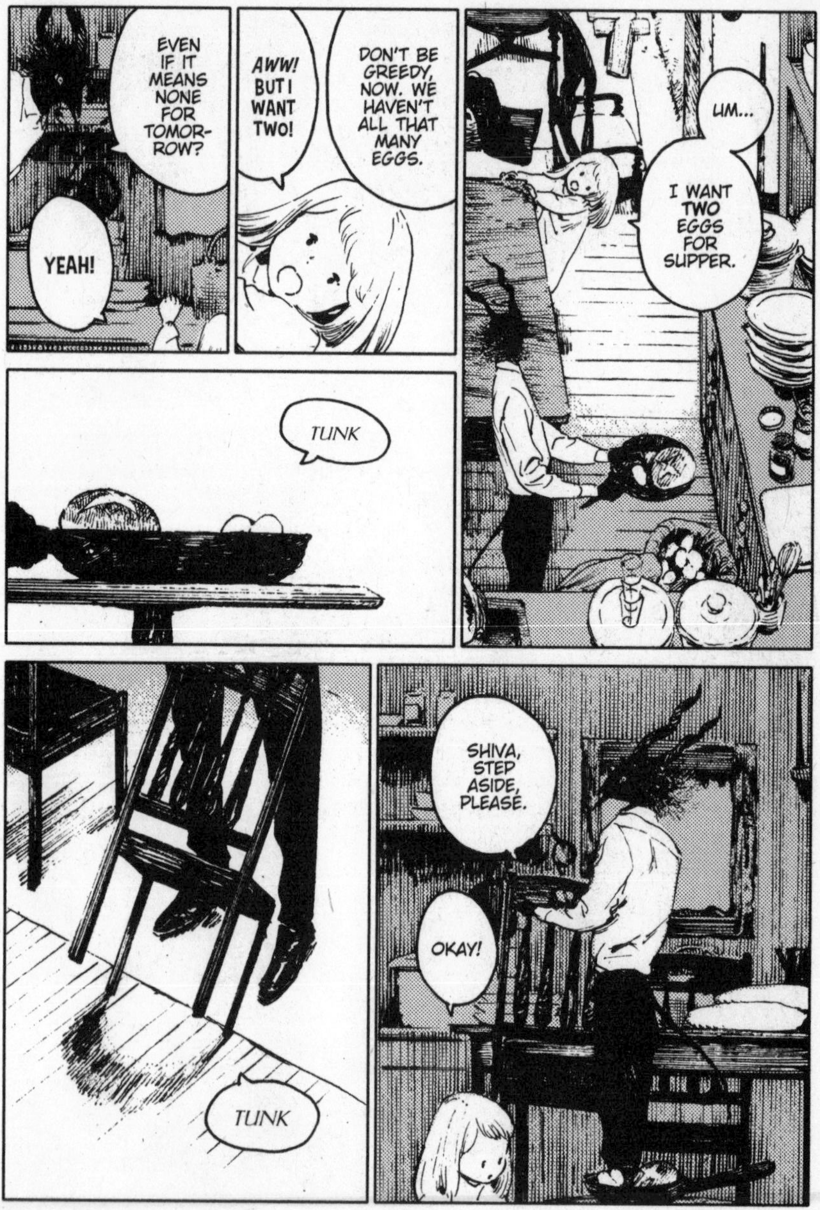
UM...
I WANT TWO EGGS FOR SUPPER.
DON'T BE GREEDY, NOW. WE HAVEN'T ALL THAT MANY EGGS.
AWW! BUT I WANT TWO!
EVEN IF IT MEANS NONE FOR TOMORROW?
YEAH!
TUNK
SHIVA, STEP ASIDE, PLEASE.
OKAY!
TUNK

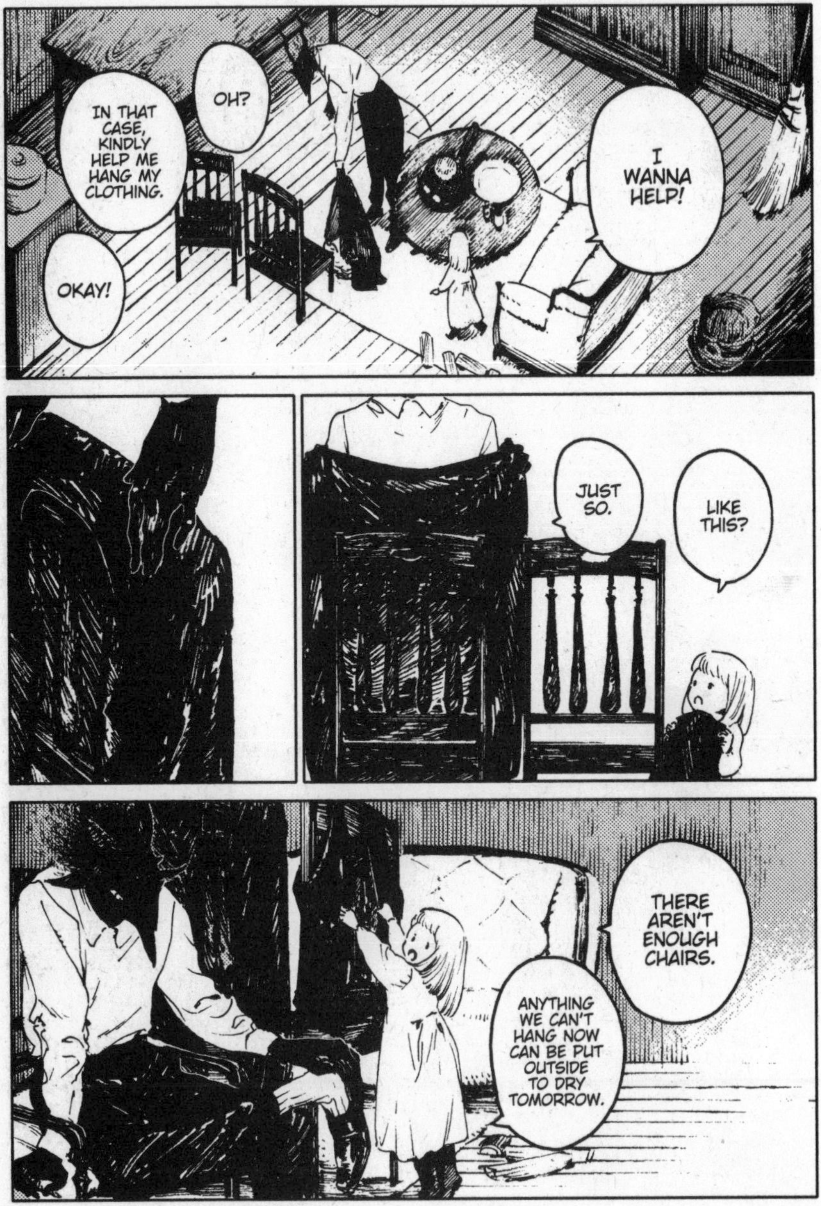
I WANNA HELP!
OH?
IN THAT CASE, KINDLY HELP ME HANG MY CLOTHING.
OKAY!
LIKE THIS?
JUST SO.
THERE AREN'T ENOUGH CHAIRS.
ANYTHING WE CAN'T HANG NOW CAN BE PUT OUTSIDE TO DRY TOMORROW.

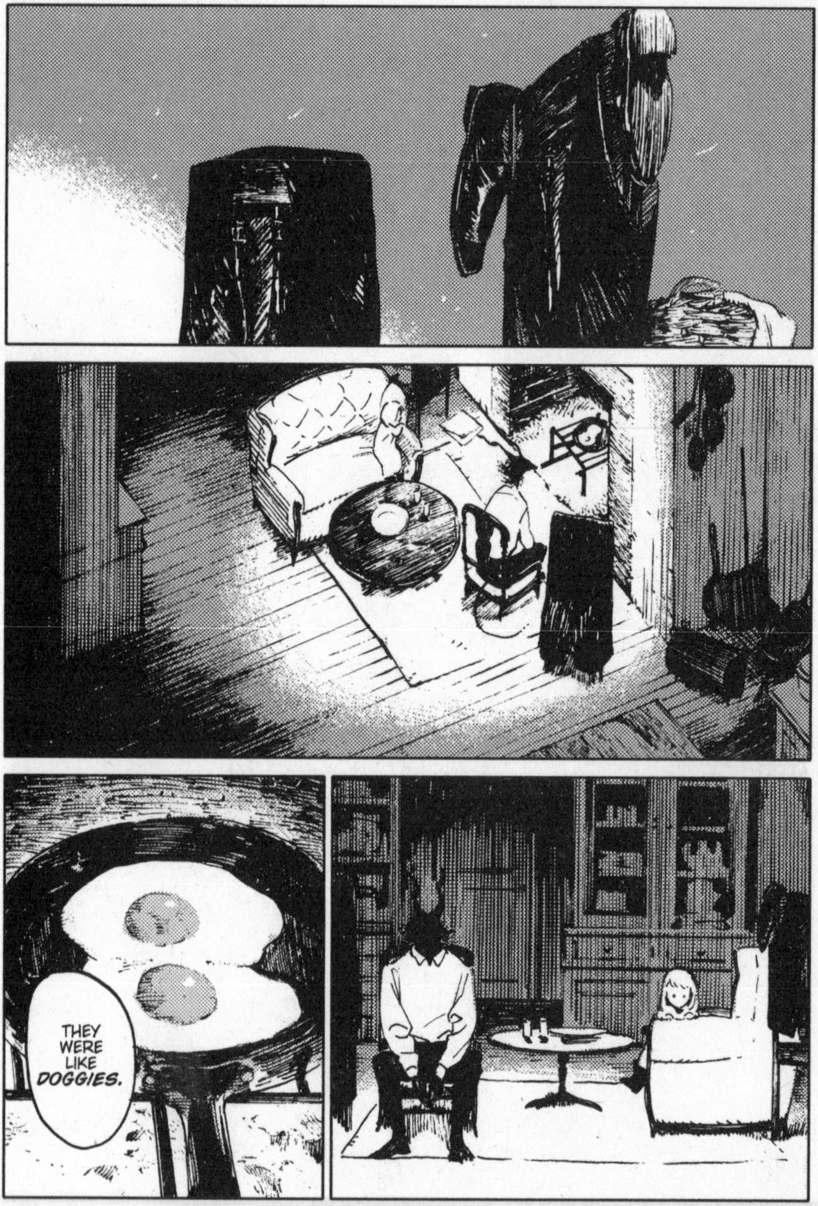
THEY WERE LIKE DOGGIES.

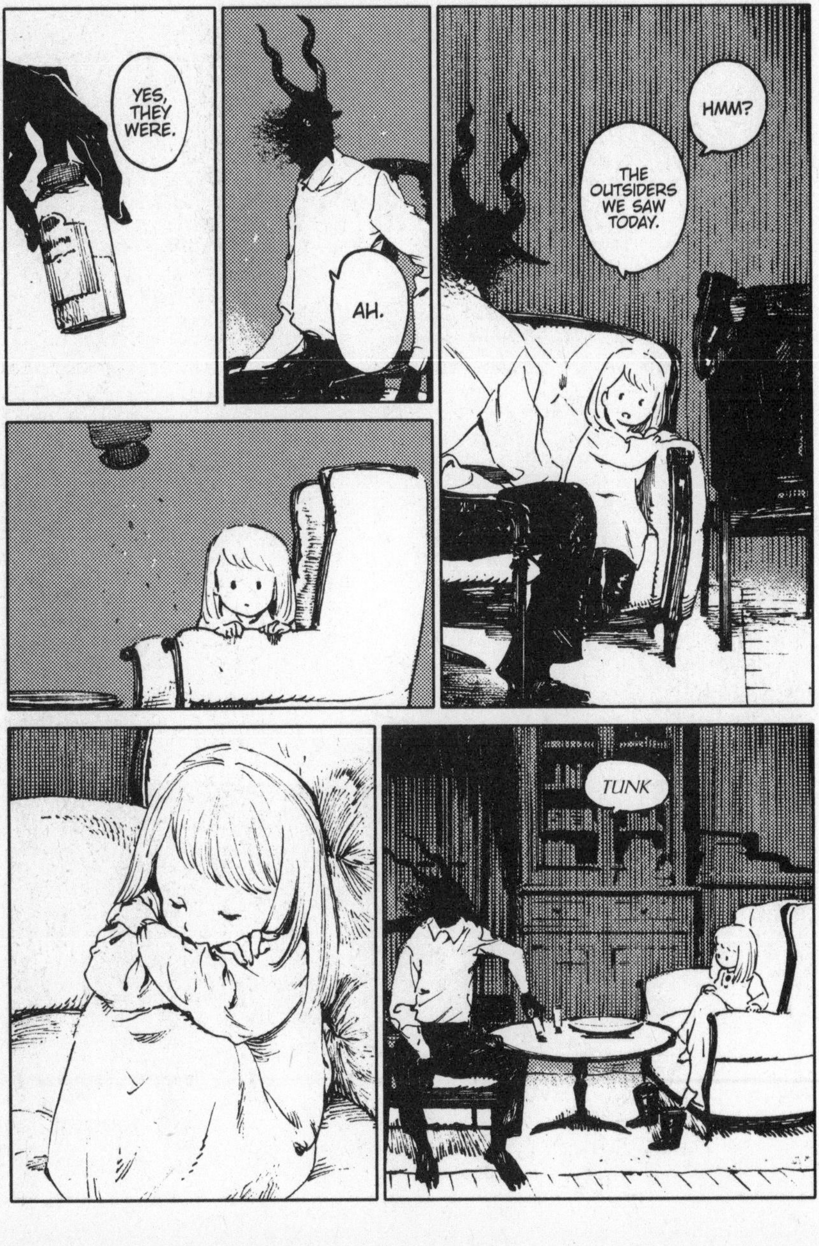
HMM?
THE OUTSIDERS WE SAW TODAY.
AH.
YES, THEY WERE.
TUNK

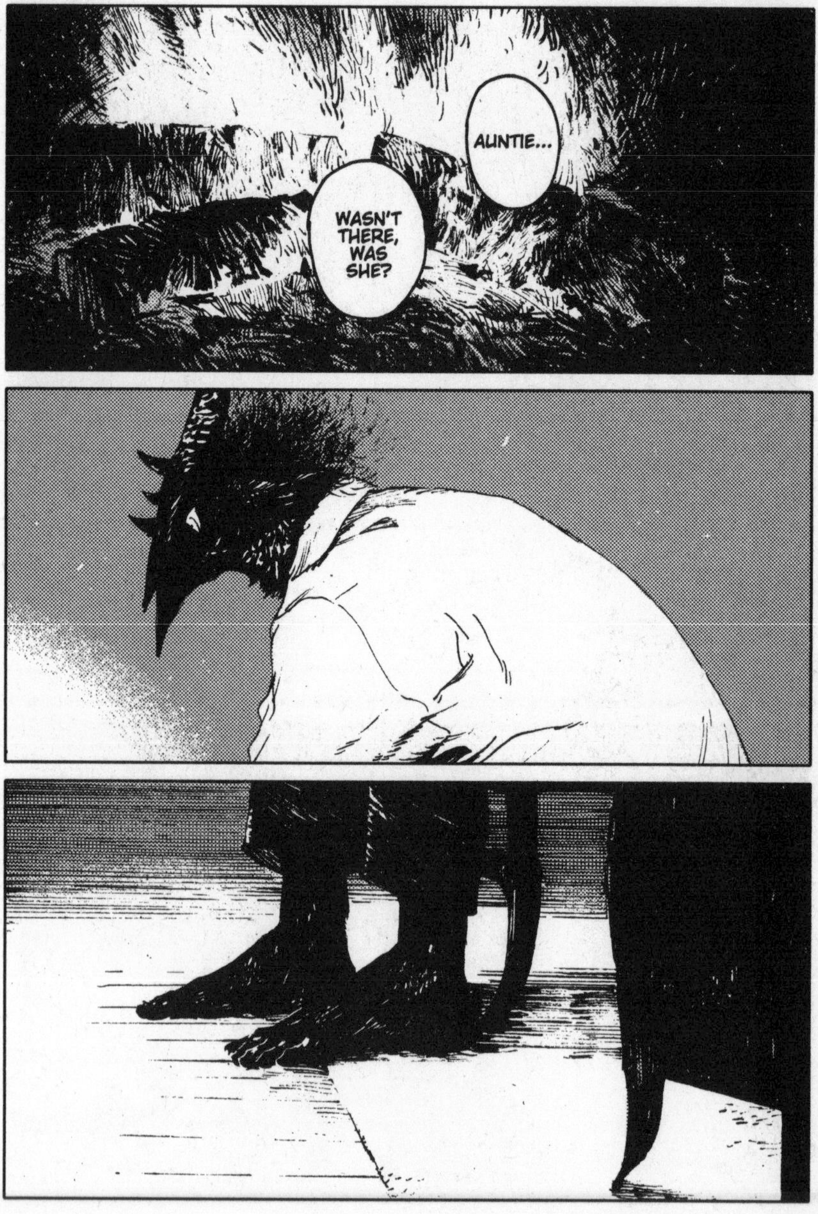
AUNTIE...
WASN'T THERE, WAS SHE?

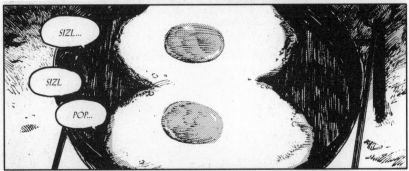

SIZL...

SIZL

POP...

TEACH-ER?

TEACHER, THE EGGS'RE GONNA BURN.

WHAT'S THE MATTER?

AH!

THAT'S RIGHT.

THE EGGS!

OH.

WHAT IS IT?

HM?

DIG IN.

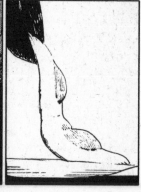

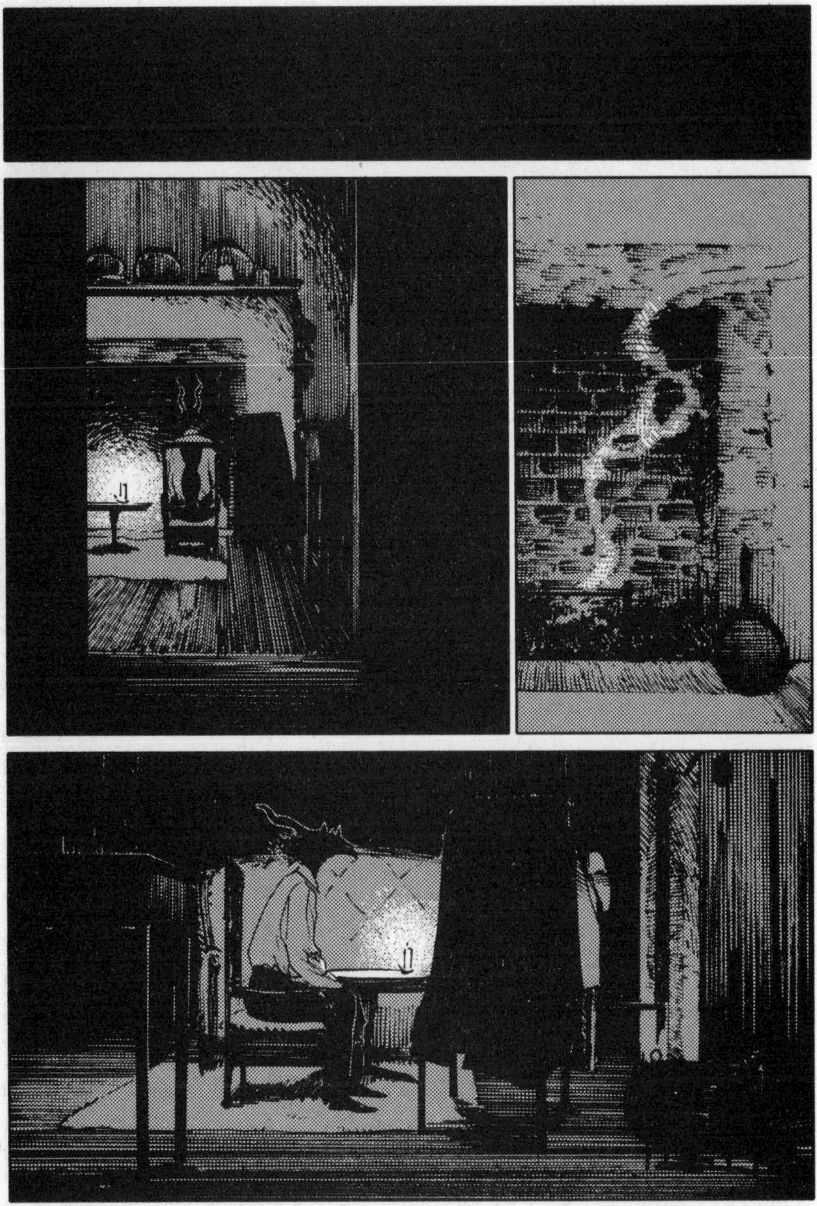

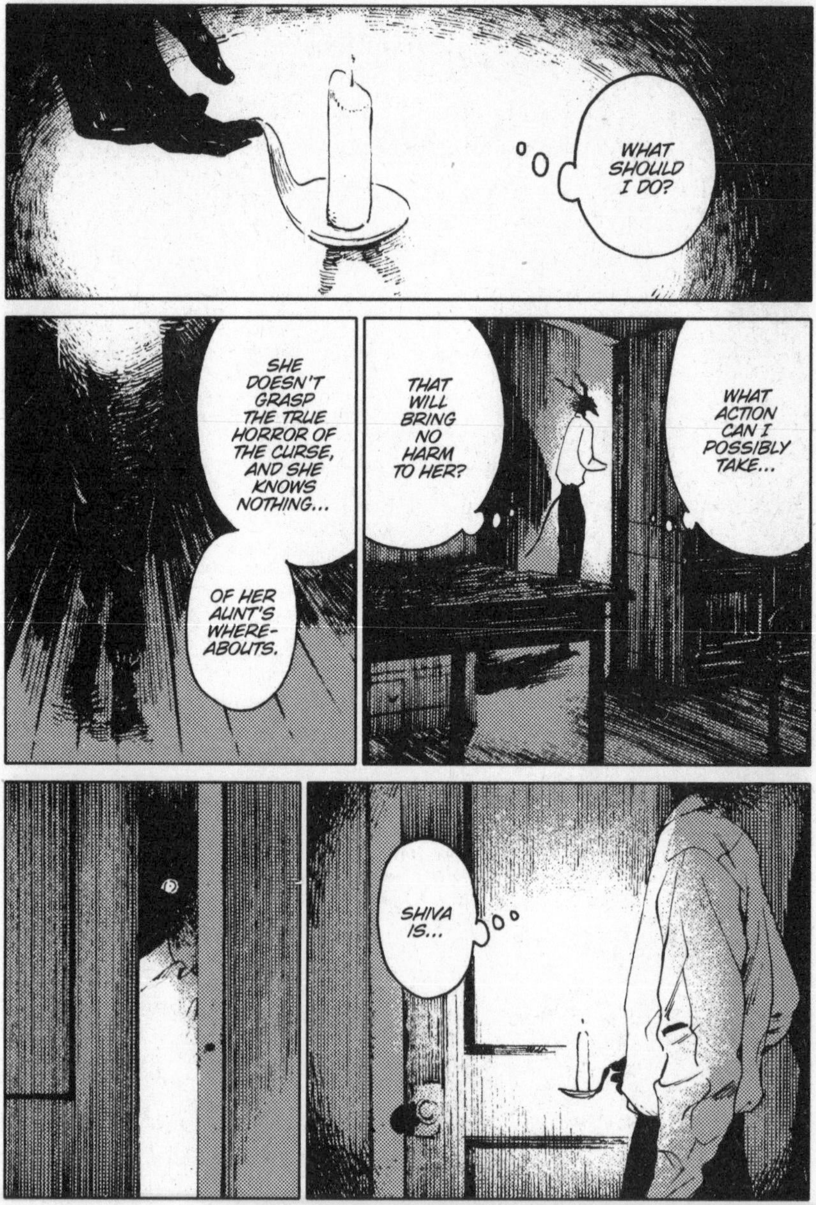
WHAT SHOULD I DO?
WHAT ACTION CAN I POSSIBLY TAKE...
THAT WILL BRING NO HARM TO HER?
SHE DOESN'T GRASP THE TRUE HORROR OF THE CURSE, AND SHE KNOWS NOTHING...
OF HER AUNT'S WHERE-ABOUTS.
SHIVA IS...

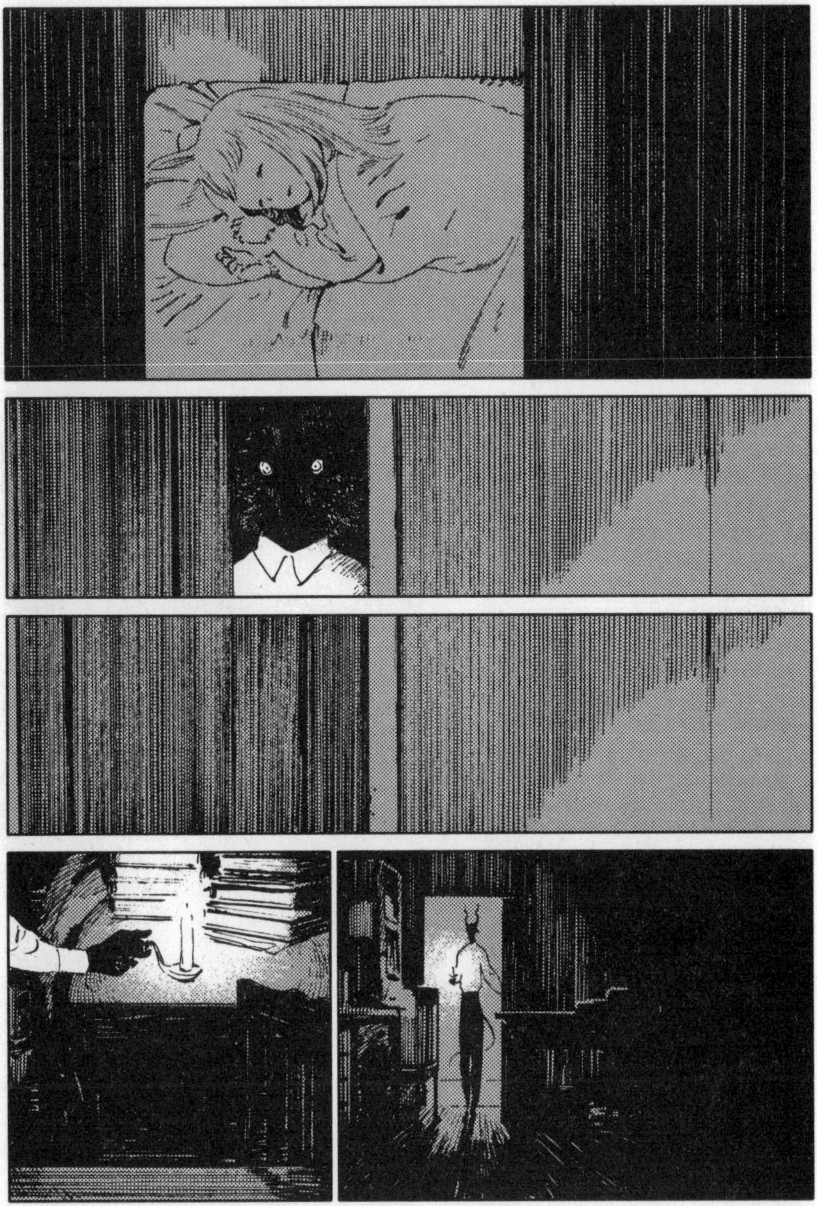

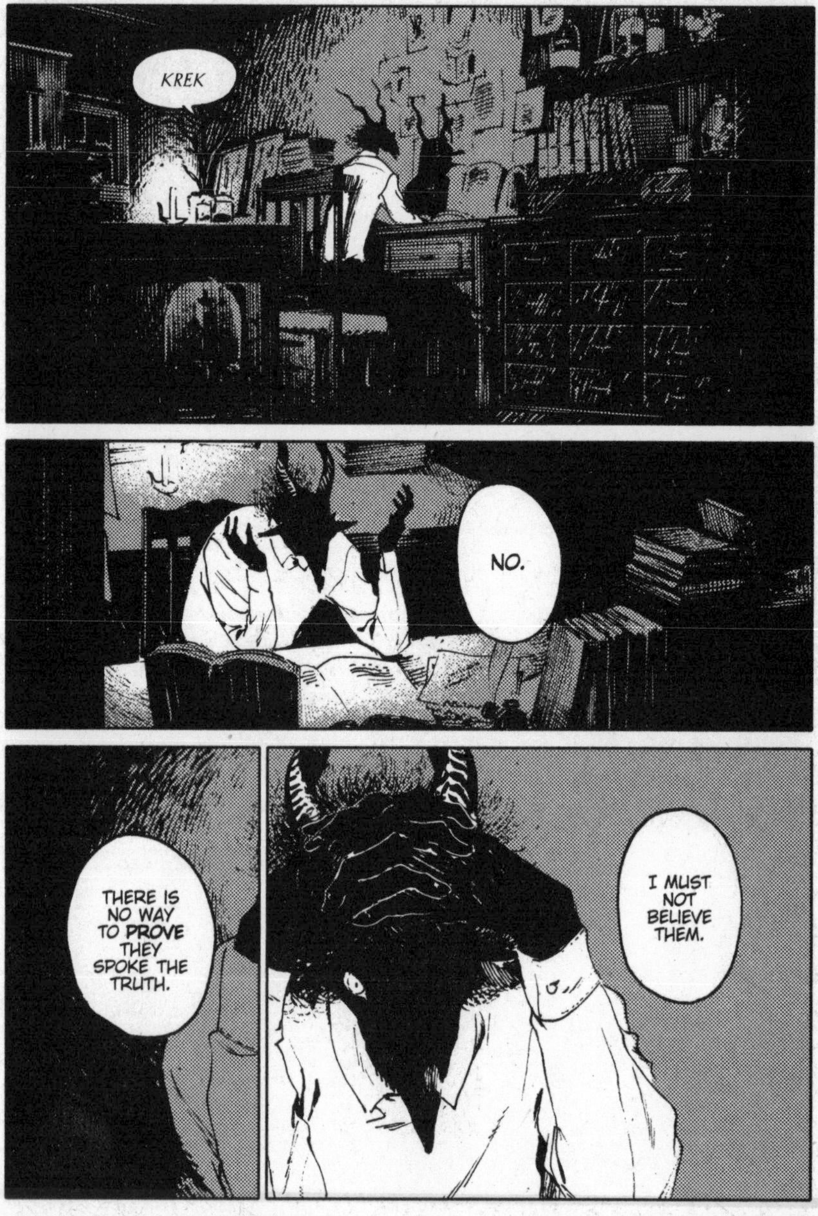
KREK
NO.
I MUST NOT BELIEVE THEM.
THERE IS NO WAY TO **PROVE** THEY SPOKE THE TRUTH.

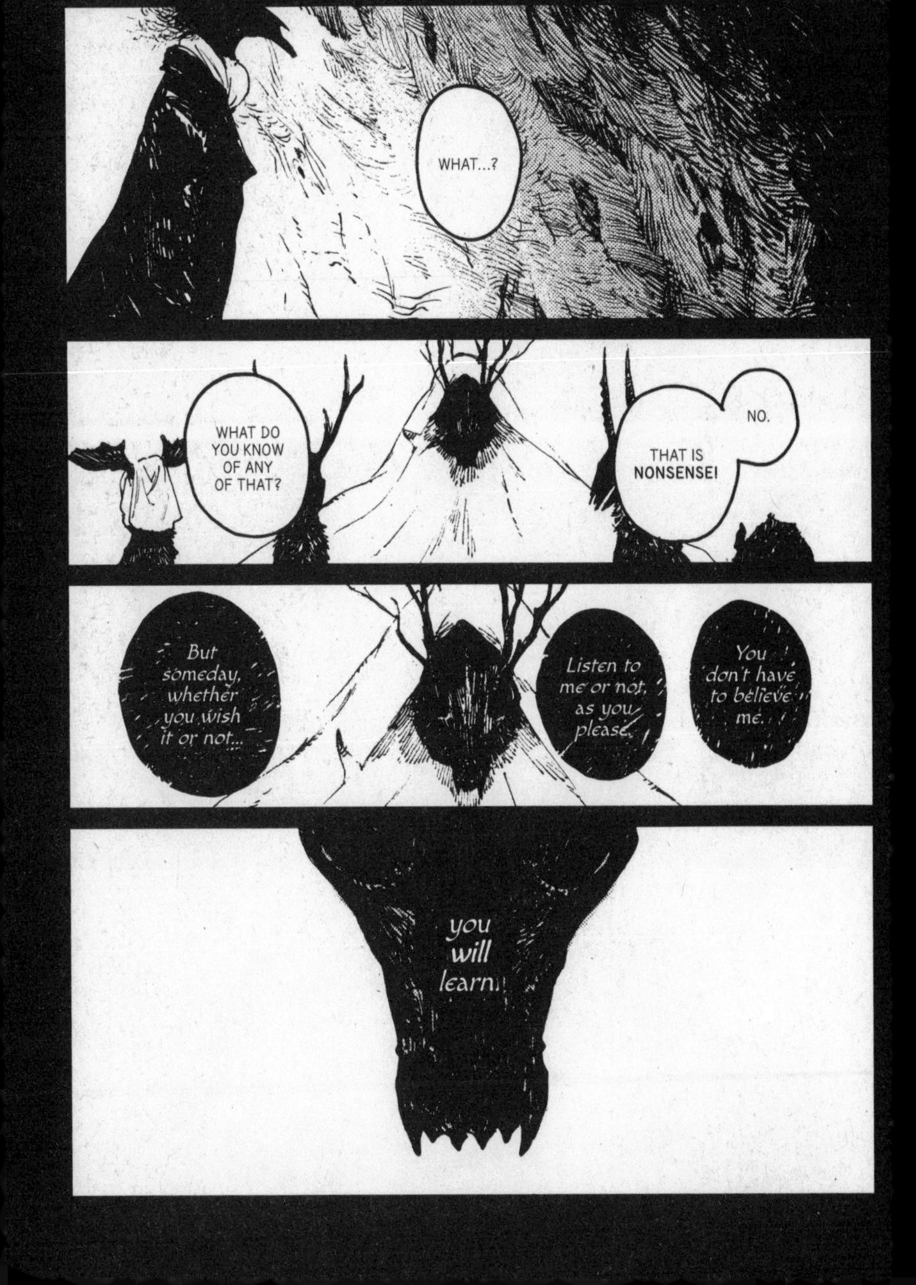
WHAT...?
NO.
THAT IS **NONSENSE!**
WHAT DO YOU KNOW OF ANY OF THAT?
You don't have to believe me.
Listen to me or not, as you please.
But someday, whether you wish it or not...
you will learn.

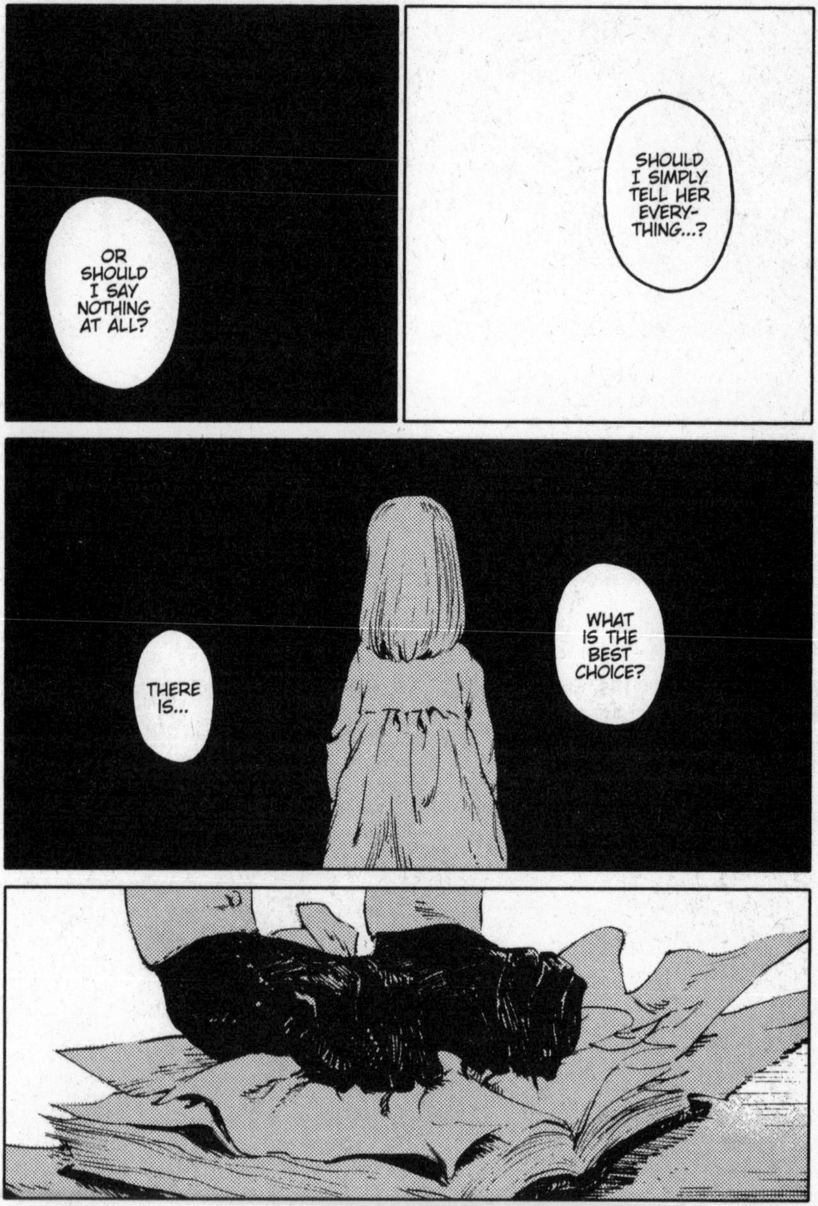
SHOULD I SIMPLY TELL HER EVERY-THING...?
OR SHOULD I SAY NOTHING AT ALL?
WHAT IS THE BEST CHOICE?
THERE IS...

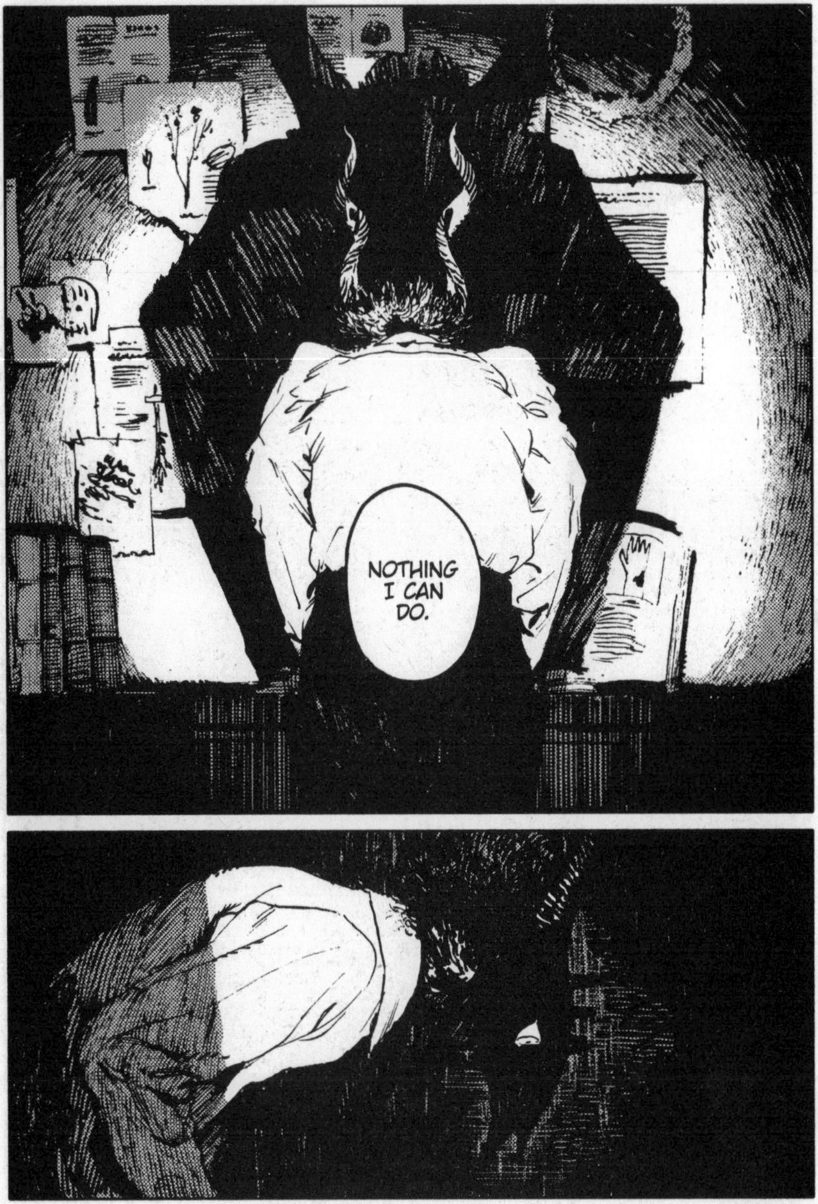
NOTHING I CAN DO.

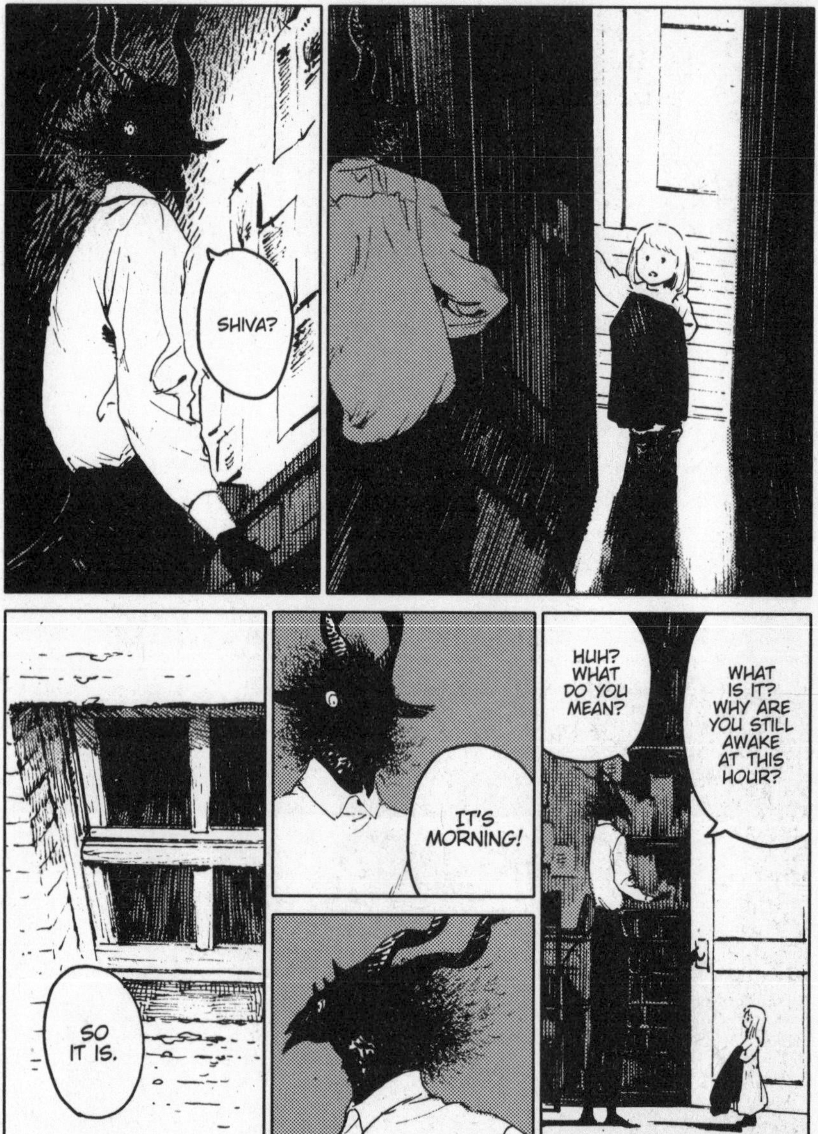
SHIVA?
WHAT IS IT? WHY ARE YOU STILL AWAKE AT THIS HOUR?
HUH? WHAT DO YOU MEAN?
IT'S MORNING!
SO IT IS.

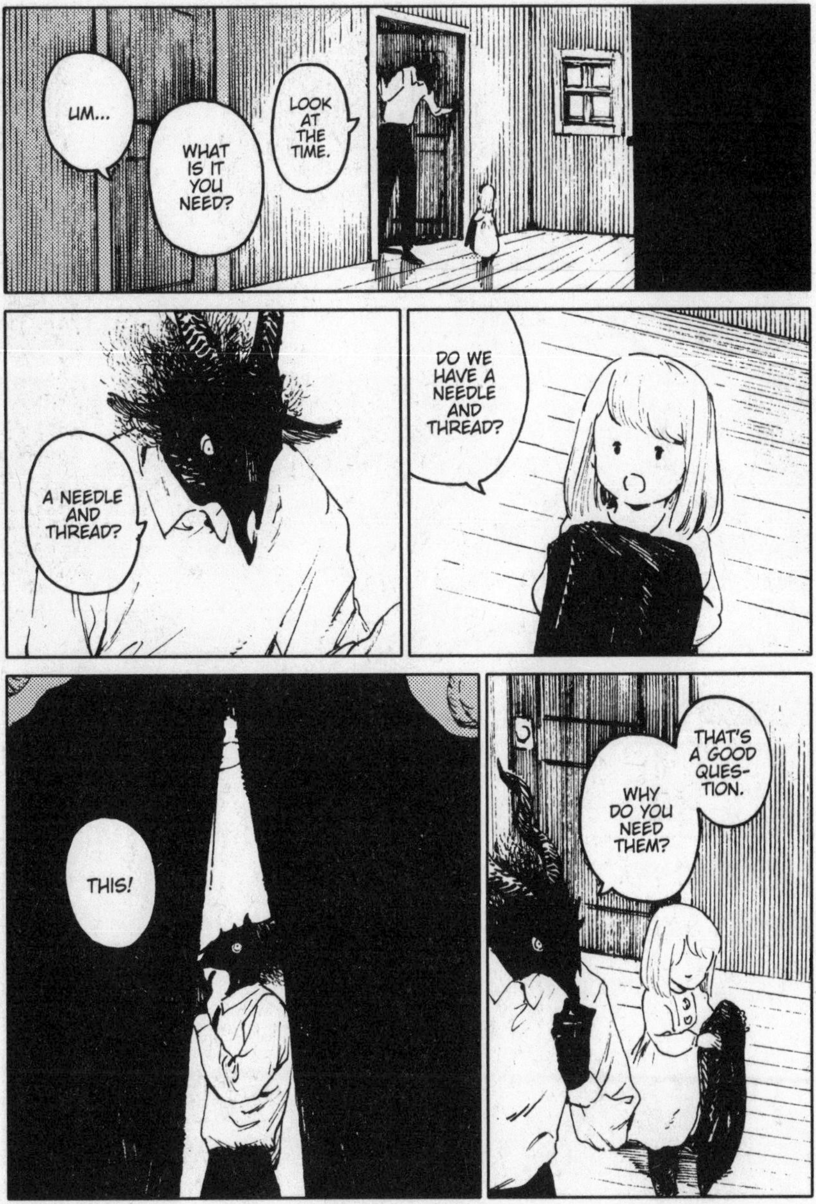
LOOK AT THE TIME.
WHAT IS IT YOU NEED?
UM...
DO WE HAVE A NEEDLE AND THREAD?
A NEEDLE AND THREAD?
THAT'S A GOOD QUESTION.
WHY DO YOU NEED THEM?
THIS!

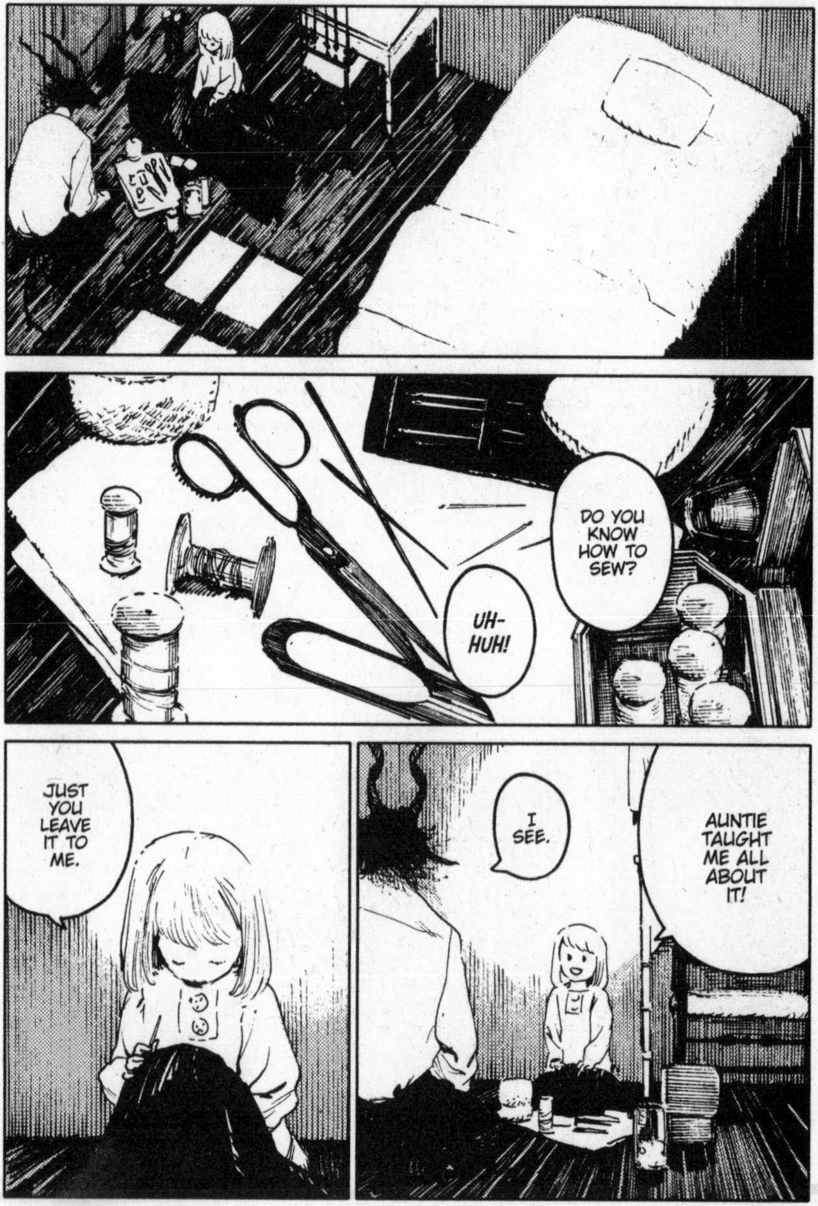
DO YOU KNOW HOW TO SEW?
UH-HUH!
AUNTIE TAUGHT ME ALL ABOUT IT!
I SEE.
JUST YOU LEAVE IT TO ME.

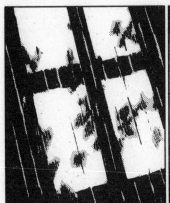

OW!

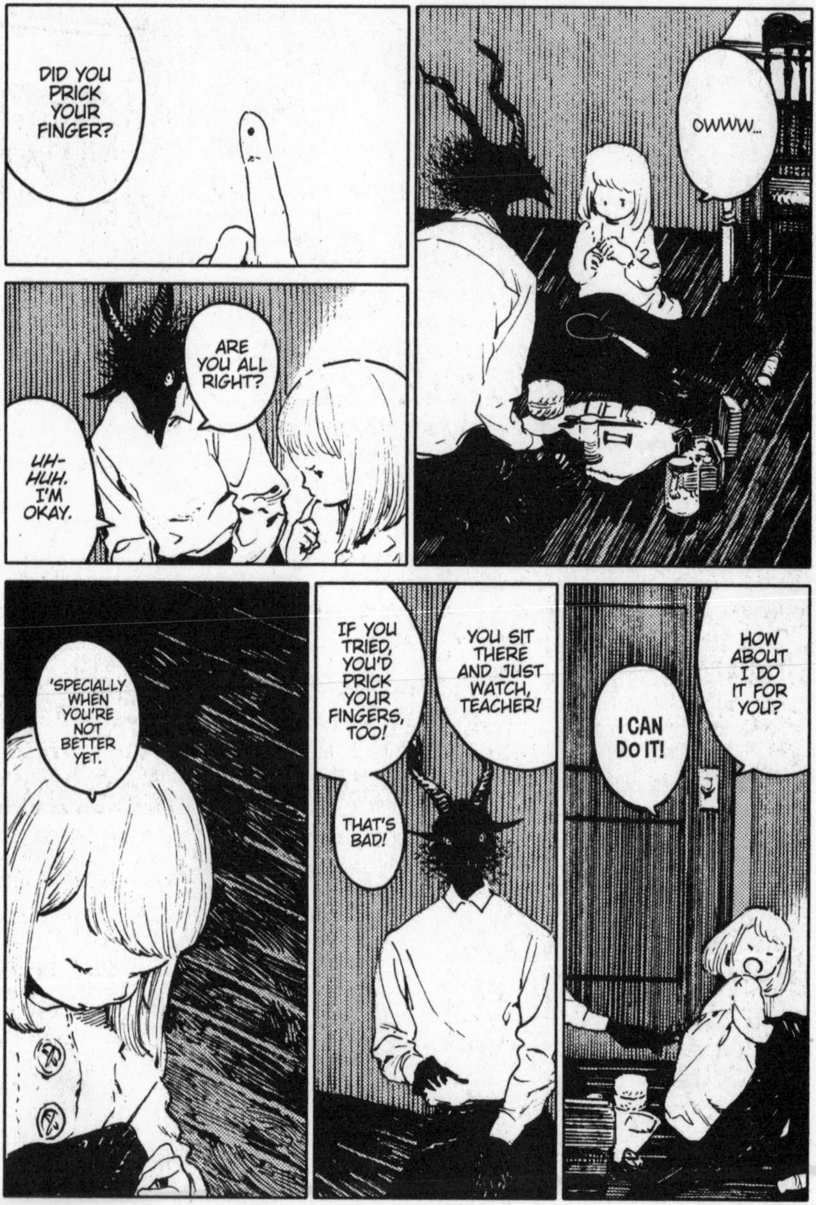
OWWW...
DID YOU PRICK YOUR FINGER?
ARE YOU ALL RIGHT?
UH-HUH. I'M OKAY.
HOW ABOUT I DO IT FOR YOU?
I CAN DO IT!
YOU SIT THERE AND JUST WATCH, TEACHER!
IF YOU TRIED, YOU'D PRICK YOUR FINGERS, TOO!
THAT'S BAD!
'SPECIALLY WHEN YOU'RE NOT BETTER YET.

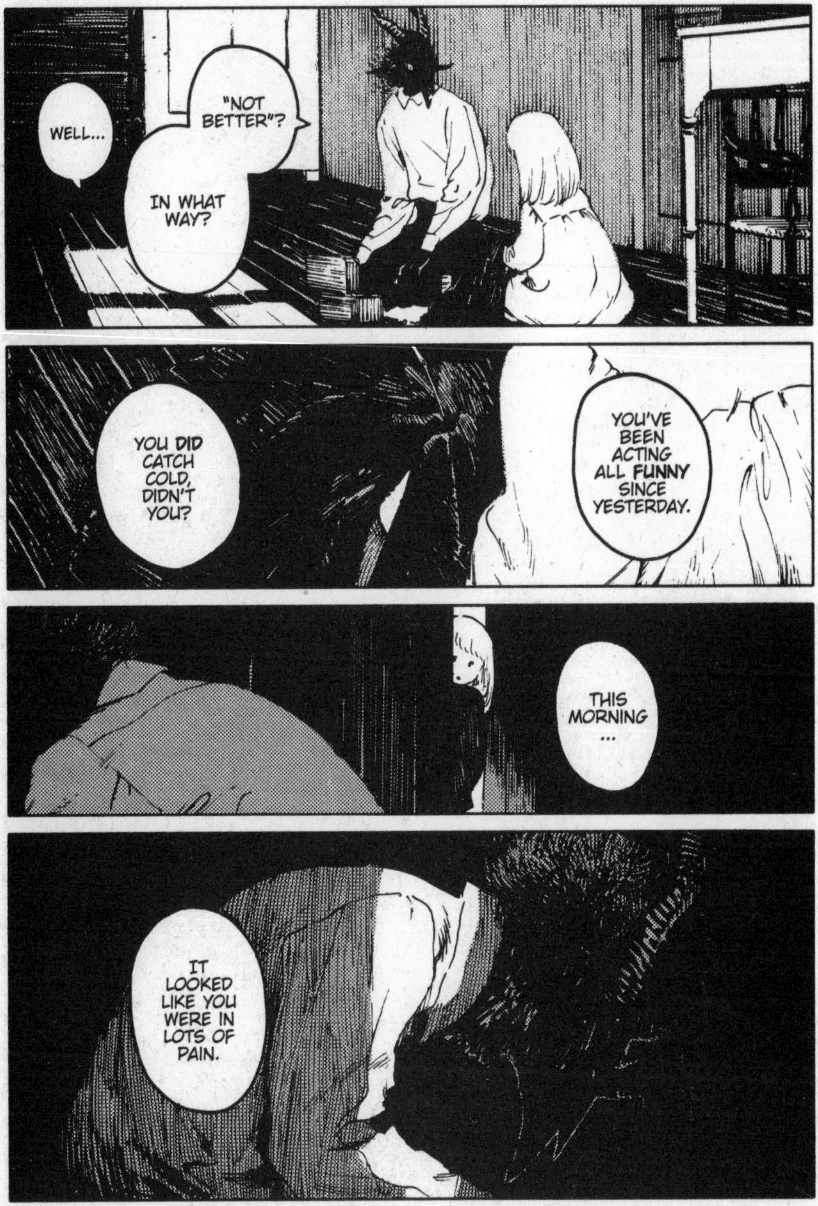
"NOT BETTER"?
IN WHAT WAY?
WELL...
YOU'VE BEEN ACTING ALL FUNNY SINCE YESTERDAY.
YOU DID CATCH COLD, DIDN'T YOU?
THIS MORNING...
IT LOOKED LIKE YOU WERE IN LOTS OF PAIN.

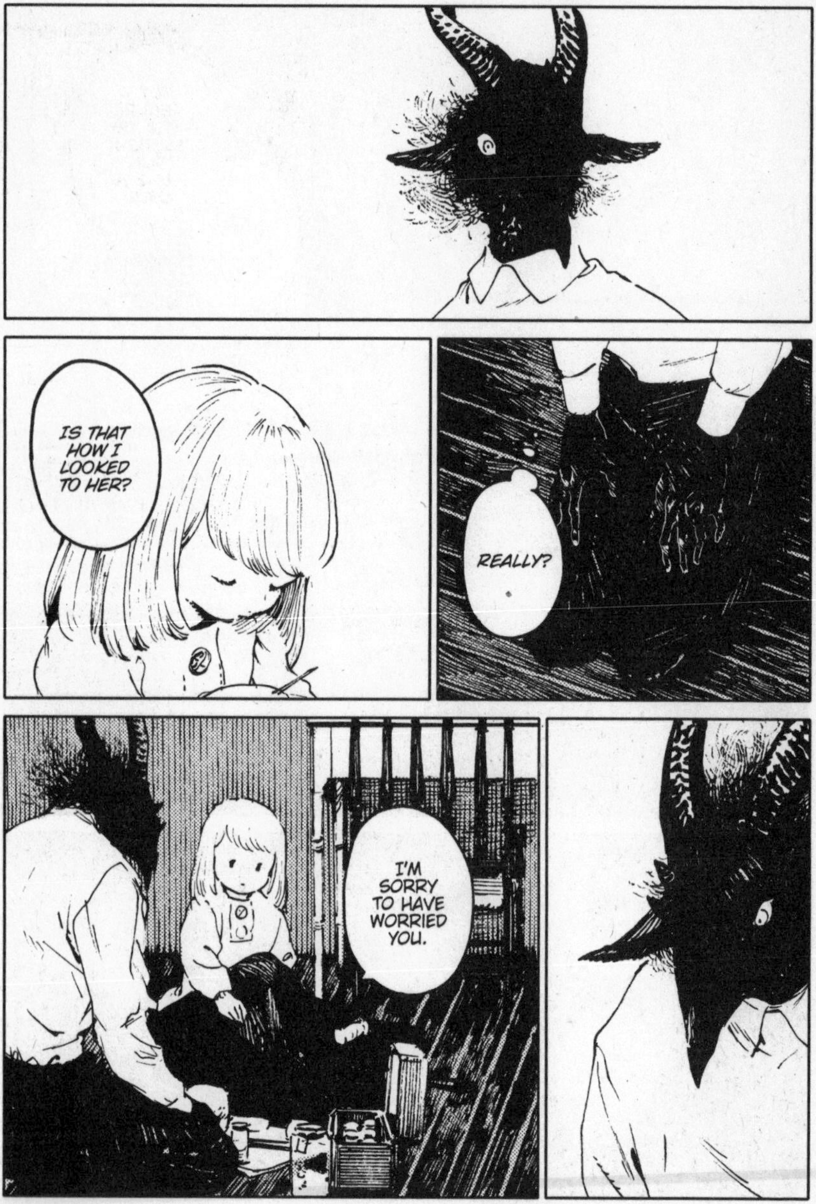
REALLY?
IS THAT HOW I LOOKED TO HER?
I'M SORRY TO HAVE WORRIED YOU.

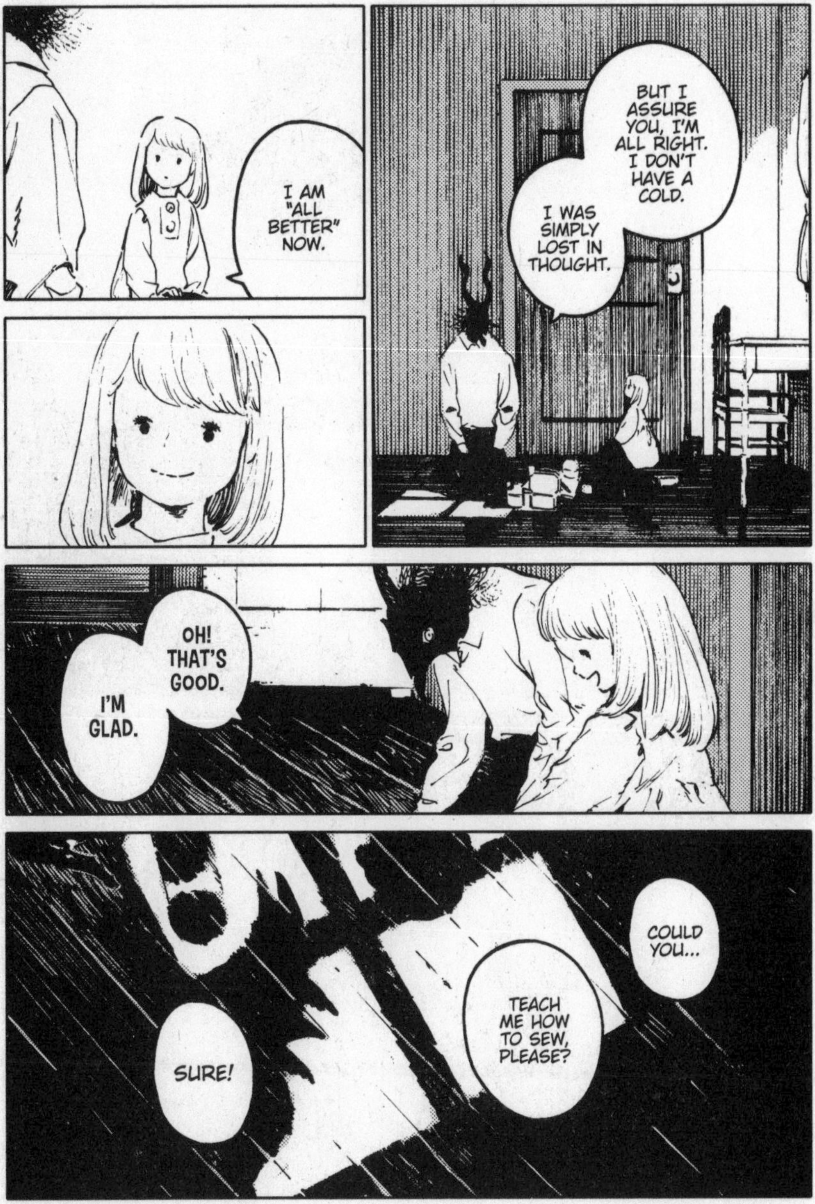
BUT I ASSURE YOU, I'M ALL RIGHT. I DON'T HAVE A COLD.
I WAS SIMPLY LOST IN THOUGHT.
I AM "ALL BETTER" NOW.
OH! THAT'S GOOD.
I'M GLAD.
COULD YOU...
TEACH ME HOW TO SEW, PLEASE?
SURE!

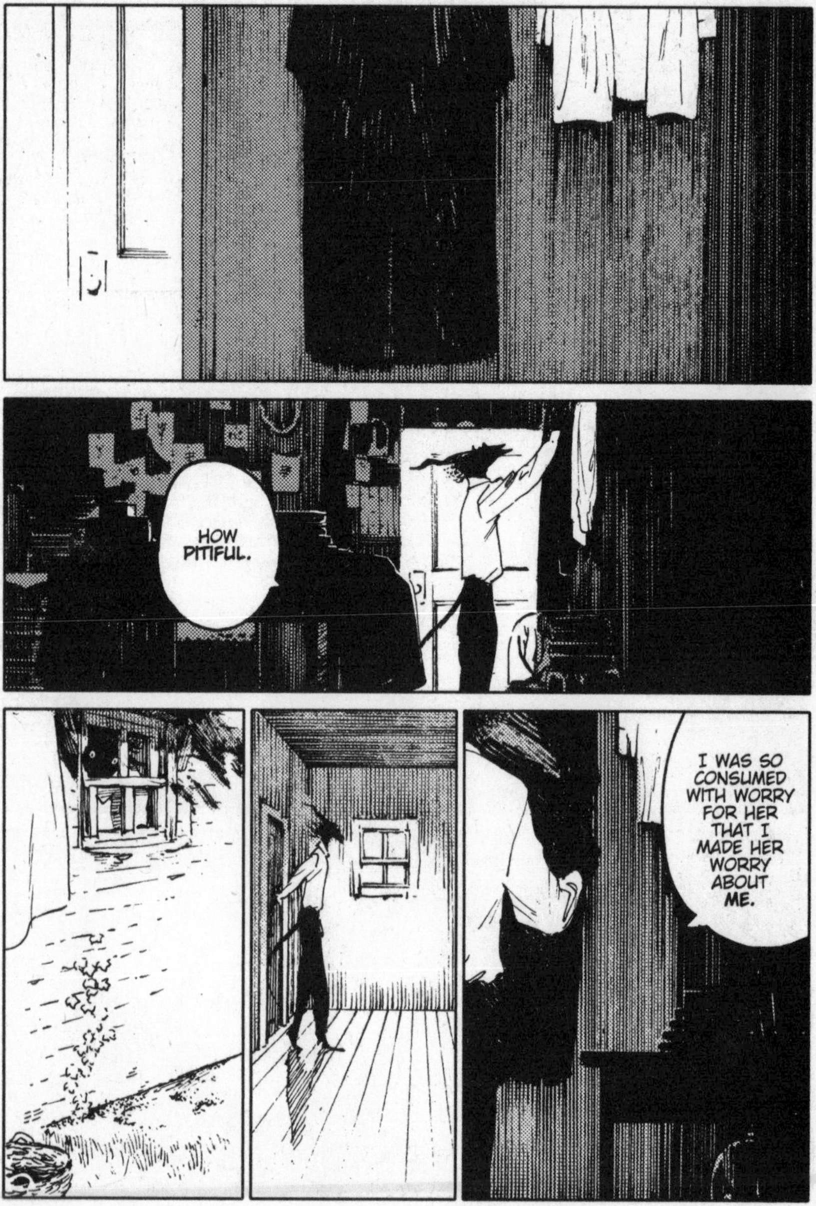
HOW PITIFUL.
I WAS SO CONSUMED WITH WORRY FOR HER THAT I MADE HER WORRY ABOUT ME.

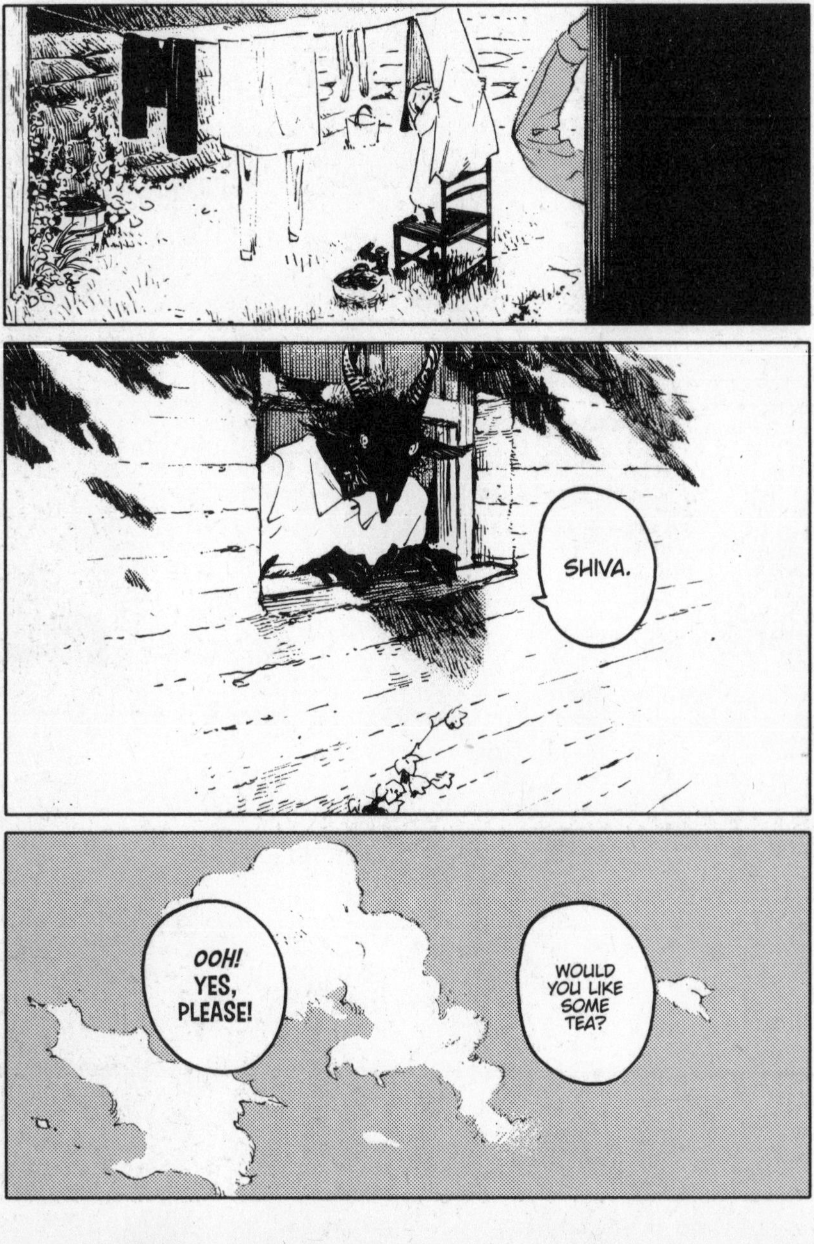
SHIVA.
WOULD YOU LIKE SOME TEA?
OOH! YES, PLEASE!

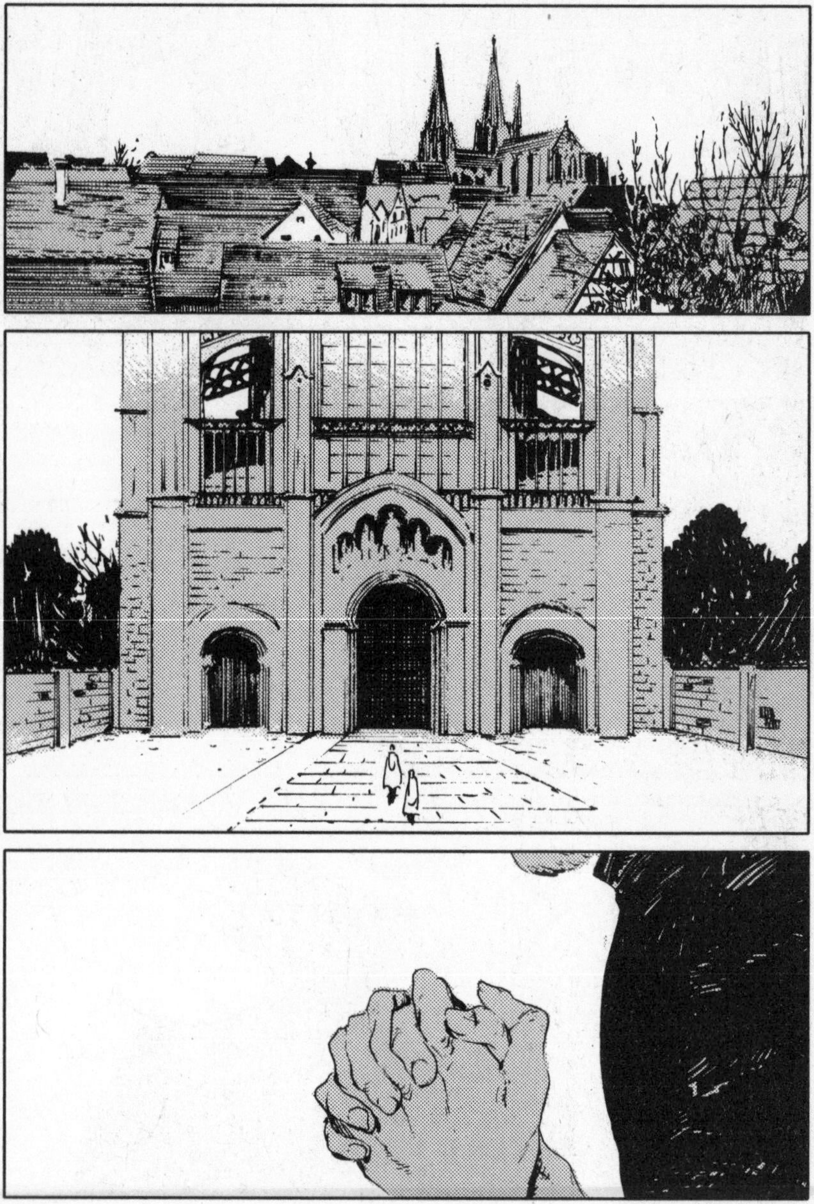

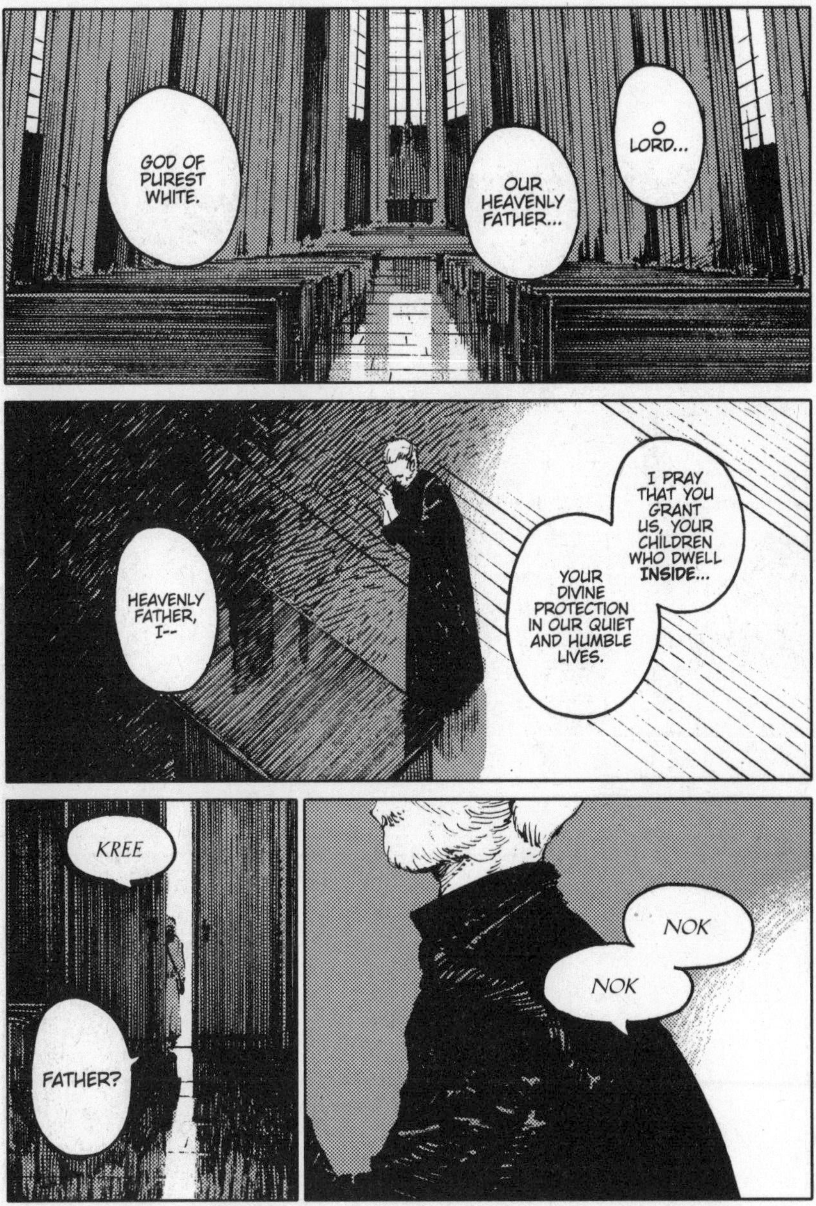
O LORD...
OUR HEAVENLY FATHER...
GOD OF PUREST WHITE.
I PRAY THAT YOU GRANT US, YOUR CHILDREN WHO DWELL **INSIDE**...
YOUR DIVINE PROTECTION IN OUR QUIET AND HUMBLE LIVES.
HEAVENLY FATHER, I--
NOK
NOK
KREE
FATHER?

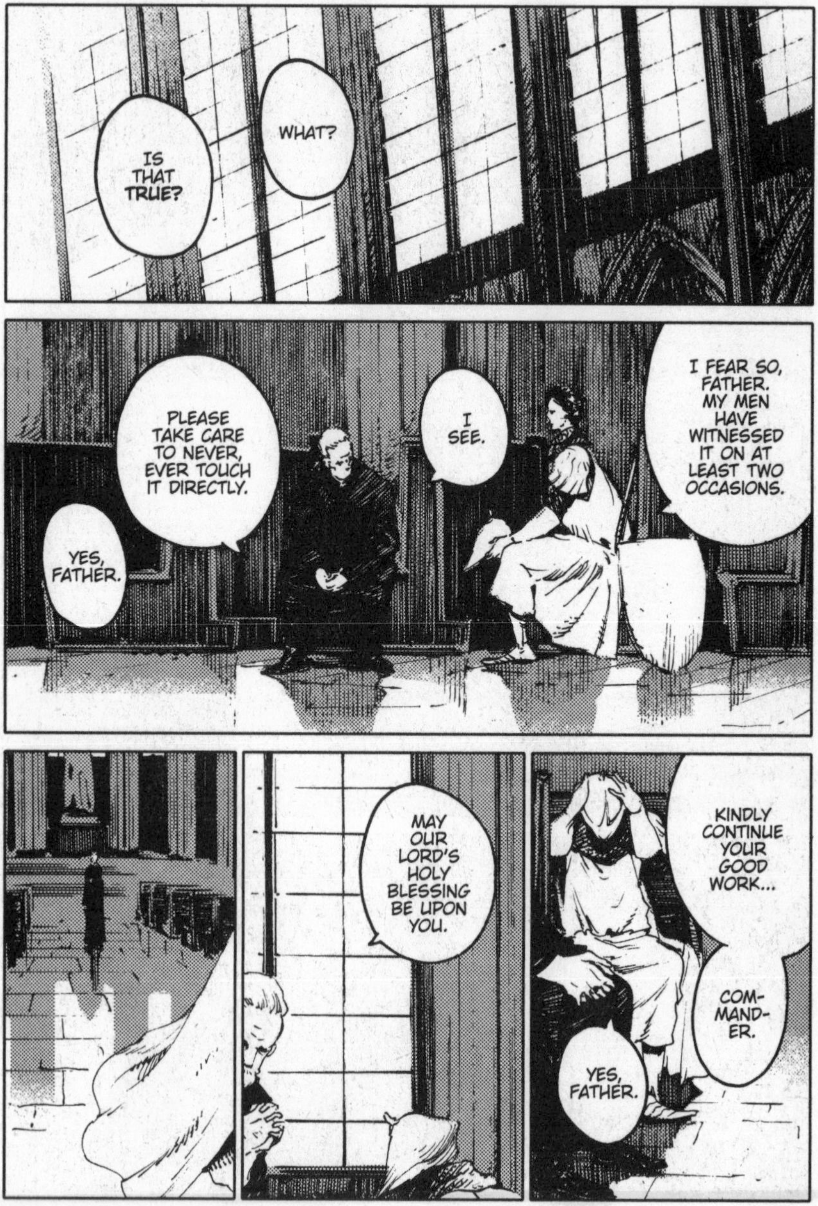
WHAT?
IS THAT TRUE?
I FEAR SO, FATHER. MY MEN HAVE WITNESSED IT ON AT LEAST TWO OCCASIONS.
I SEE.
PLEASE TAKE CARE TO NEVER, EVER TOUCH IT DIRECTLY.
YES, FATHER.
KINDLY CONTINUE YOUR GOOD WORK...
COM-MAND-ER.
YES, FATHER.
MAY OUR LORD'S HOLY BLESSING BE UPON YOU.

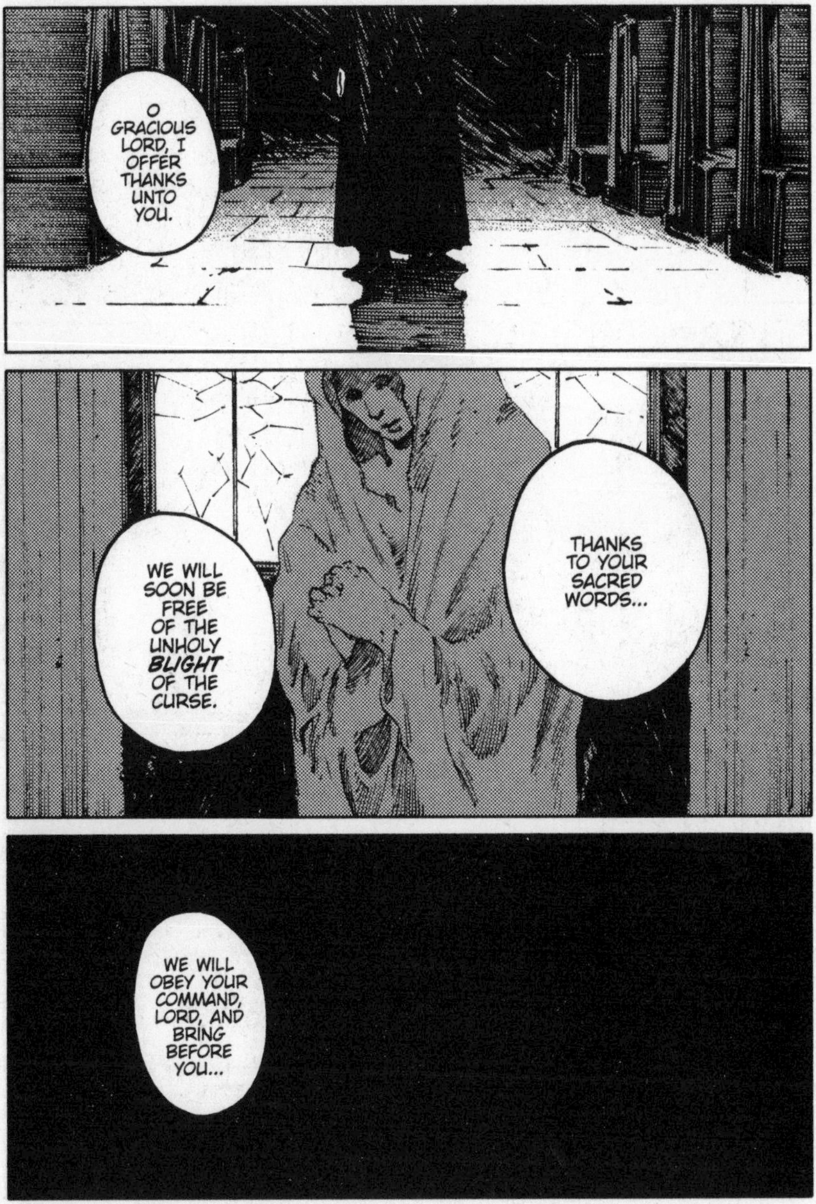
O GRACIOUS LORD, I OFFER THANKS UNTO YOU.
THANKS TO YOUR SACRED WORDS...
WE WILL SOON BE FREE OF THE UNHOLY *BLIGHT* OF THE CURSE.
WE WILL OBEY YOUR COMMAND, LORD, AND BRING BEFORE YOU...

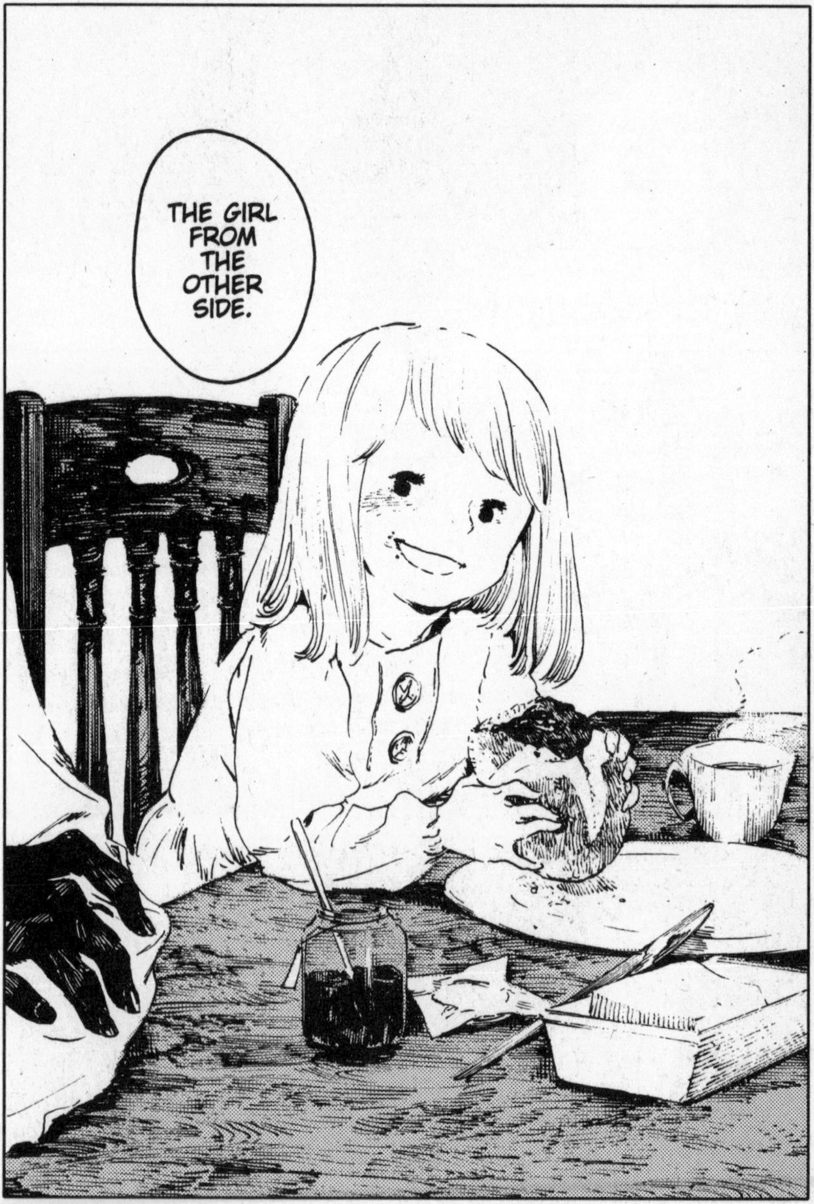
THE GIRL FROM THE OTHER SIDE.

Chapter 10

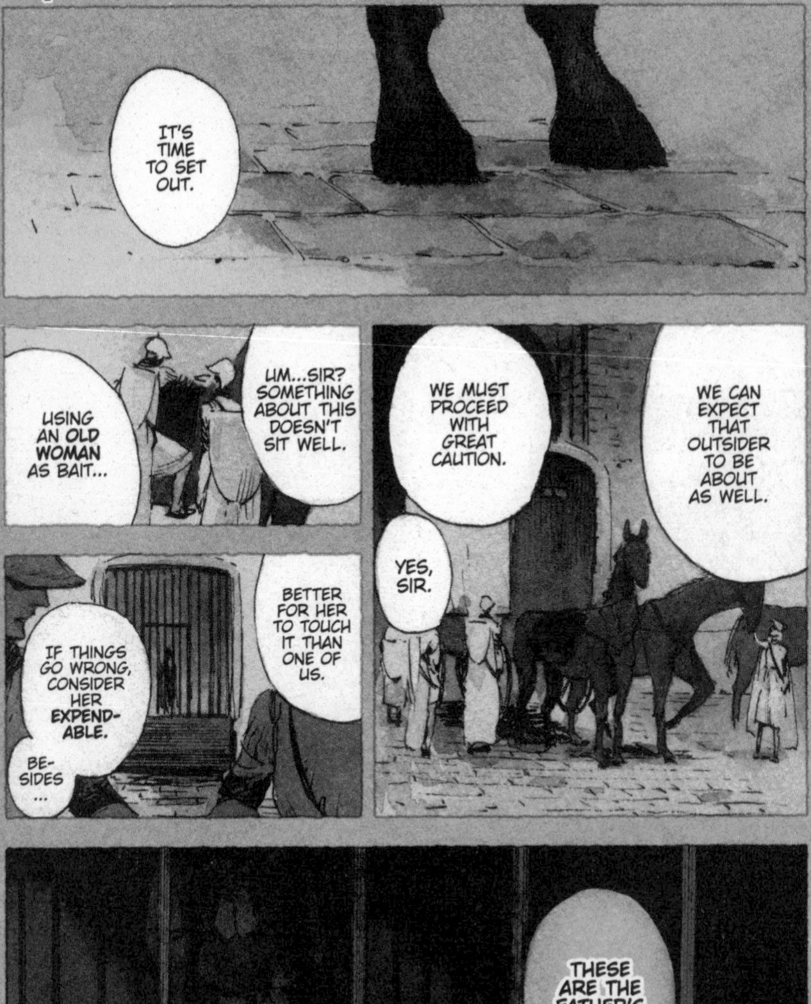
IT'S TIME TO SET OUT.
WE CAN EXPECT THAT OUTSIDER TO BE ABOUT AS WELL.
WE MUST PROCEED WITH GREAT CAUTION.
YES, SIR.
UM...SIR? SOMETHING ABOUT THIS DOESN'T SIT WELL.
USING AN OLD WOMAN AS BAIT...
BETTER FOR HER TO TOUCH IT THAN ONE OF US.
IF THINGS GO WRONG, CONSIDER HER EXPEND-ABLE.
BE-SIDES ...
THESE ARE THE FATHER'S ORDERS.

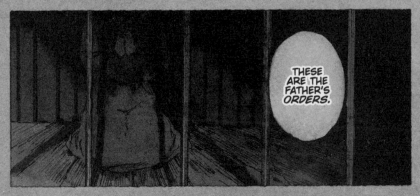

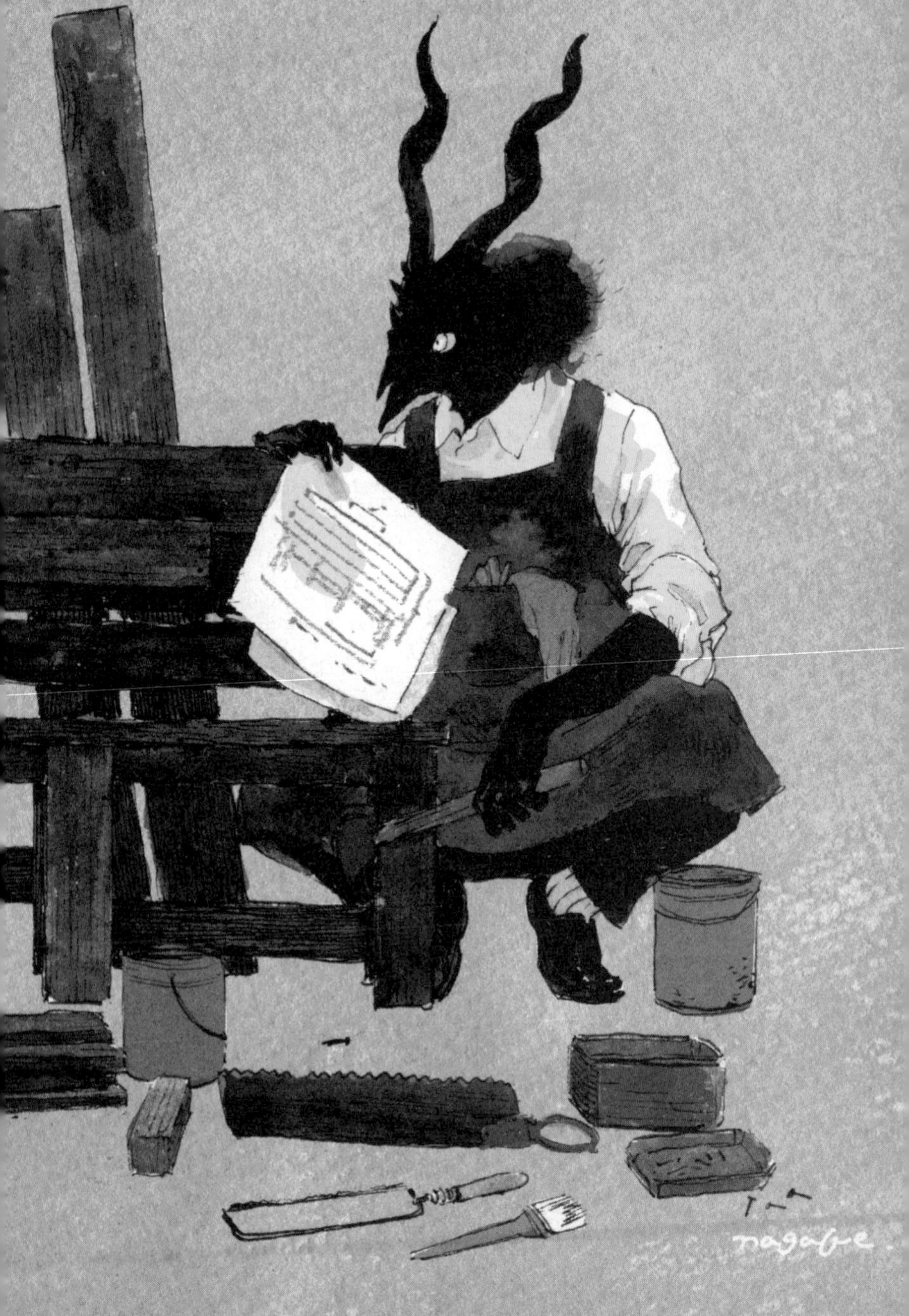
nagabe

siúil a rún

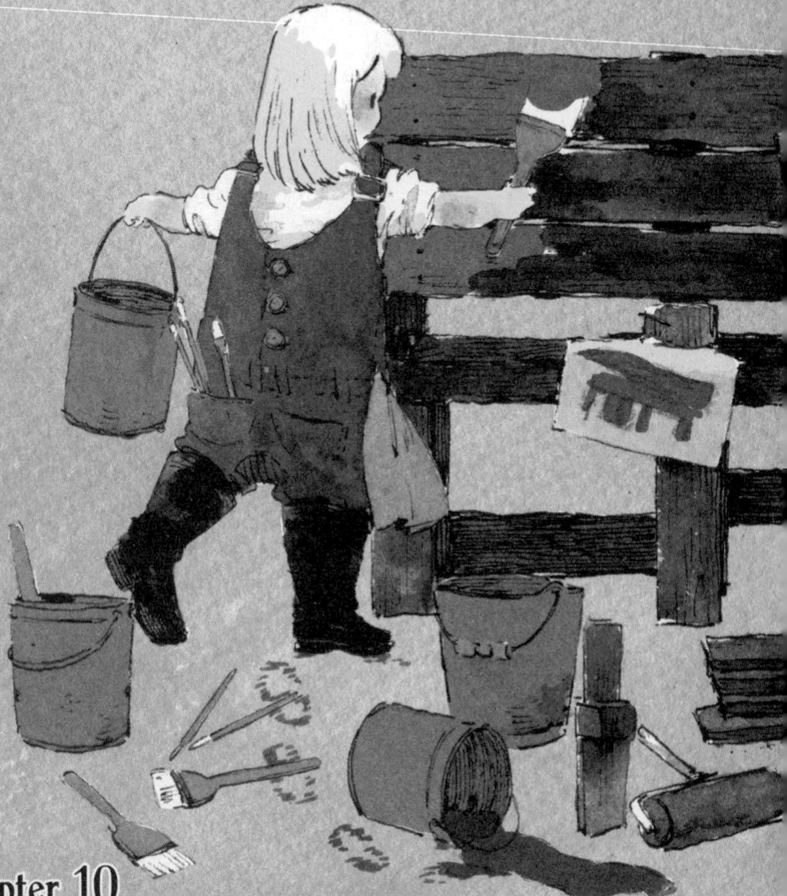

Chapter 10

Siúil, a Rún
The Girl from the Other Side

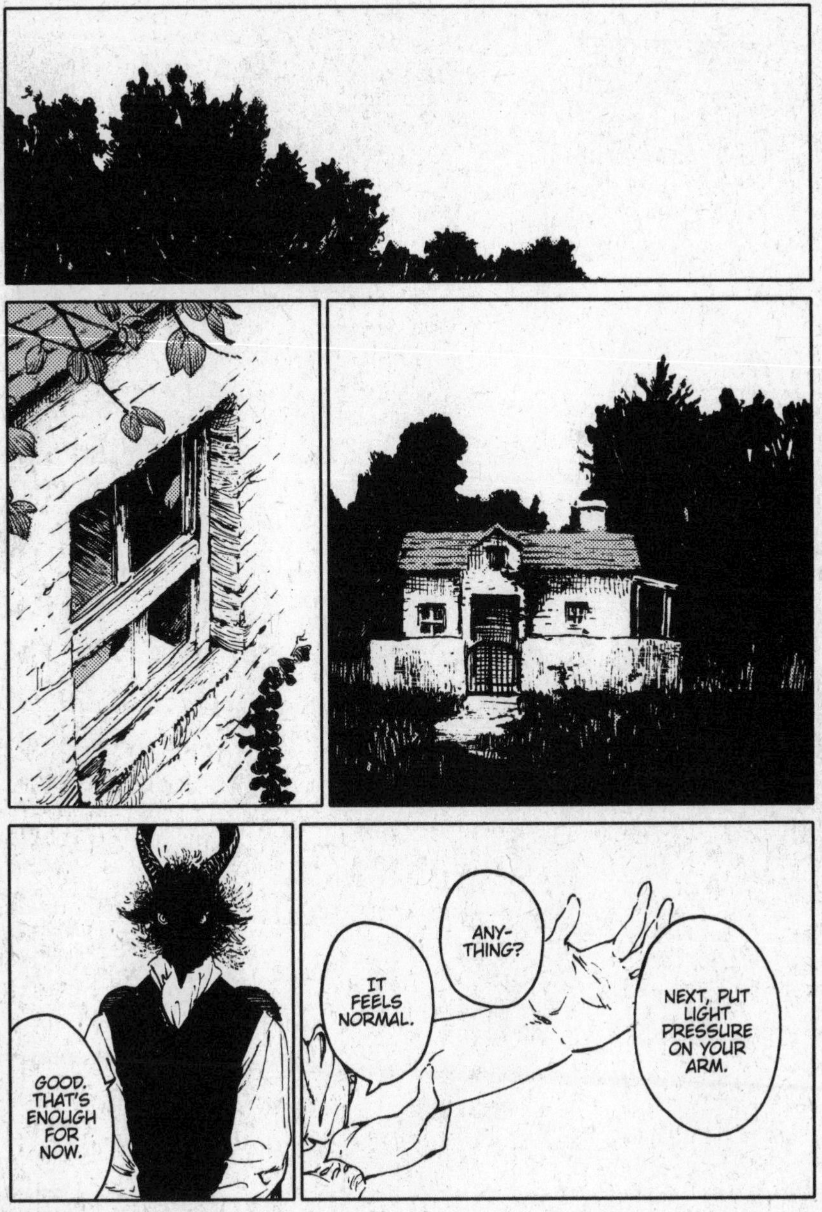
NEXT, PUT LIGHT PRESSURE ON YOUR ARM.
ANY-THING?
IT FEELS NORMAL.
GOOD. THAT'S ENOUGH FOR NOW.

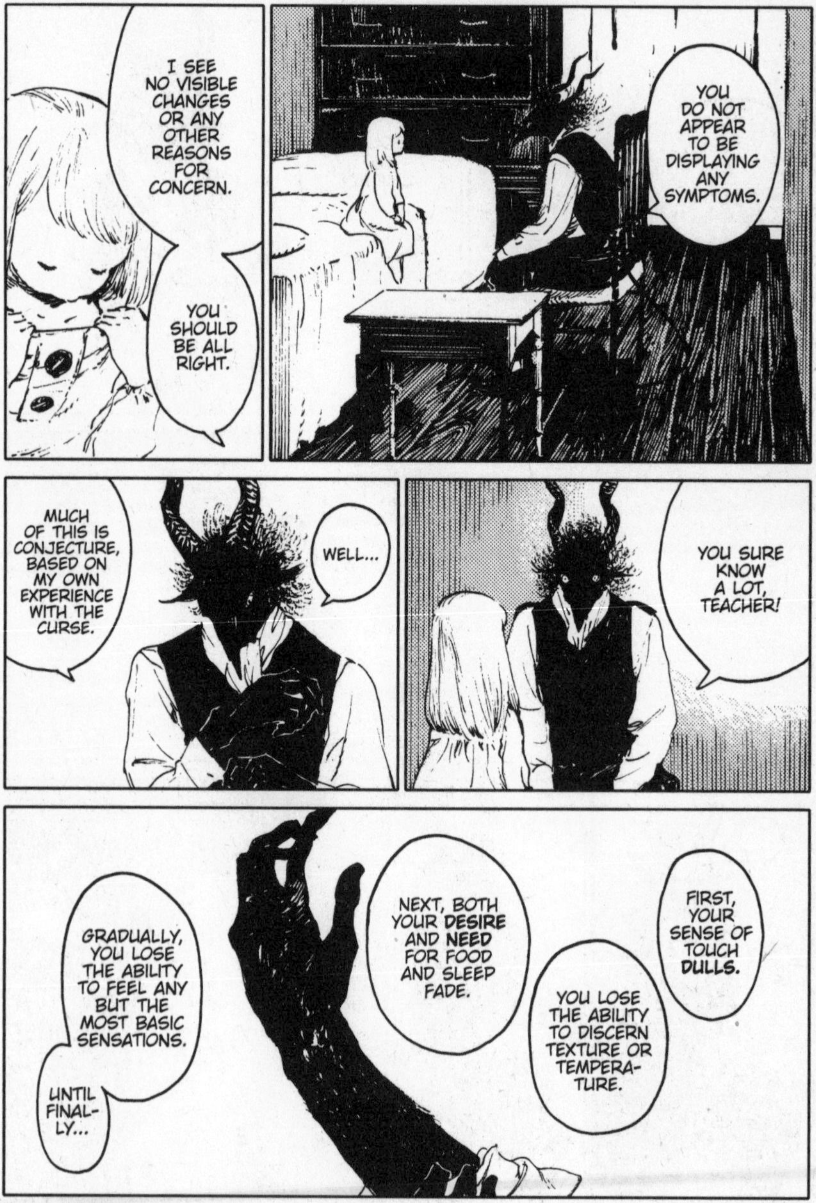
YOU DO NOT APPEAR TO BE DISPLAYING ANY SYMPTOMS.
I SEE NO VISIBLE CHANGES OR ANY OTHER REASONS FOR CONCERN.
YOU SHOULD BE ALL RIGHT.
YOU SURE KNOW A LOT, TEACHER!
WELL...
MUCH OF THIS IS CONJECTURE, BASED ON MY OWN EXPERIENCE WITH THE CURSE.
FIRST, YOUR SENSE OF TOUCH **DULLS.**
YOU LOSE THE ABILITY TO DISCERN TEXTURE OR TEMPERA-TURE.
NEXT, BOTH YOUR **DESIRE** AND **NEED** FOR FOOD AND SLEEP FADE.
GRADUALLY, YOU LOSE THE ABILITY TO FEEL ANY BUT THE MOST BASIC SENSATIONS.
UNTIL FINAL-LY...

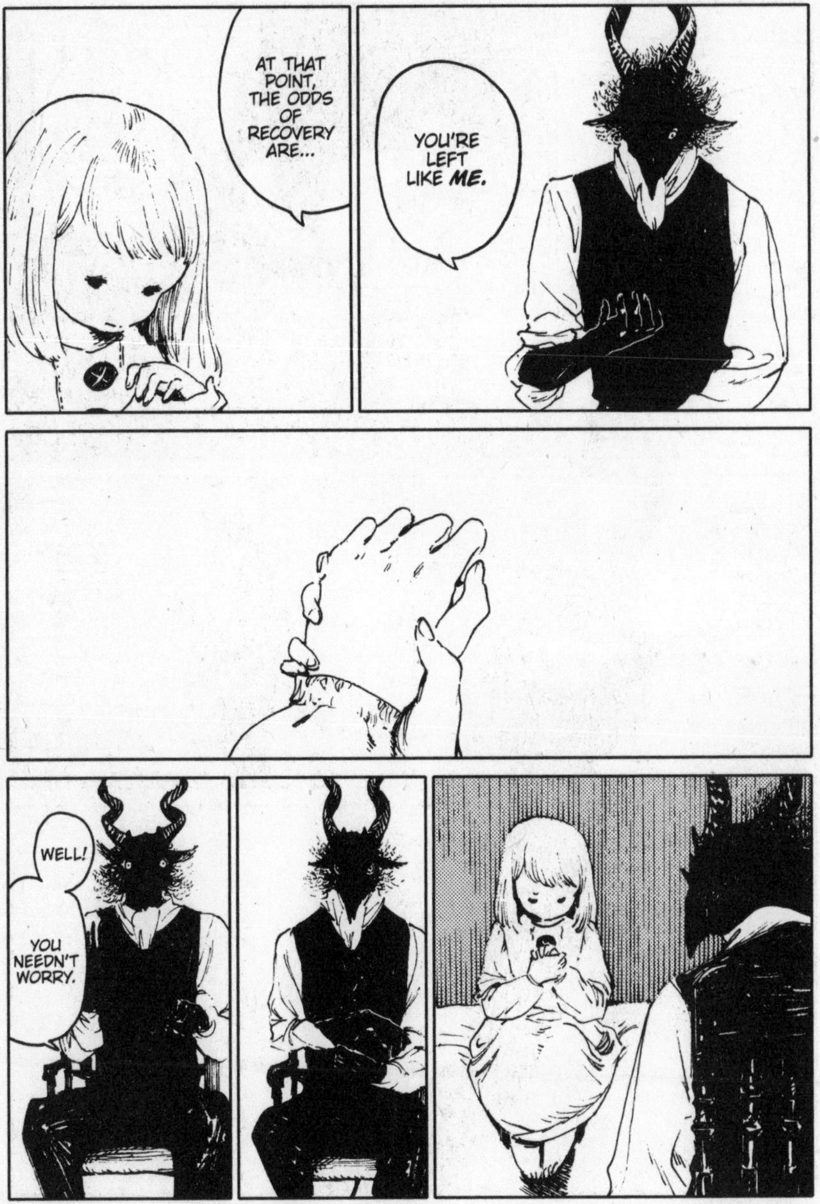
YOU'RE LEFT LIKE ME.
AT THAT POINT, THE ODDS OF RECOVERY ARE...
WELL!
YOU NEEDN'T WORRY.

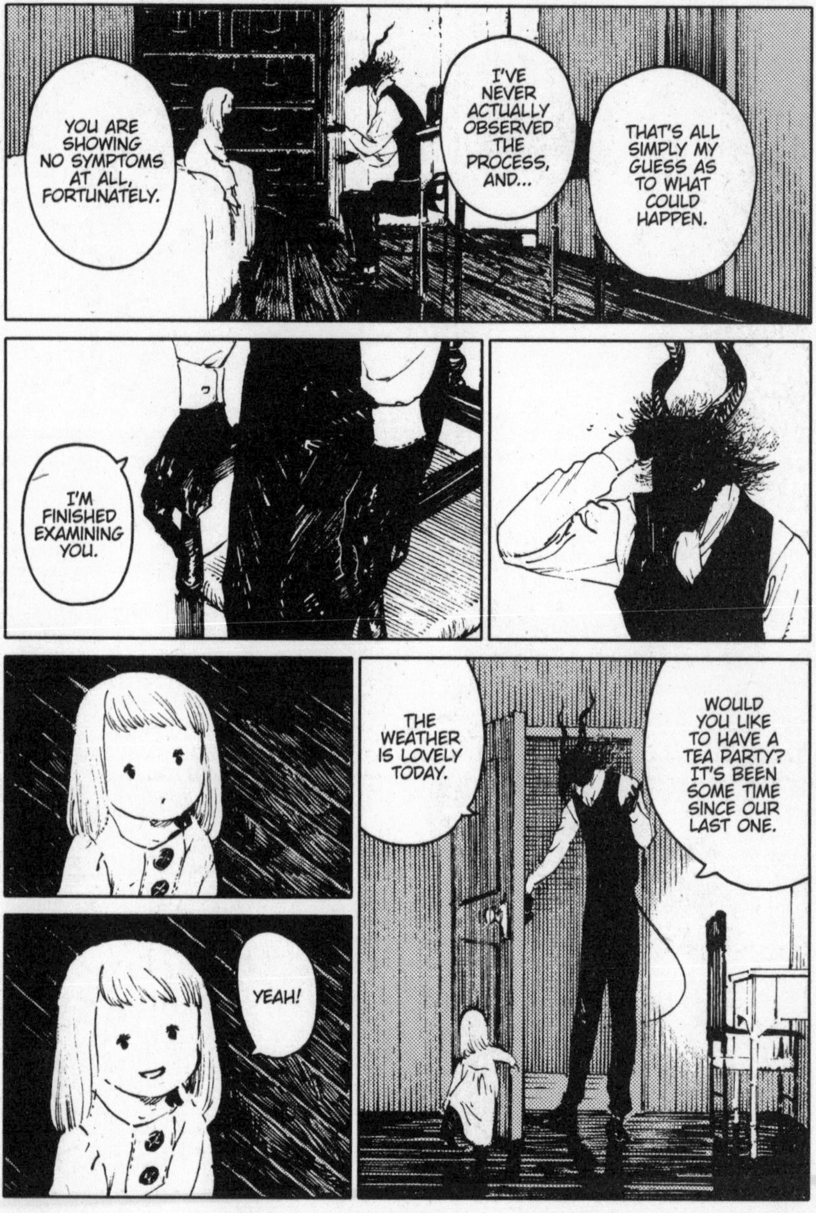
THAT'S ALL SIMPLY MY GUESS AS TO WHAT COULD HAPPEN.
I'VE NEVER ACTUALLY OBSERVED THE PROCESS, AND...
YOU ARE SHOWING NO SYMPTOMS AT ALL, FORTUNATELY.
I'M FINISHED EXAMINING YOU.
WOULD YOU LIKE TO HAVE A TEA PARTY? IT'S BEEN SOME TIME SINCE OUR LAST ONE.
THE WEATHER IS LOVELY TODAY.
YEAH!

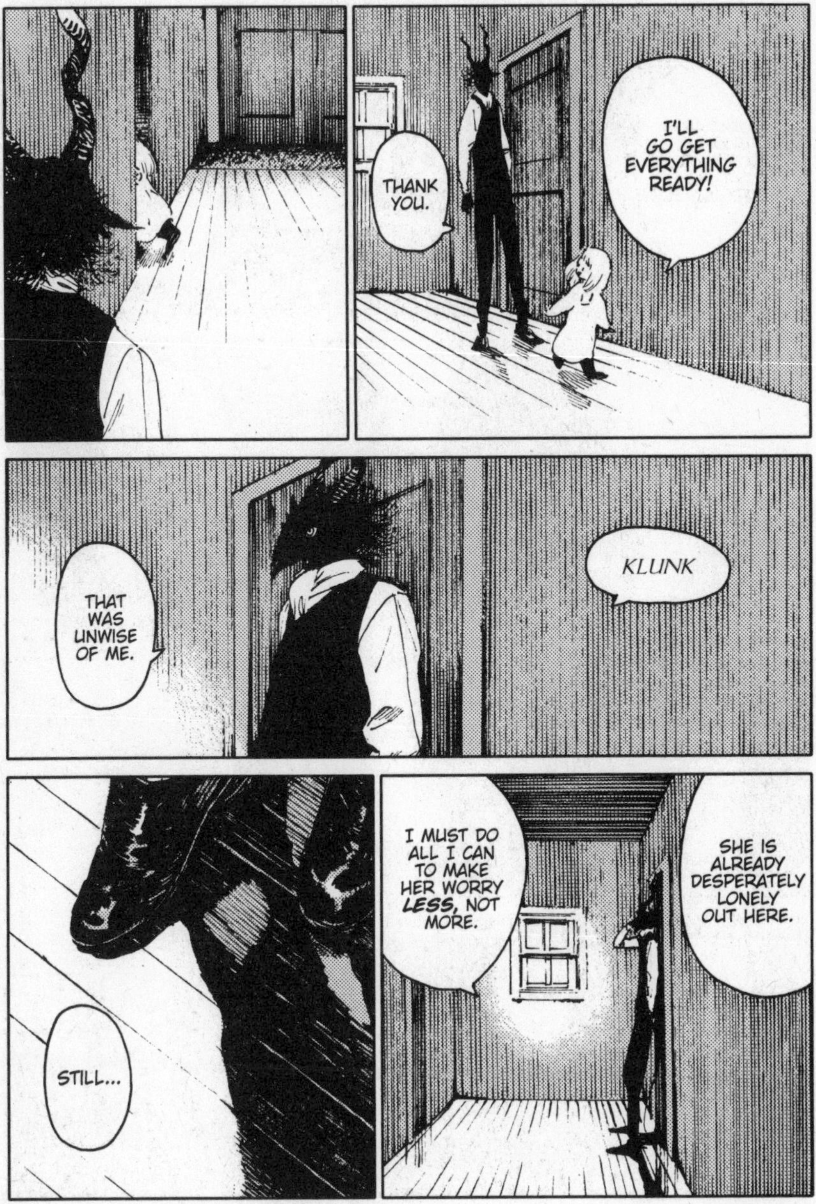
I'LL GO GET EVERYTHING READY!
THANK YOU.
KLUNK
THAT WAS UNWISE OF ME.
SHE IS ALREADY DESPERATELY LONELY OUT HERE.
I MUST DO ALL I CAN TO MAKE HER WORRY *LESS*, NOT MORE.
STILL...

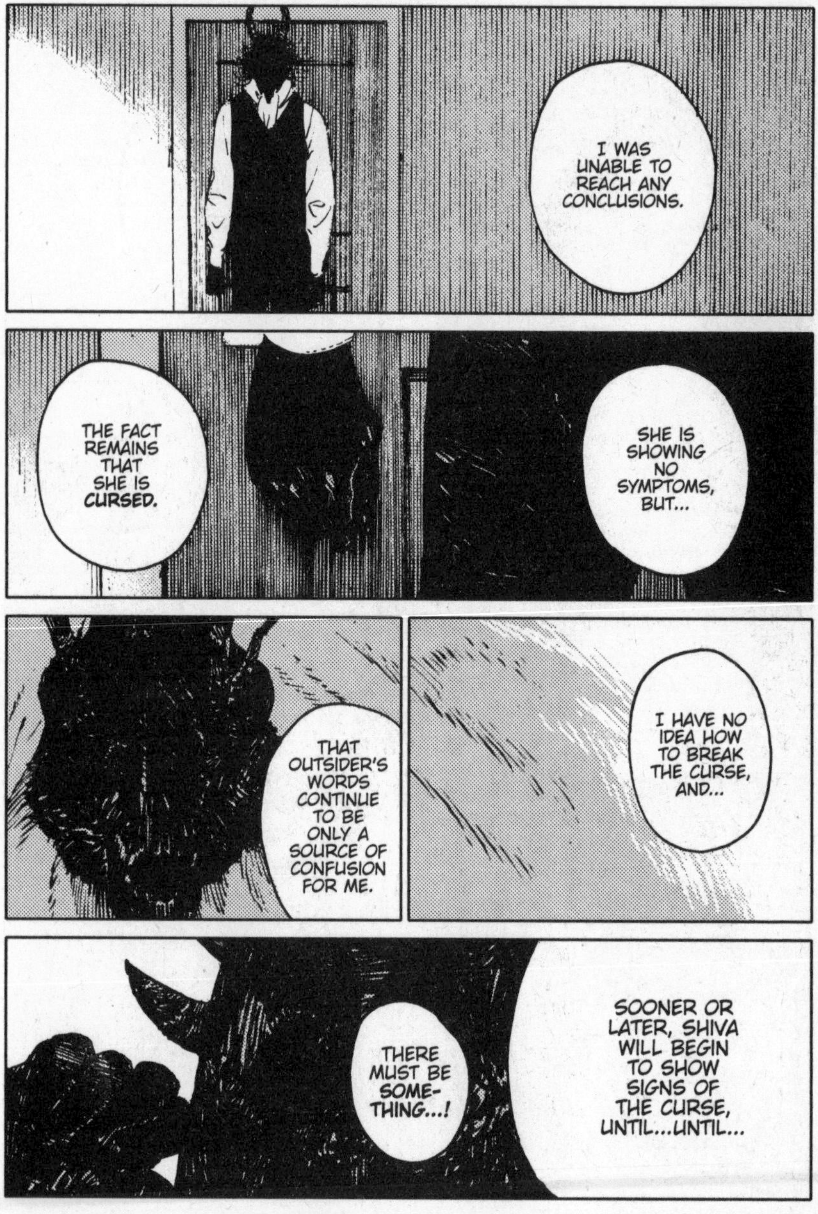
I WAS UNABLE TO REACH ANY CONCLUSIONS.
SHE IS SHOWING NO SYMPTOMS, BUT...
THE FACT REMAINS THAT SHE IS CURSED.
I HAVE NO IDEA HOW TO BREAK THE CURSE, AND...
THAT OUTSIDER'S WORDS CONTINUE TO BE ONLY A SOURCE OF CONFUSION FOR ME.
SOONER OR LATER, SHIVA WILL BEGIN TO SHOW SIGNS OF THE CURSE, UNTIL...UNTIL...
THERE MUST BE SOME-THING...!

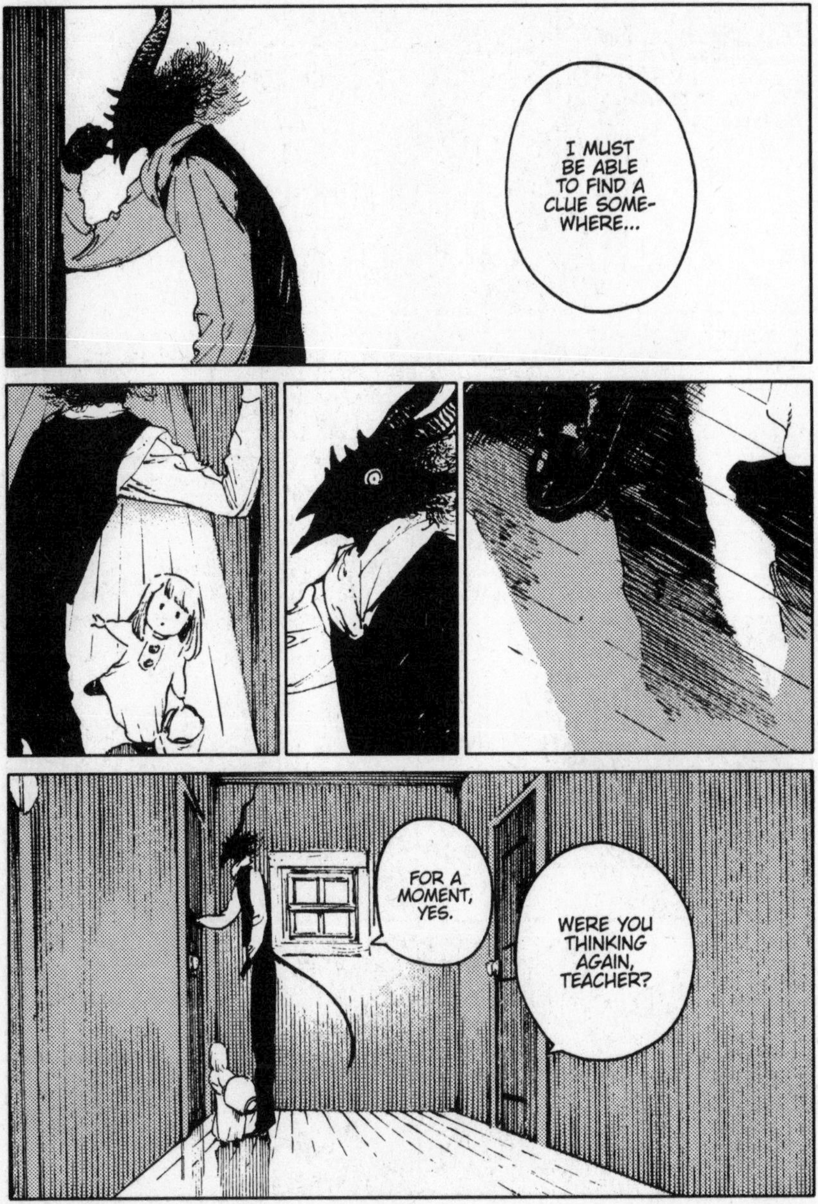
I MUST BE ABLE TO FIND A CLUE SOMEWHERE...
WERE YOU THINKING AGAIN, TEACHER?
FOR A MOMENT, YES.

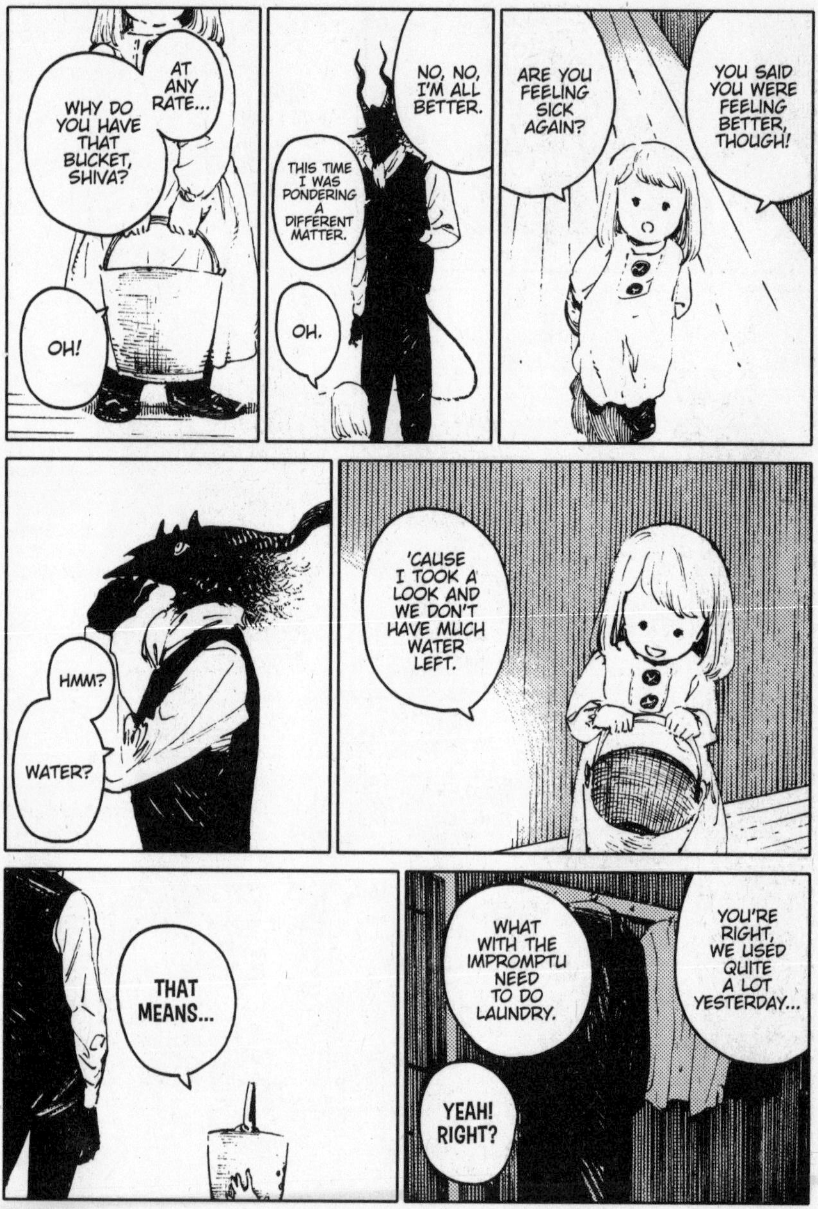
YOU SAID YOU WERE FEELING BETTER, THOUGH!
ARE YOU FEELING SICK AGAIN?
NO, NO, I'M ALL BETTER.
THIS TIME I WAS PONDERING A DIFFERENT MATTER.
OH.
AT ANY RATE...
WHY DO YOU HAVE THAT BUCKET, SHIVA?
OH!
'CAUSE I TOOK A LOOK AND WE DON'T HAVE MUCH WATER LEFT.
HMM?
WATER?
YOU'RE RIGHT, WE USED QUITE A LOT YESTERDAY...
WHAT WITH THE IMPROMPTU NEED TO DO LAUNDRY.
YEAH! RIGHT?
THAT MEANS...

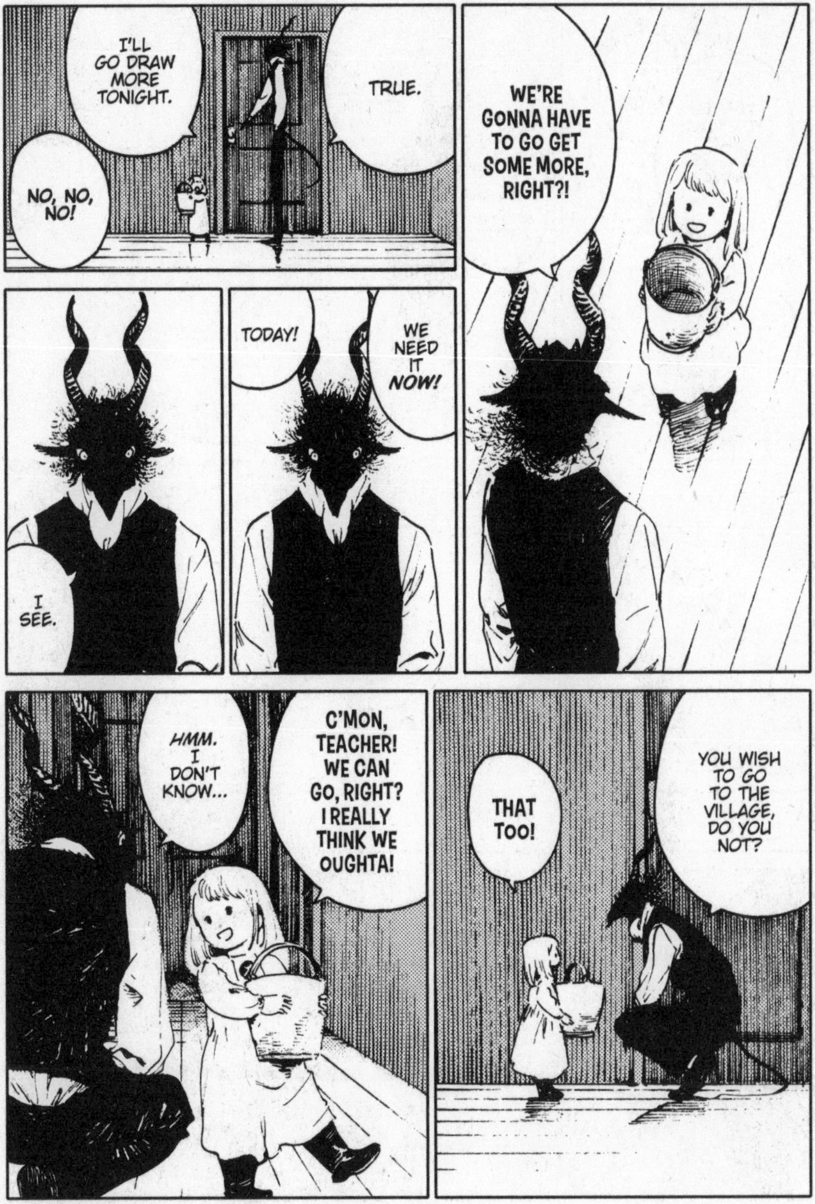
WE'RE GONNA HAVE TO GO GET SOME MORE, RIGHT?!
TRUE.
I'LL GO DRAW MORE TONIGHT.
NO, NO, NO!
WE NEED IT *NOW!*
TODAY!
I SEE.
YOU WISH TO GO TO THE VILLAGE, DO YOU NOT?
THAT TOO!
C'MON, TEACHER! WE CAN GO, RIGHT? I REALLY THINK WE OUGHTA!
HMM. I DON'T KNOW...

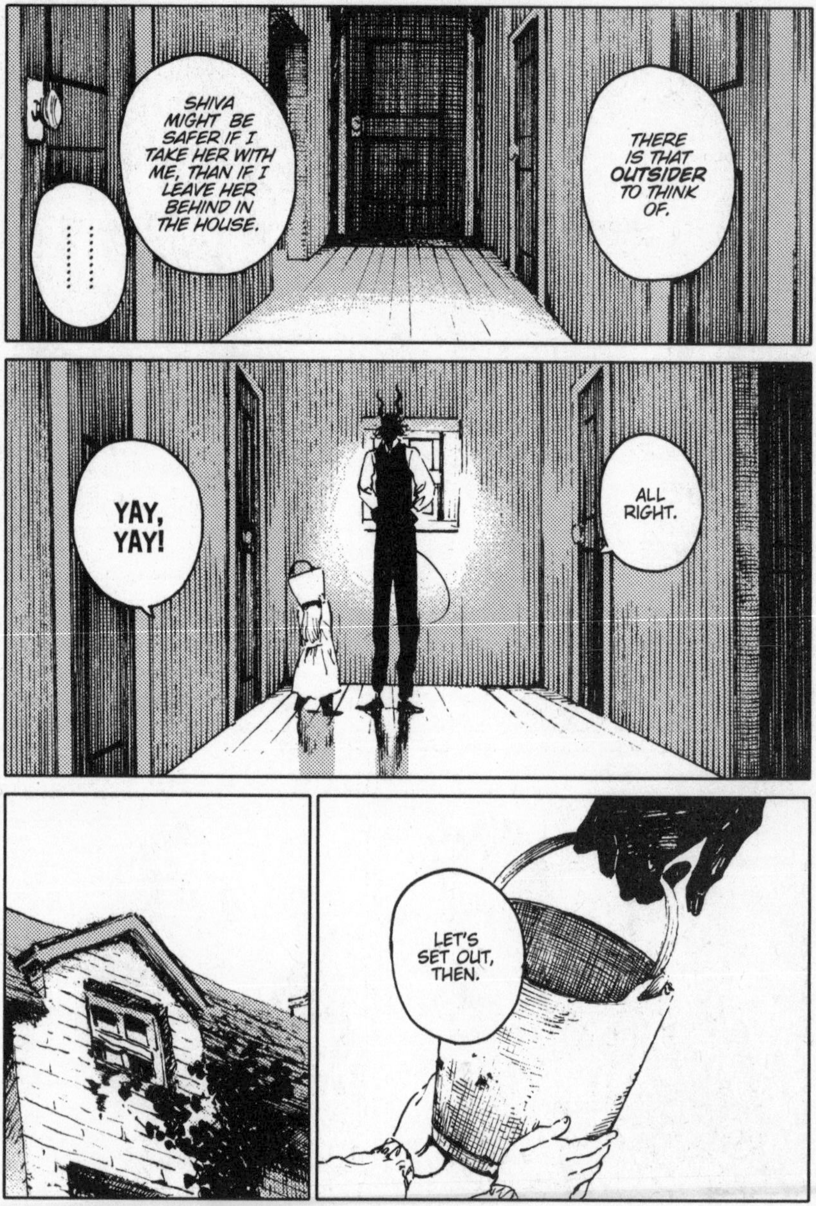
THERE IS THAT OUTSIDER TO THINK OF.
SHIVA MIGHT BE SAFER IF I TAKE HER WITH ME, THAN IF I LEAVE HER BEHIND IN THE HOUSE.
......
ALL RIGHT.
YAY, YAY!
LET'S SET OUT, THEN.

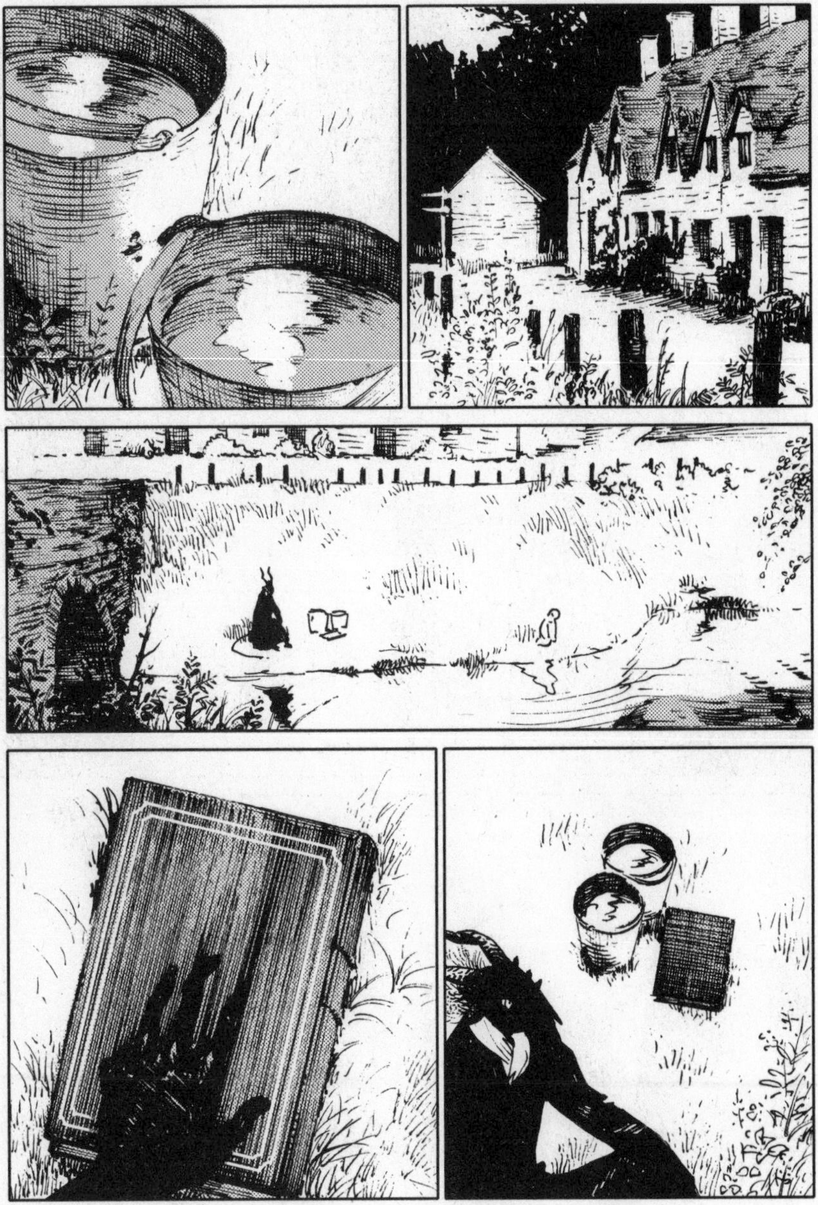

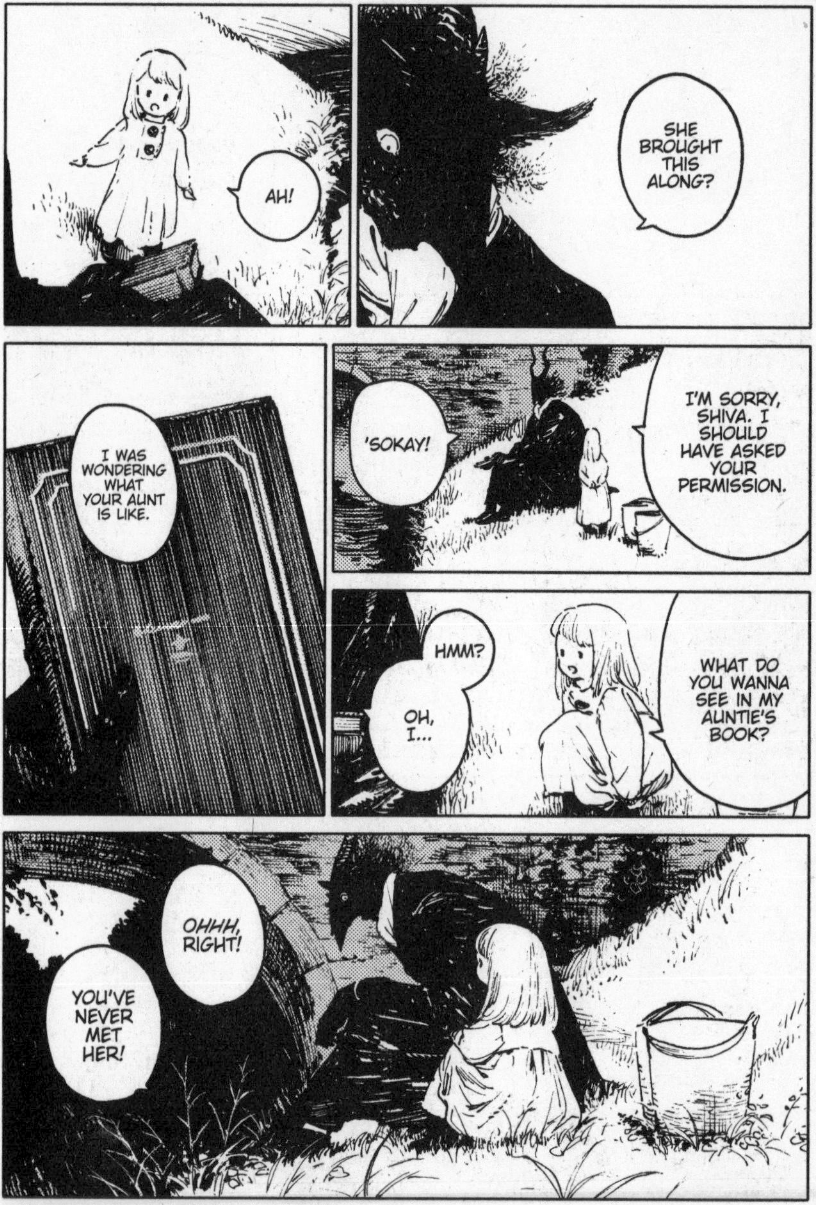
SHE BROUGHT THIS ALONG?
AH!
I'M SORRY, SHIVA. I SHOULD HAVE ASKED YOUR PERMISSION.
'SOKAY!
WHAT DO YOU WANNA SEE IN MY AUNTIE'S BOOK?
HMM?
OH, I...
I WAS WONDERING WHAT YOUR AUNT IS LIKE.
OHHH, RIGHT!
YOU'VE NEVER MET HER!

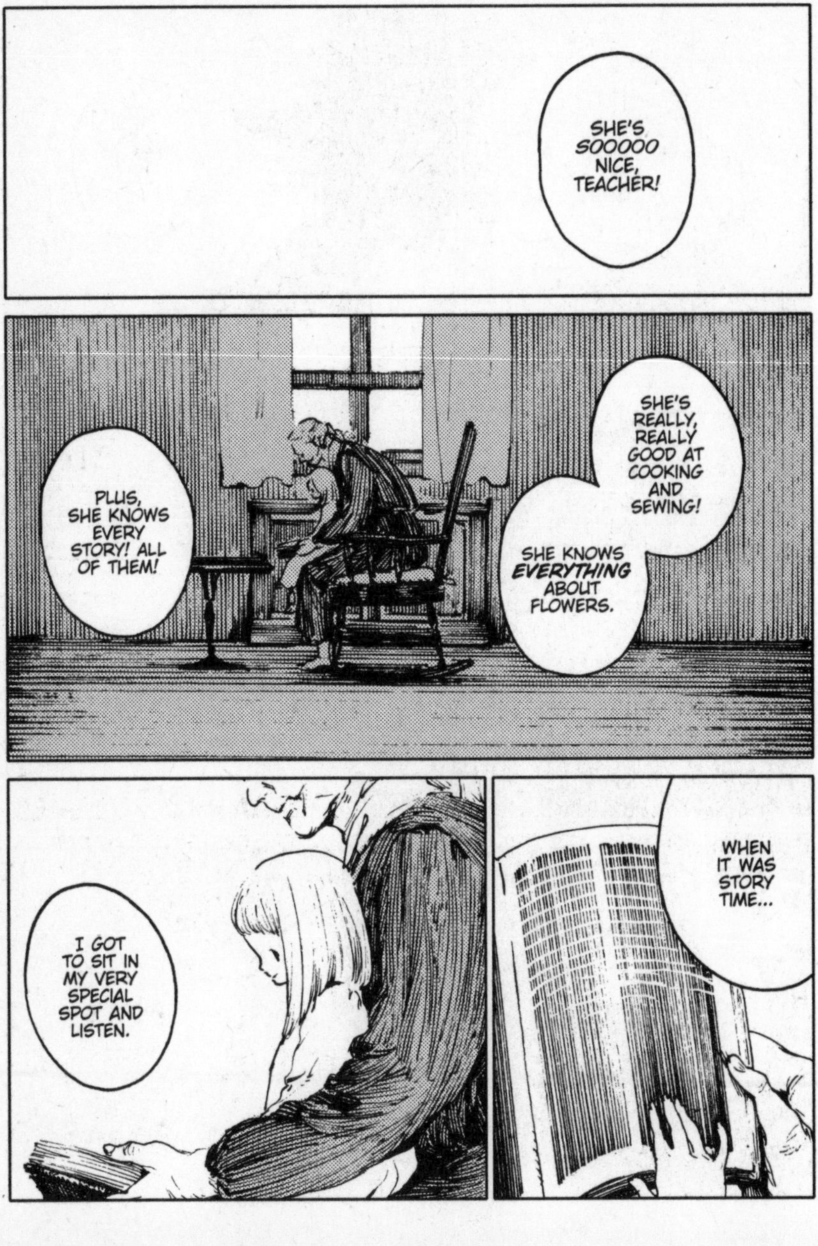
SHE'S SOOOOO NICE, TEACHER!
SHE'S REALLY, REALLY GOOD AT COOKING AND SEWING!
SHE KNOWS **EVERYTHING** ABOUT FLOWERS.
PLUS, SHE KNOWS EVERY STORY! ALL OF THEM!
WHEN IT WAS STORY TIME...
I GOT TO SIT IN MY VERY SPECIAL SPOT AND LISTEN.

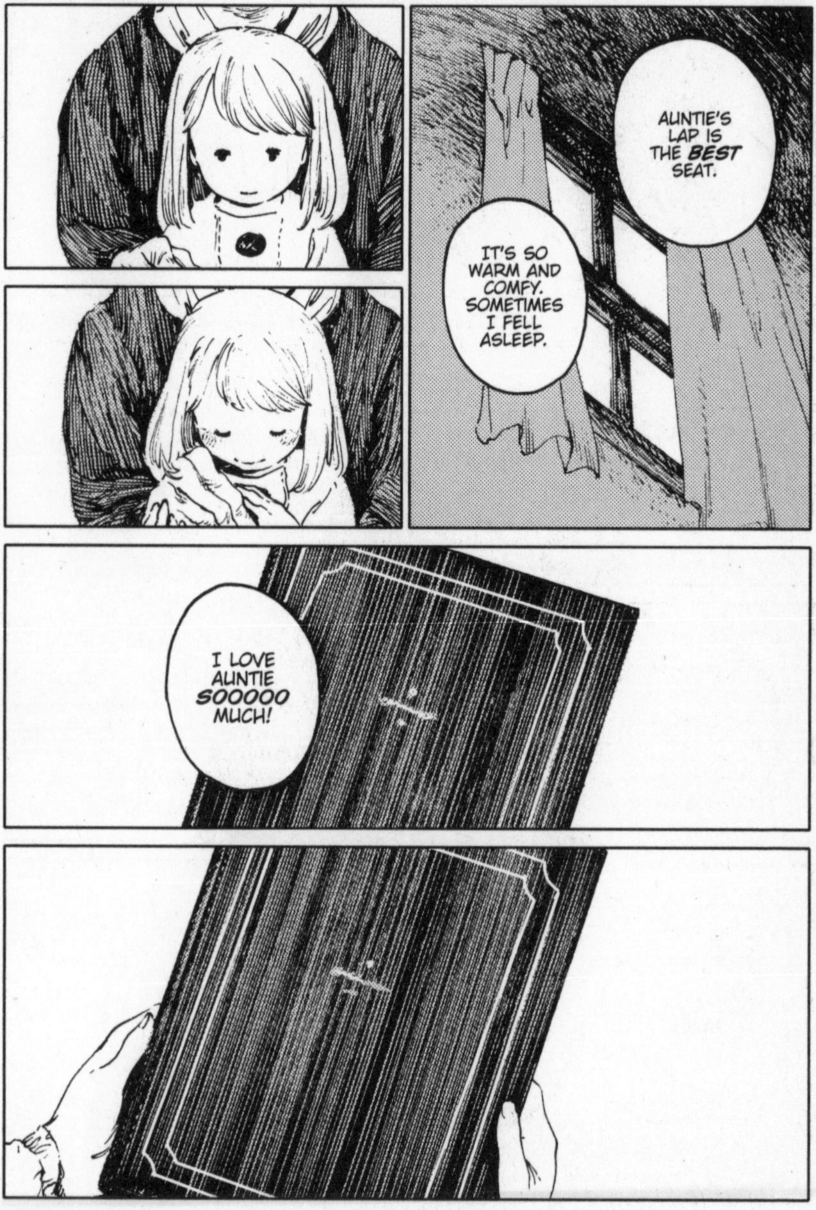
AUNTIE'S LAP IS THE ***BEST*** SEAT.
IT'S SO WARM AND COMFY. SOMETIMES I FELL ASLEEP.
I LOVE AUNTIE ***SOOOOO*** MUCH!

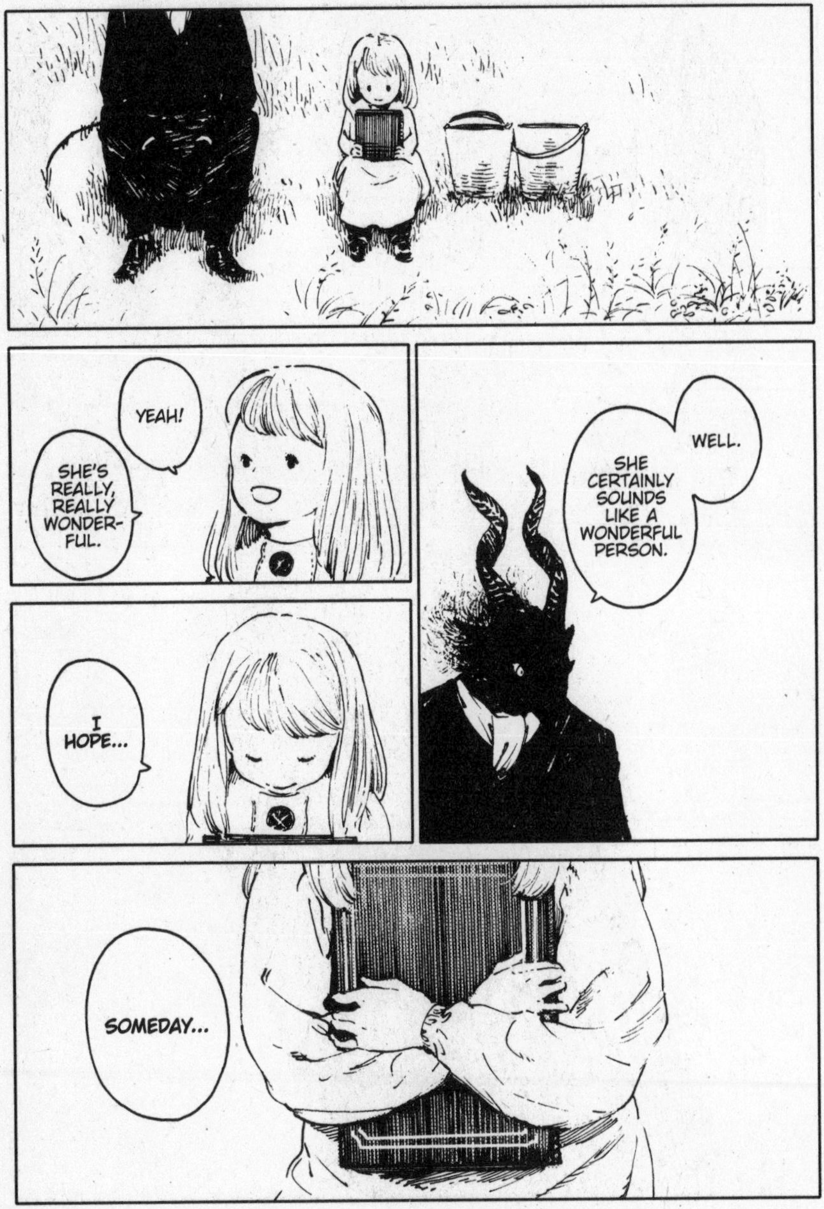
WELL.
SHE CERTAINLY SOUNDS LIKE A WONDERFUL PERSON.
YEAH!
SHE'S REALLY, REALLY WONDER-FUL.
I HOPE...
SOMEDAY...

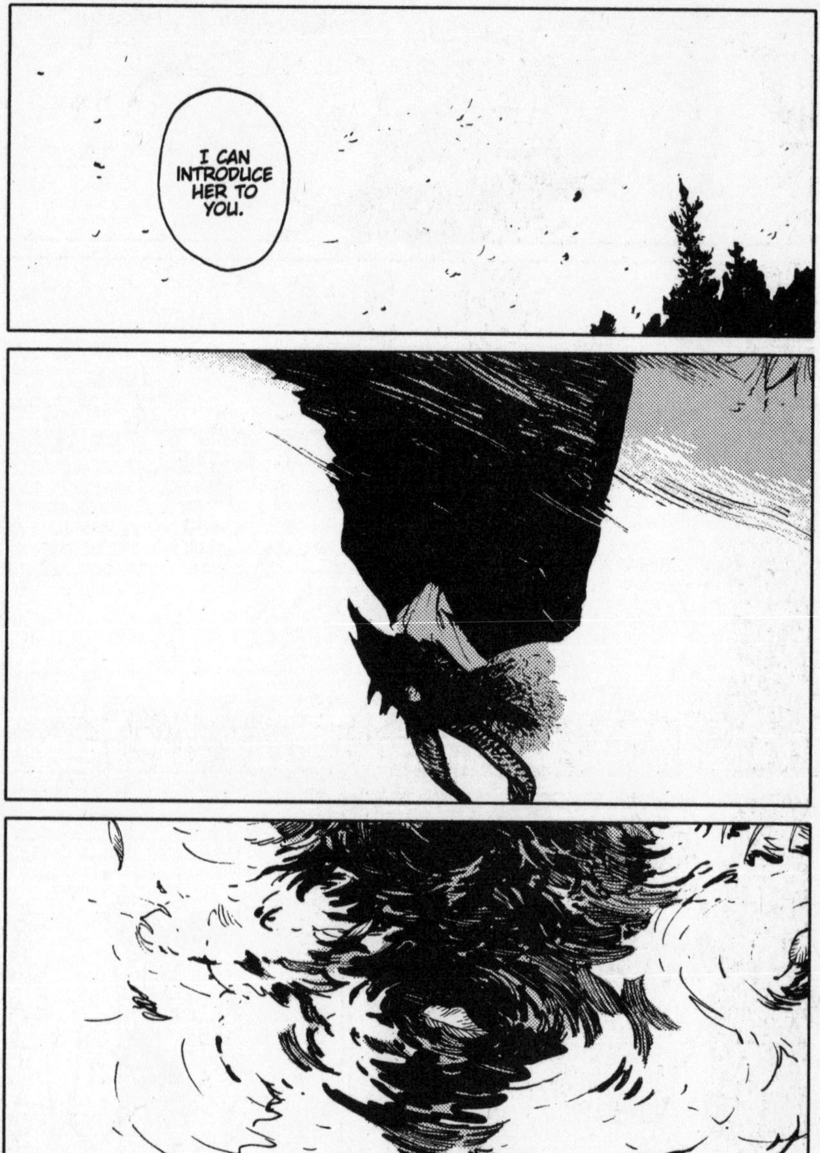
I CAN INTRODUCE HER TO YOU.

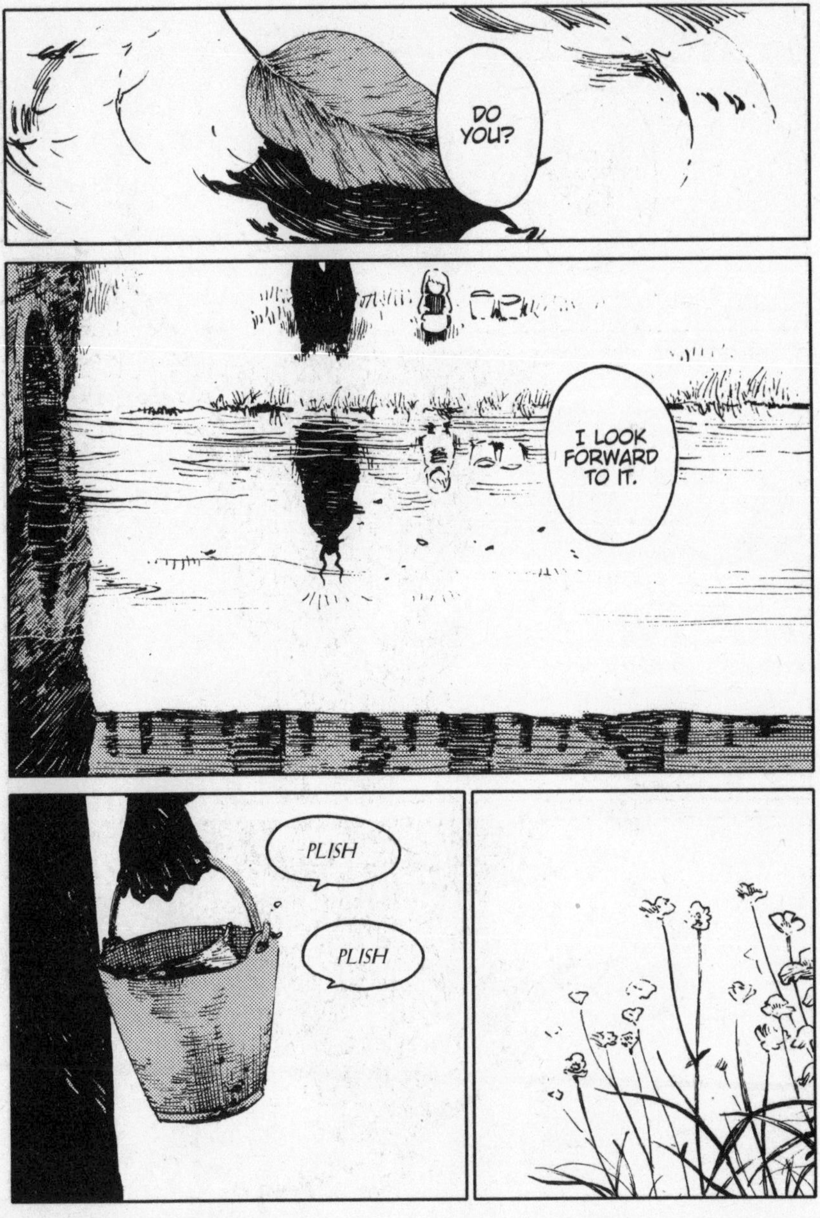
DO YOU?
I LOOK FORWARD TO IT.
PLISH
PLISH

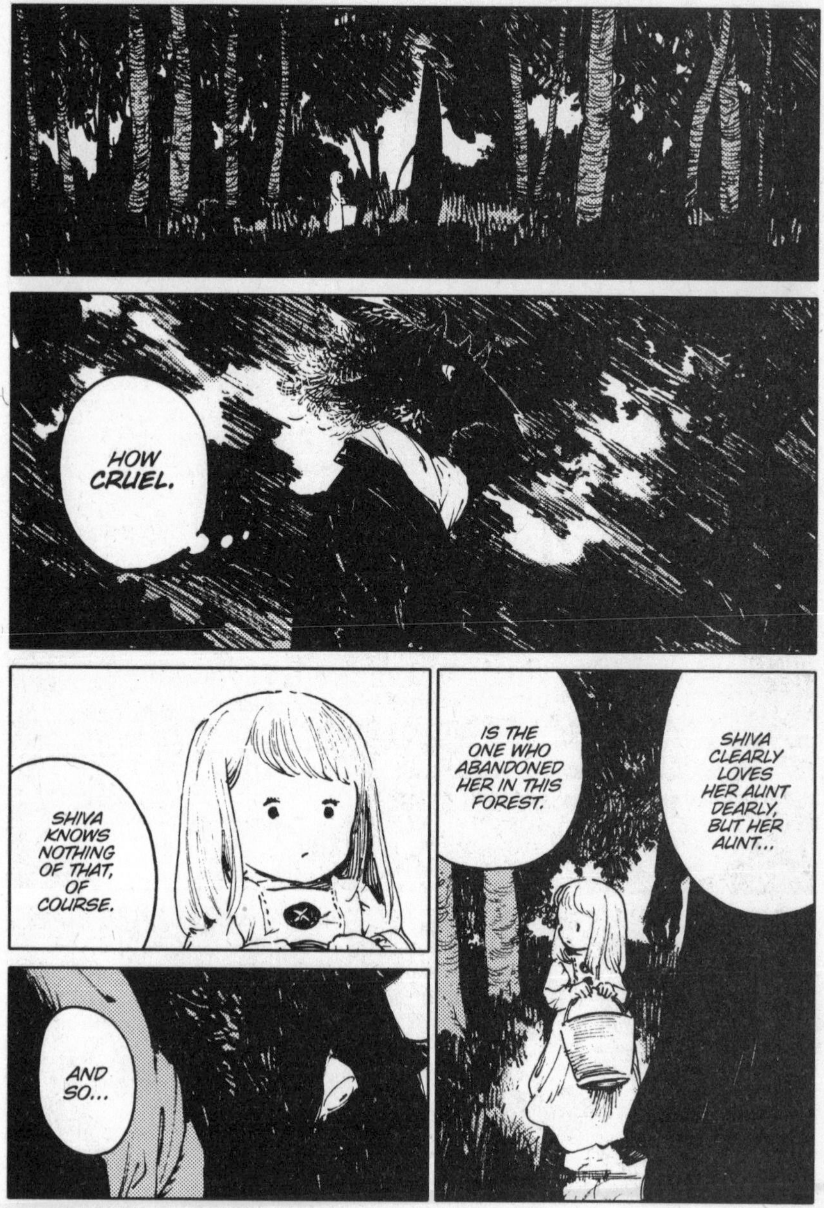
HOW CRUEL.
SHIVA CLEARLY LOVES HER AUNT DEARLY, BUT HER AUNT...
IS THE ONE WHO ABANDONED HER IN THIS FOREST.
SHIVA KNOWS NOTHING OF THAT, OF COURSE.
AND SO...

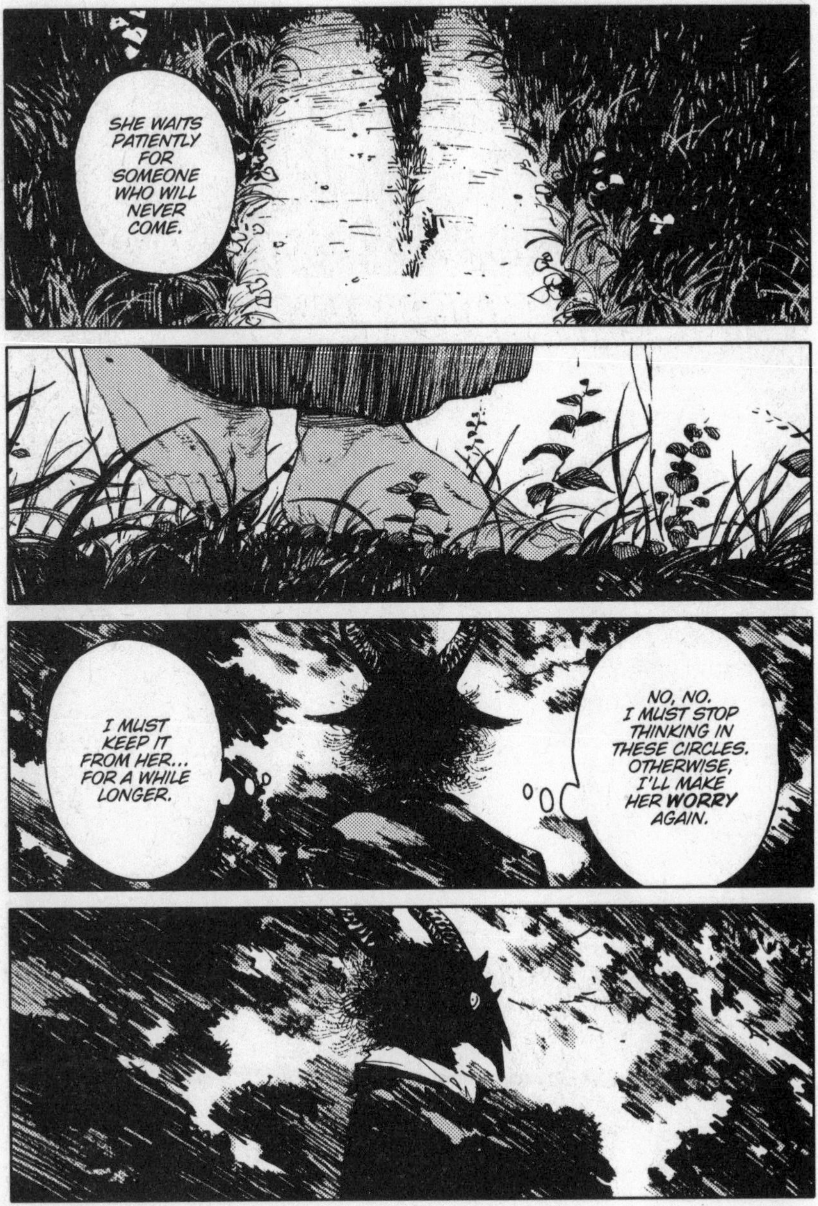
SHE WAITS PATIENTLY FOR SOMEONE WHO WILL NEVER COME.
NO, NO. I MUST STOP THINKING IN THESE CIRCLES. OTHERWISE, I'LL MAKE HER **WORRY** AGAIN.
I MUST KEEP IT FROM HER... FOR A WHILE LONGER.

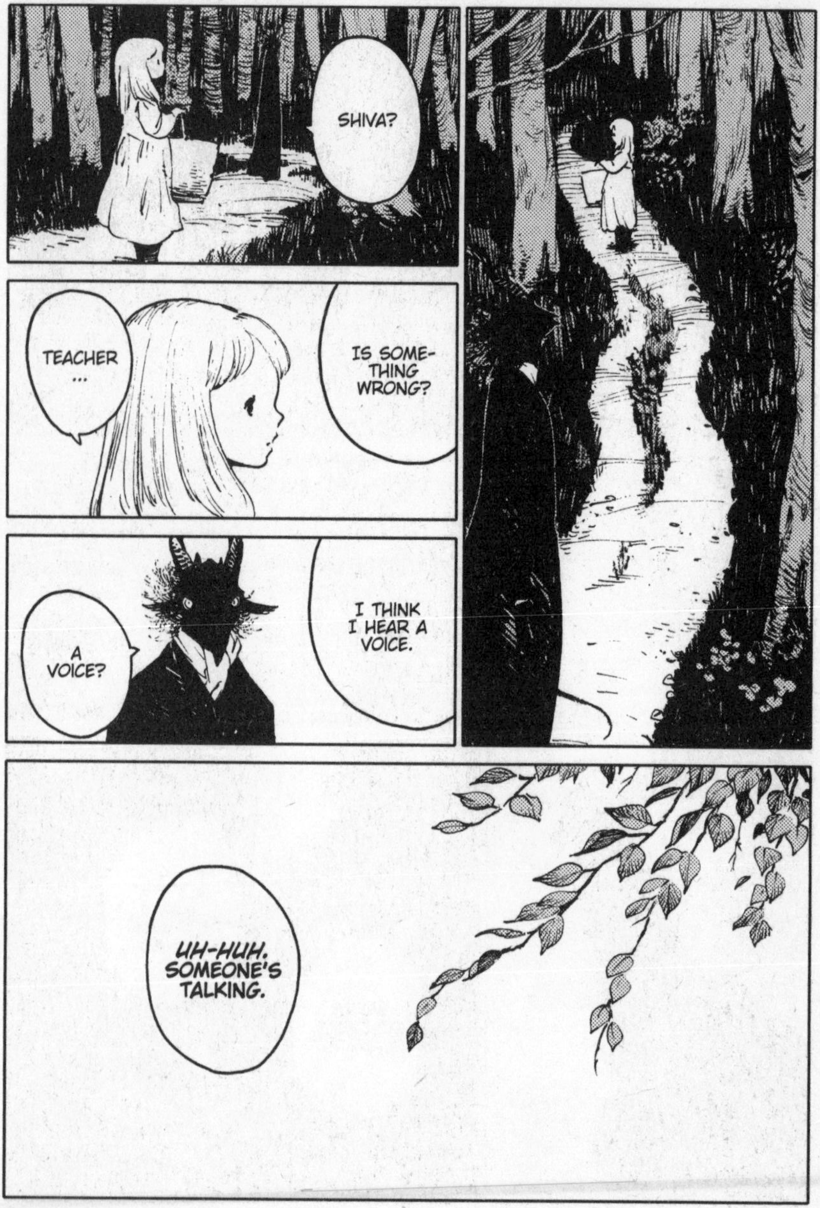
SHIVA?
IS SOME-THING WRONG?
TEACHER ...
I THINK I HEAR A VOICE.
A VOICE?
UH-HUH. SOMEONE'S TALKING.

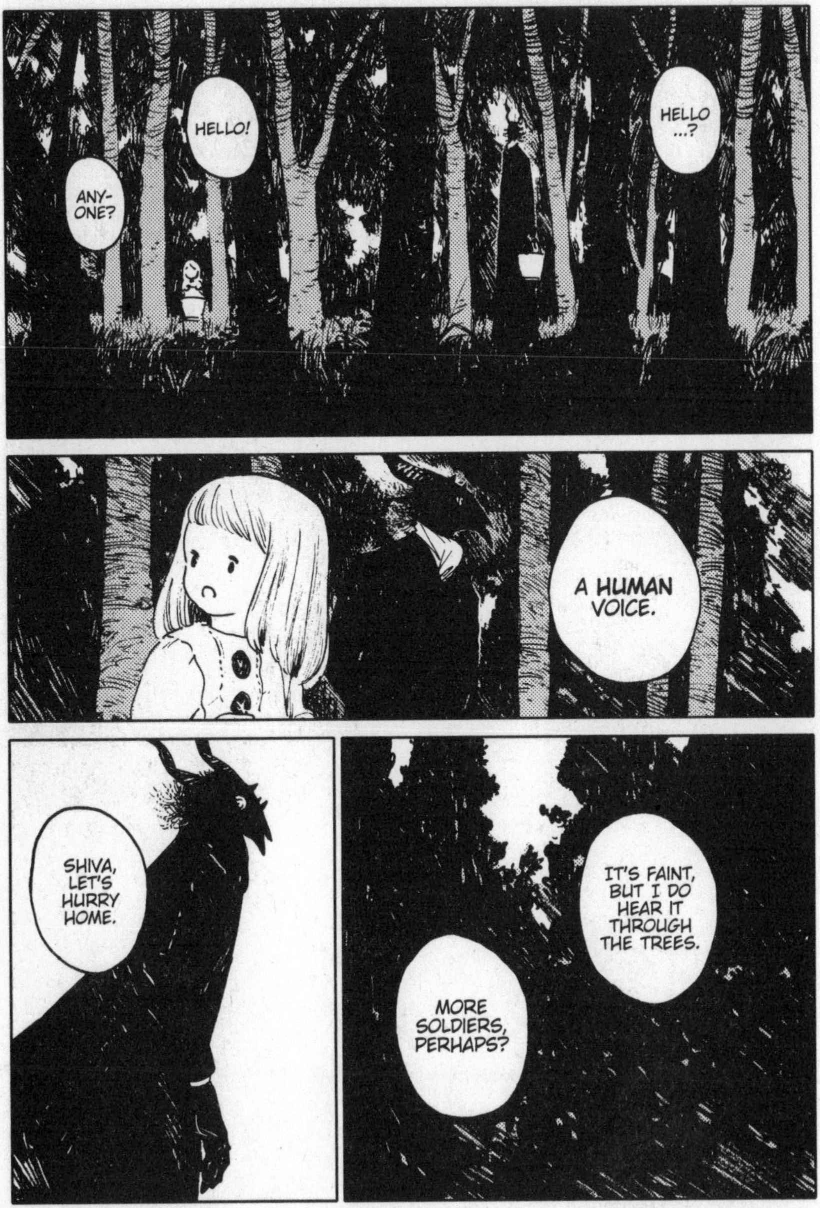
HELLO ...?
HELLO!
ANY-ONE?
A HUMAN VOICE.
IT'S FAINT, BUT I DO HEAR IT THROUGH THE TREES.
MORE SOLDIERS, PERHAPS?
SHIVA, LET'S HURRY HOME.

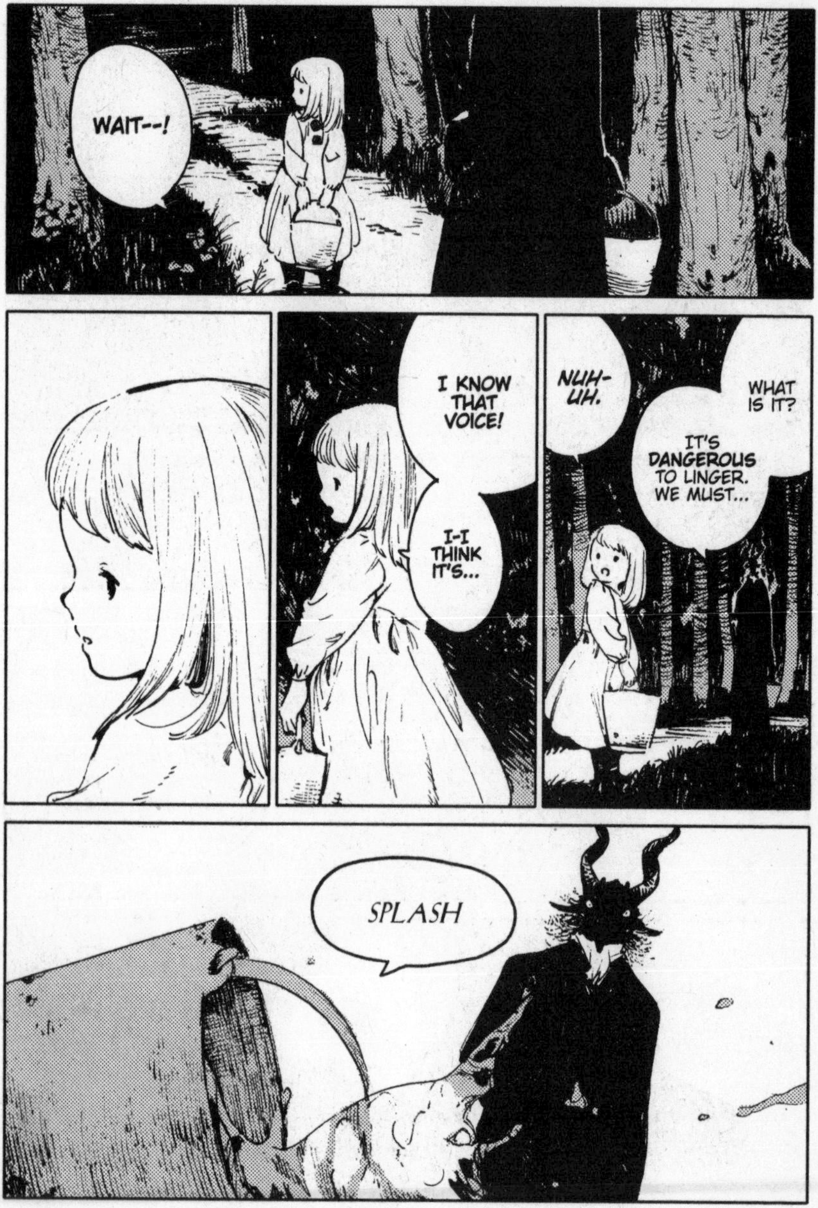
WAIT--!
WHAT IS IT?
NUH-UH.
IT'S DANGEROUS TO LINGER. WE MUST...
I KNOW THAT VOICE!
I-I THINK IT'S...
SPLASH

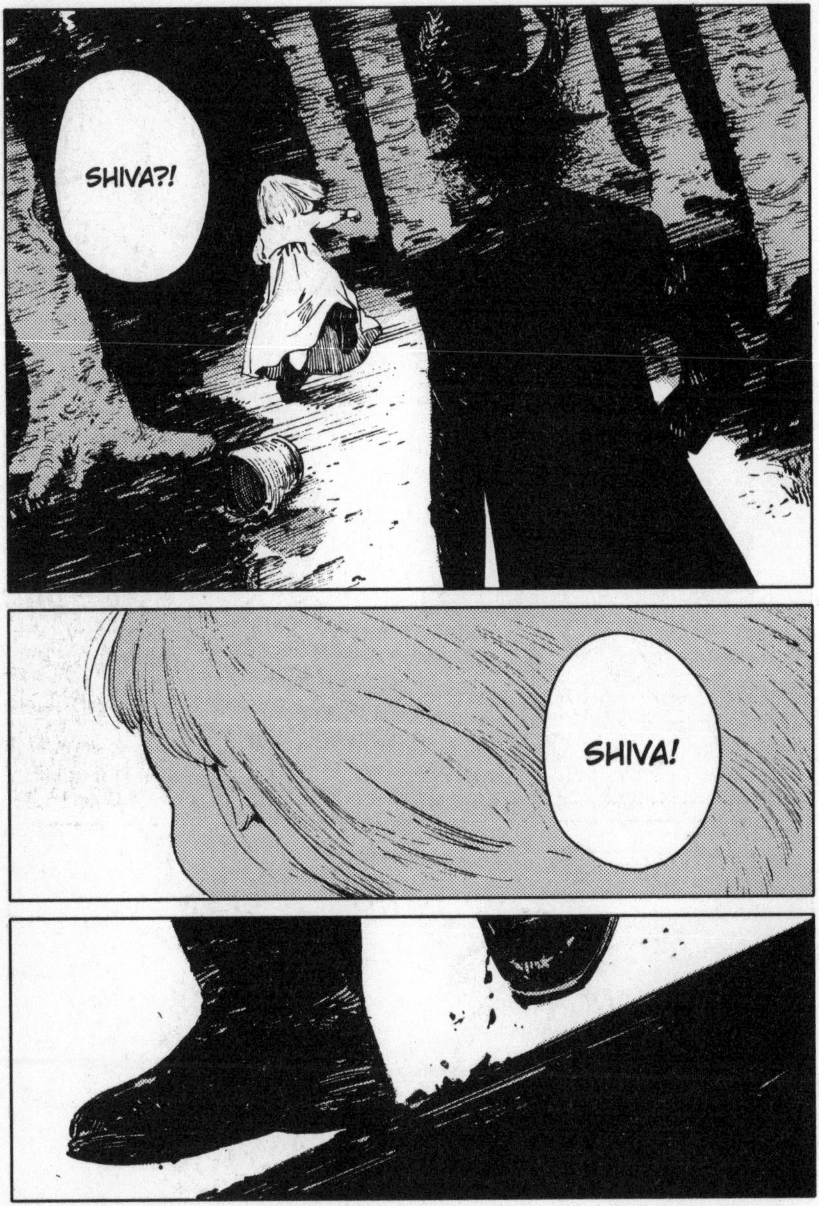
SHIVA?!
SHIVA!

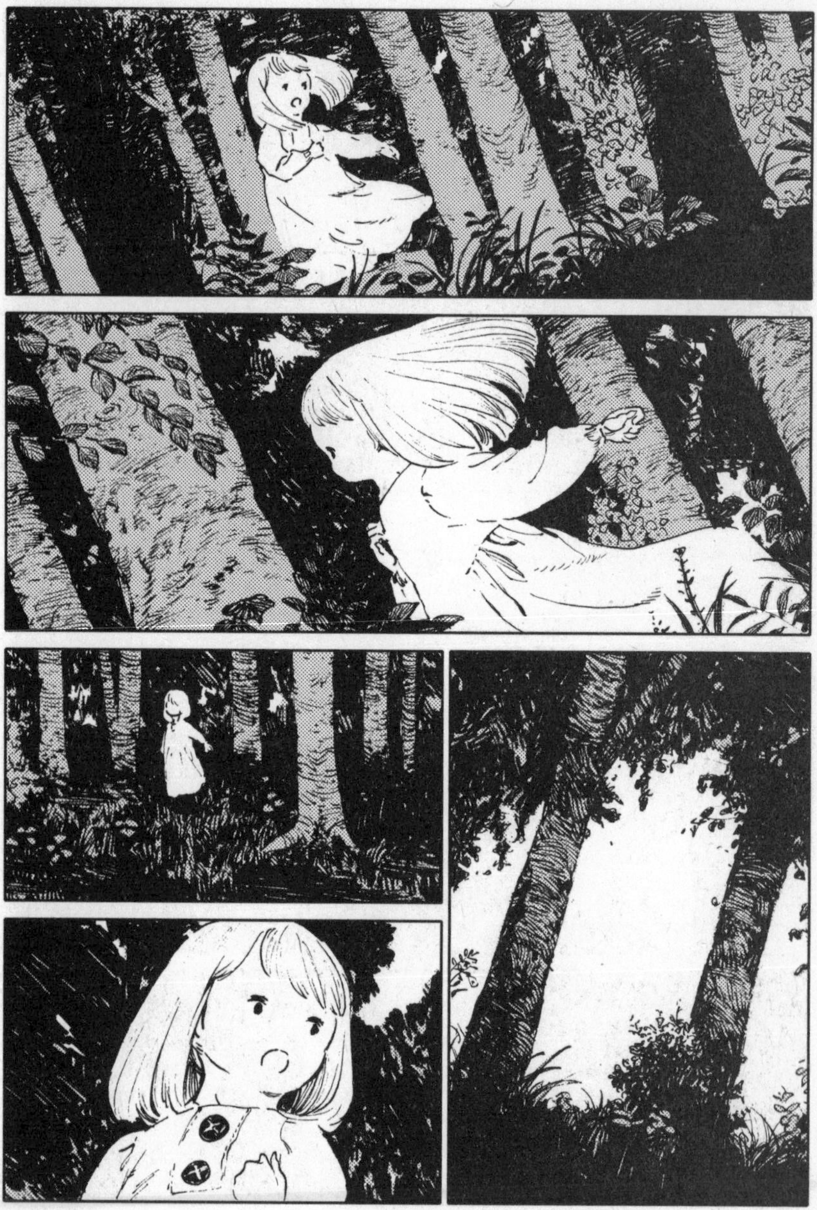

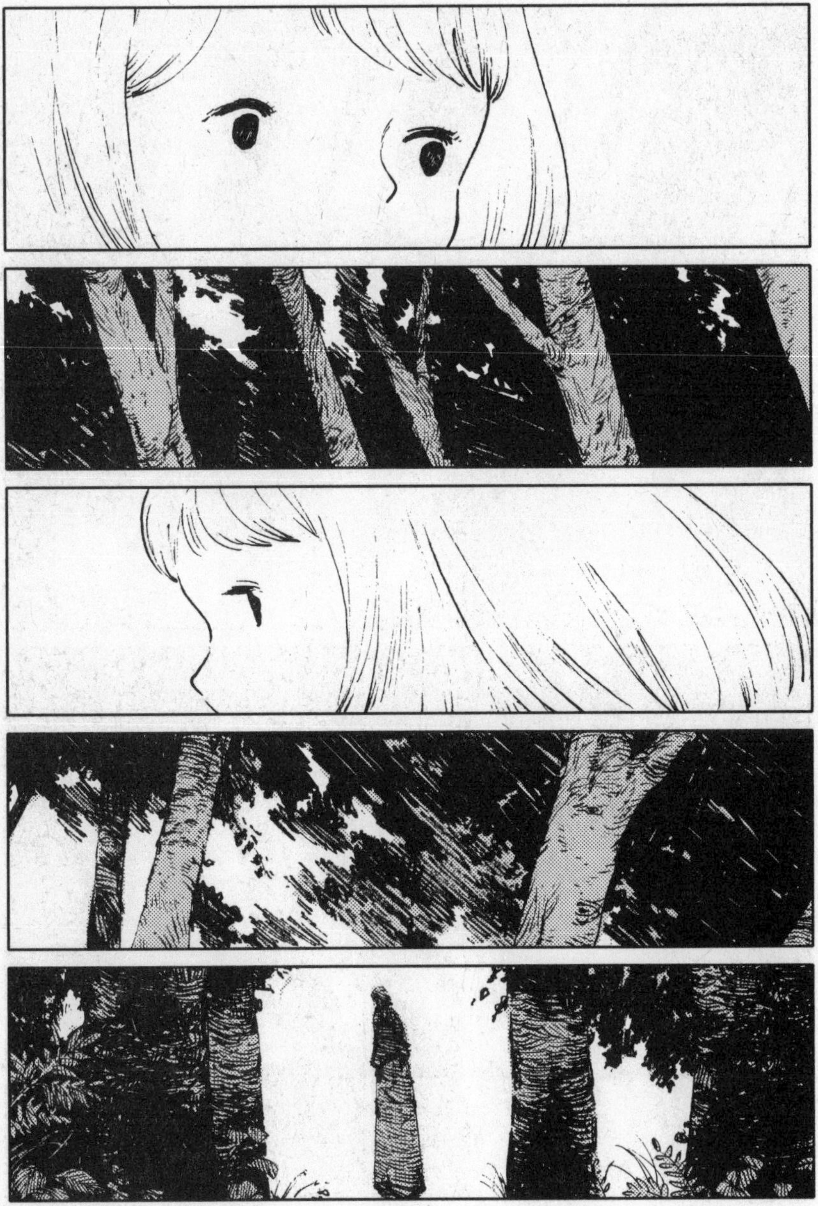

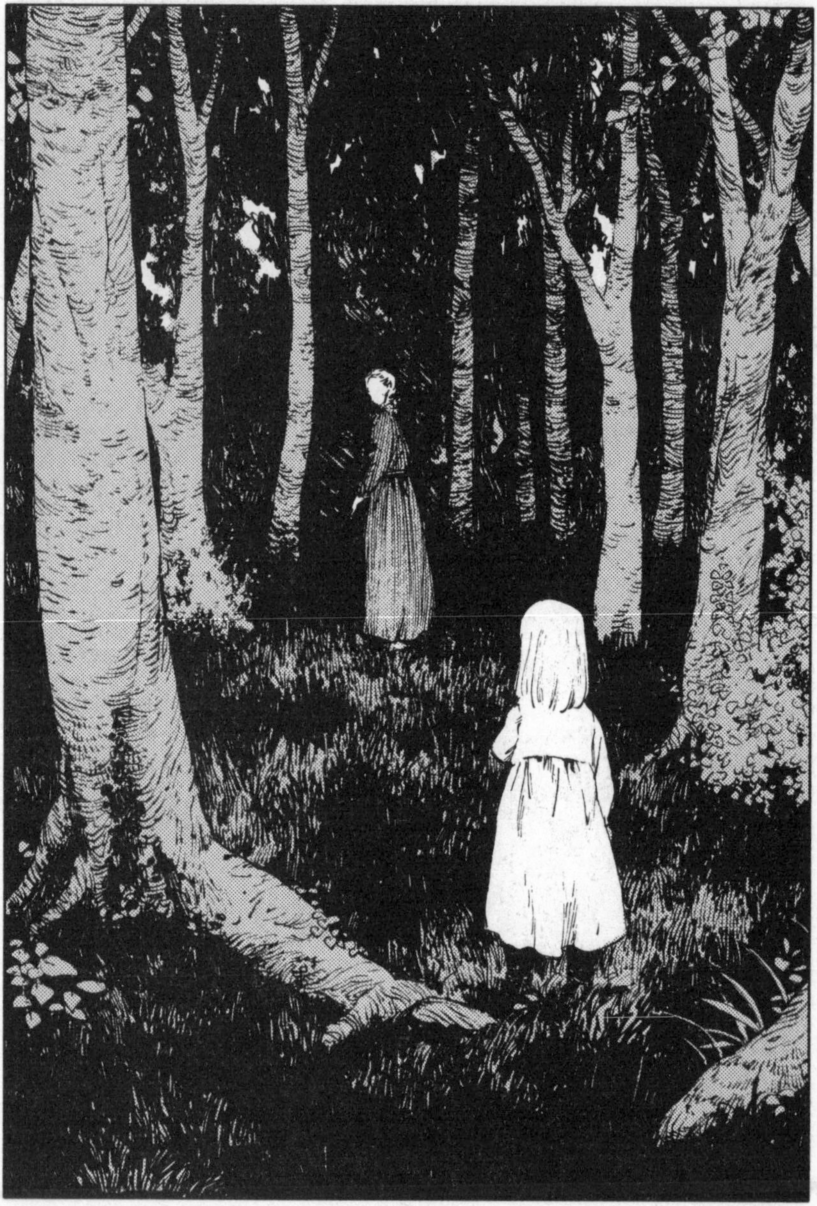

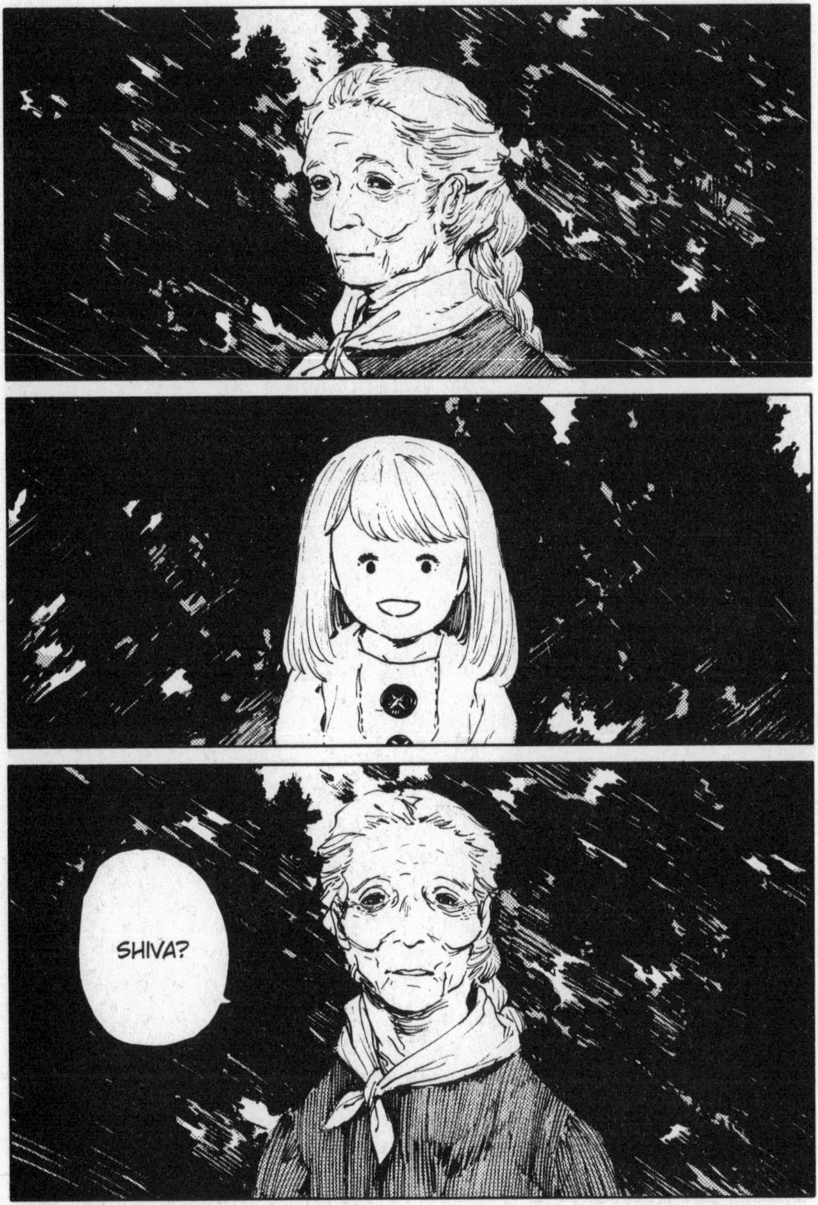
SHIVA?

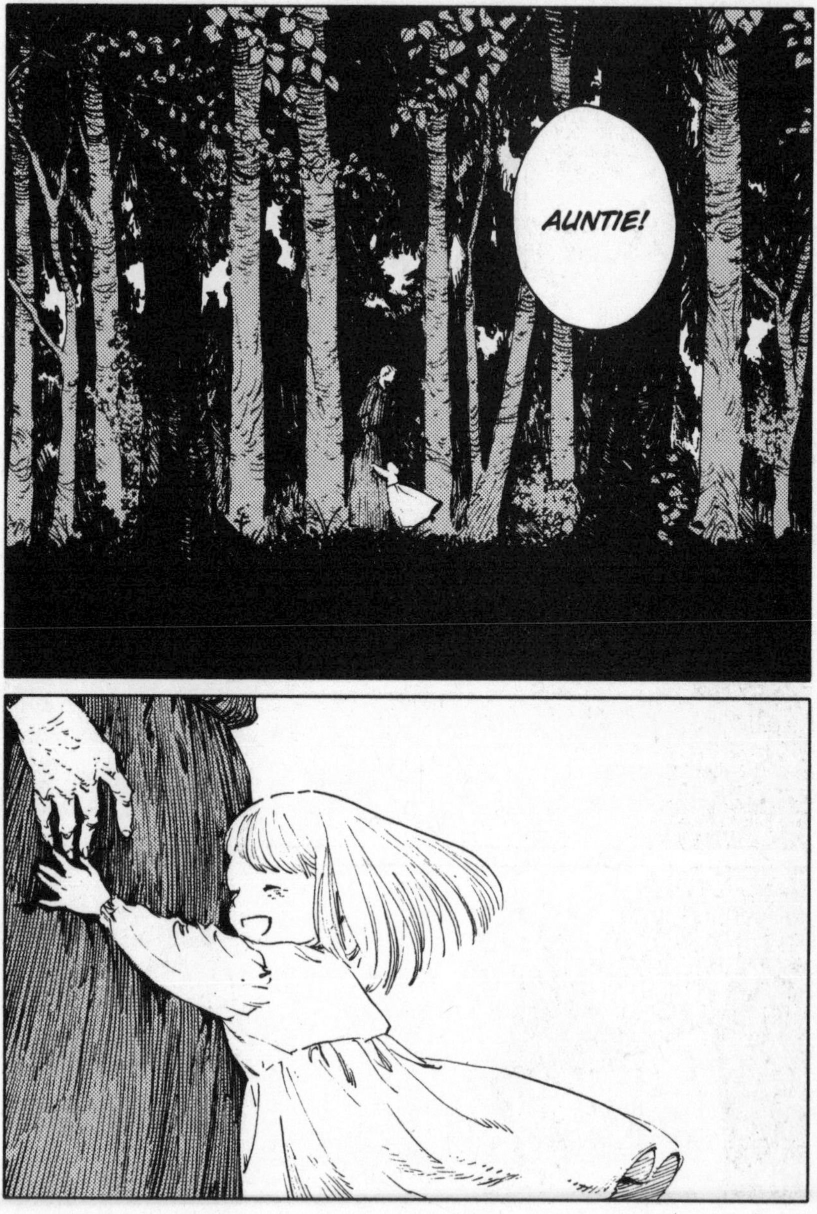
AUNTIE!

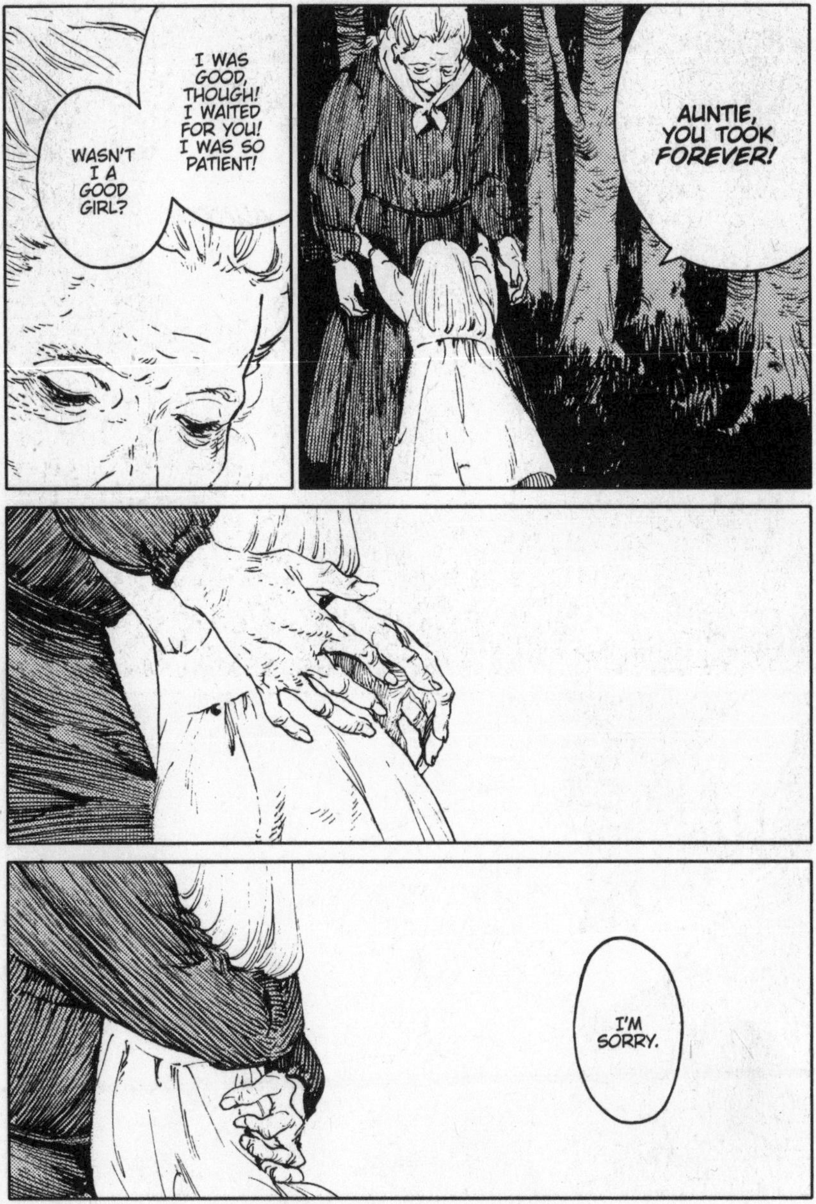
AUNTIE, YOU TOOK *FOREVER!*
I WAS GOOD, THOUGH! I WAITED FOR YOU! I WAS SO PATIENT!
WASN'T I A GOOD GIRL?
I'M SORRY.

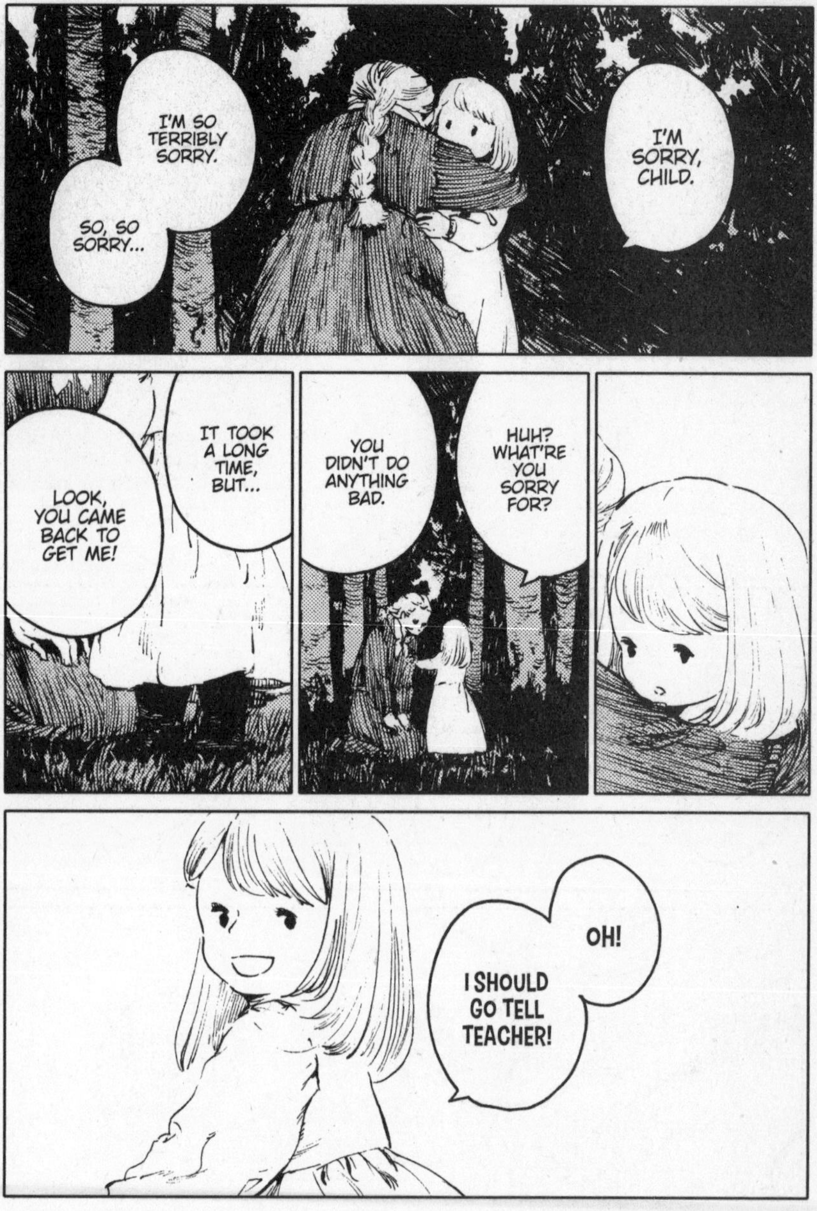
I'M SORRY, CHILD.
I'M SO TERRIBLY SORRY.
SO, SO SORRY...
HUH? WHAT'RE YOU SORRY FOR?
YOU DIDN'T DO ANYTHING BAD.
IT TOOK A LONG TIME, BUT...
LOOK, YOU CAME BACK TO GET ME!
OH!
I SHOULD GO TELL TEACHER!

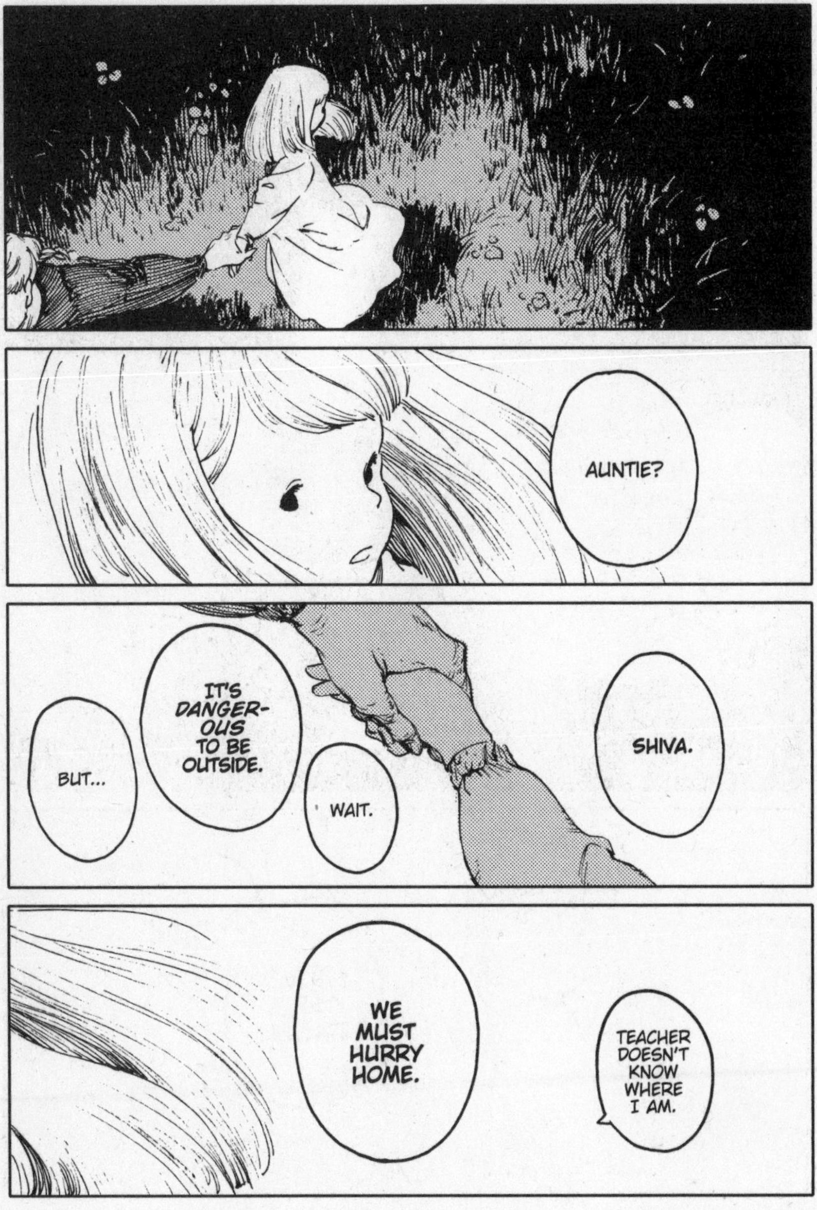
AUNTIE?
SHIVA.
WAIT.
IT'S DANGER-OUS TO BE OUTSIDE.
BUT...
TEACHER DOESN'T KNOW WHERE I AM.
WE MUST HURRY HOME.

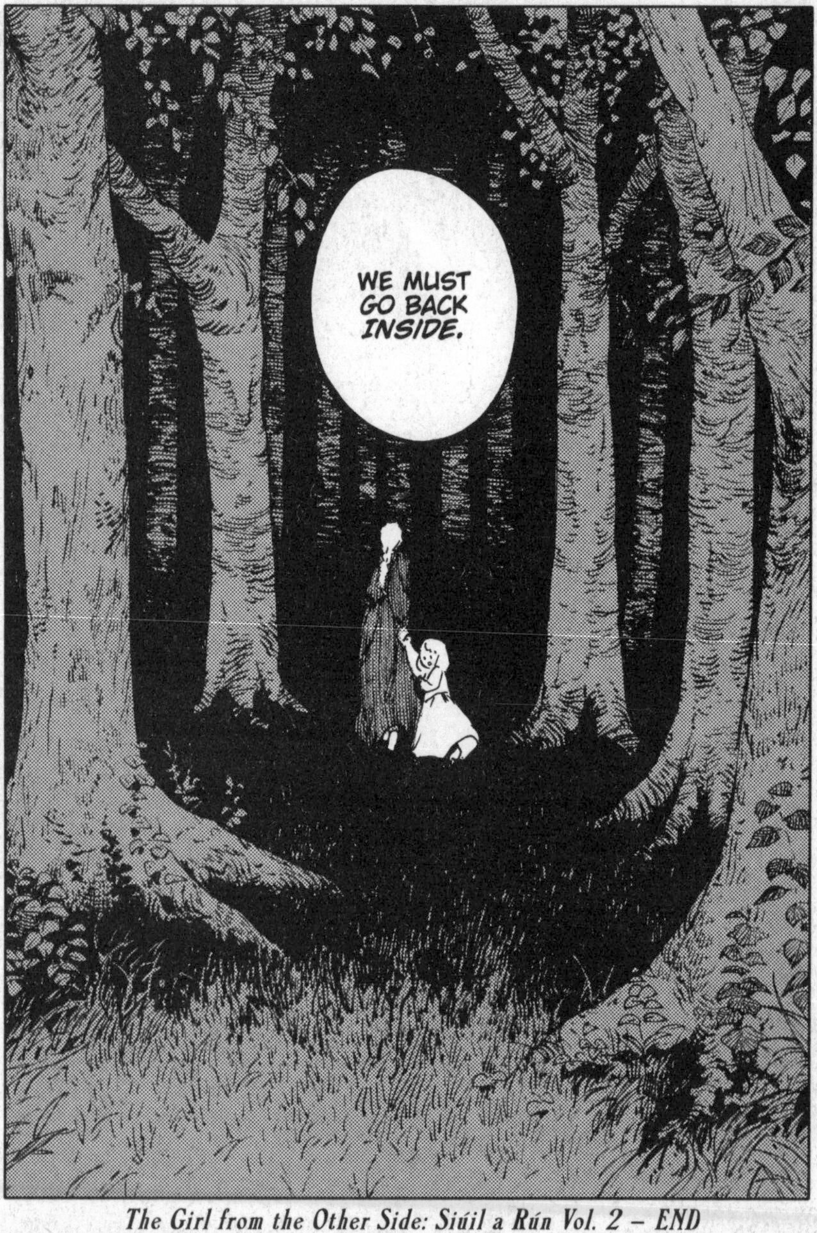
WE MUST
GO BACK
INSIDE.

The Girl from the Other Side: Siúil a Rún Vol. 2 – END

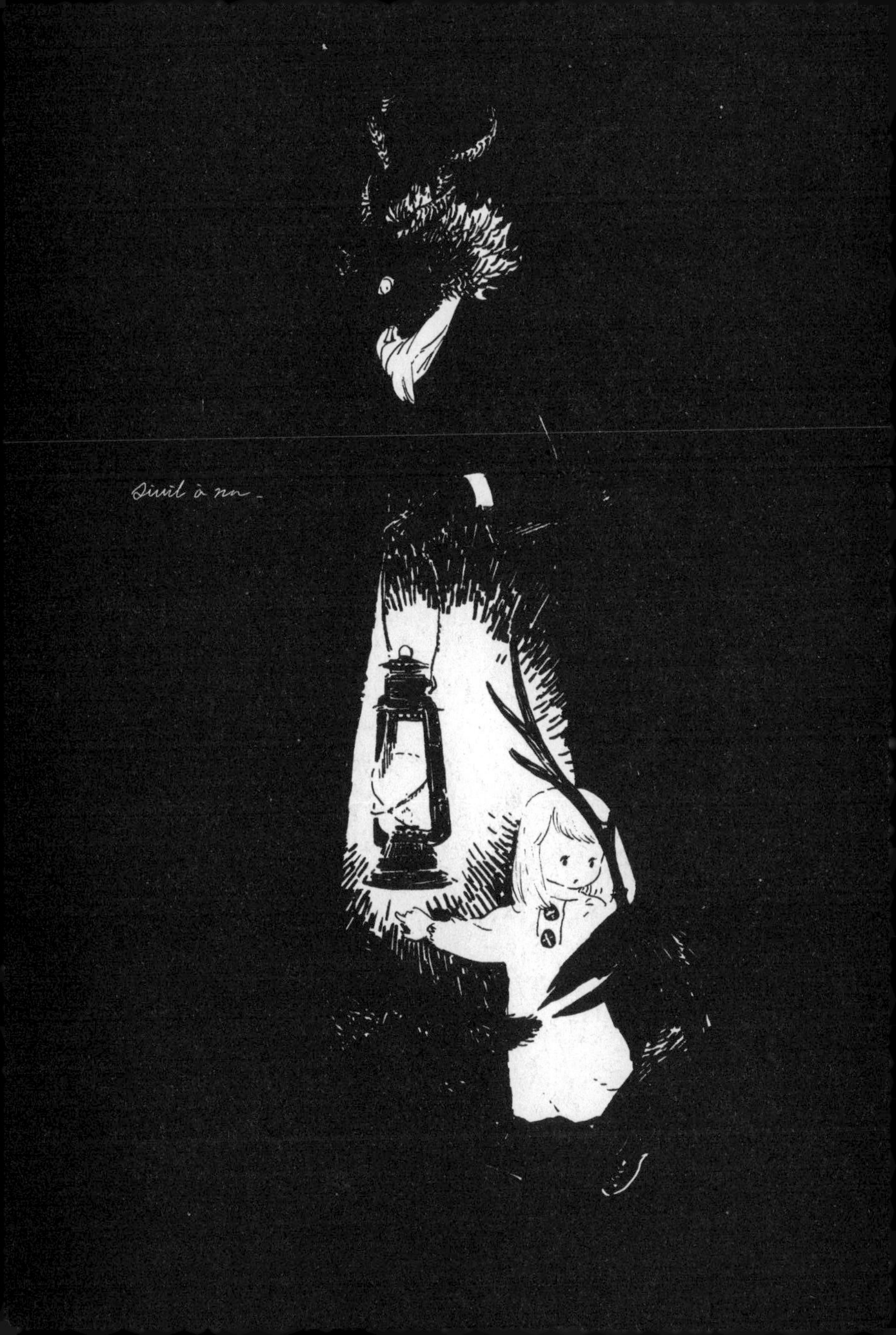

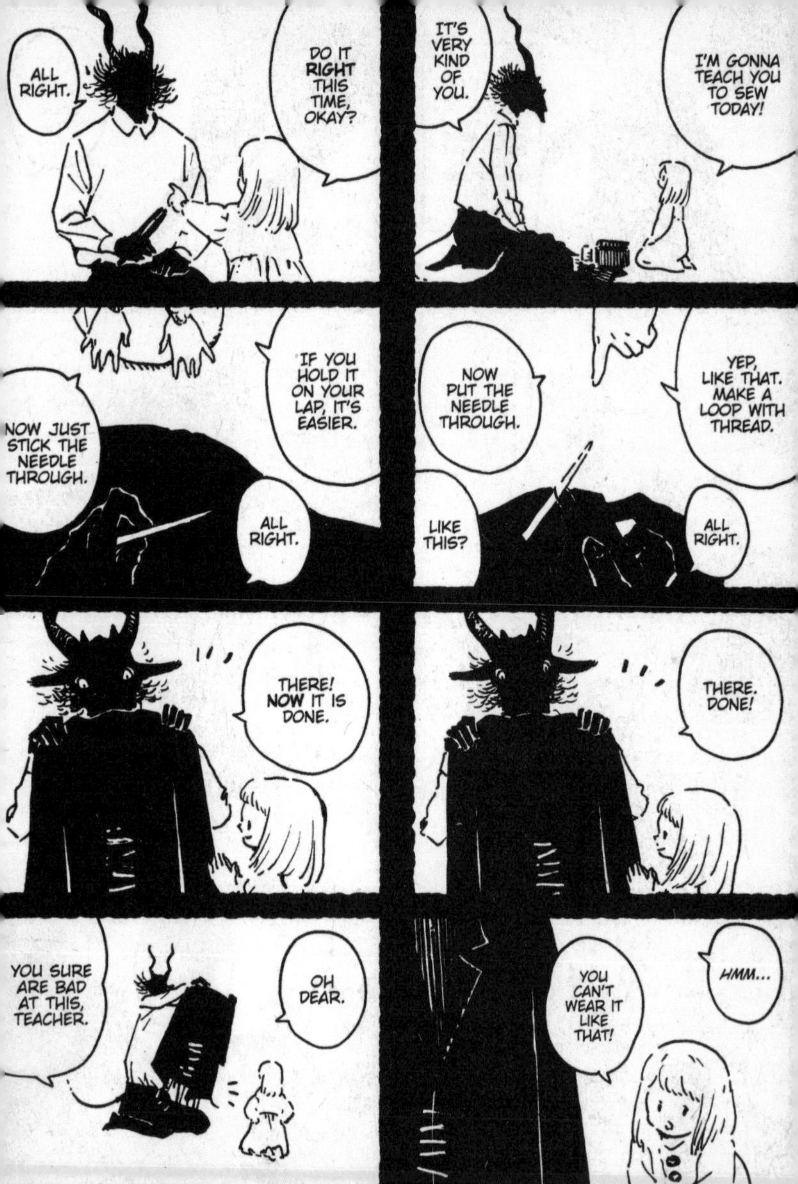
I'M GONNA TEACH YOU TO SEW TODAY!
IT'S VERY KIND OF YOU.
DO IT **RIGHT** THIS TIME, OKAY?
ALL RIGHT.
YEP, LIKE THAT. MAKE A LOOP WITH THREAD.
NOW PUT THE NEEDLE THROUGH.
ALL RIGHT.
LIKE THIS?
IF YOU HOLD IT ON YOUR LAP, IT'S EASIER.
NOW JUST STICK THE NEEDLE THROUGH.
ALL RIGHT.
THERE. DONE!
THERE! **NOW** IT IS DONE.
HMM...
YOU CAN'T WEAR IT LIKE THAT!
OH DEAR.
YOU SURE ARE BAD AT THIS, TEACHER.

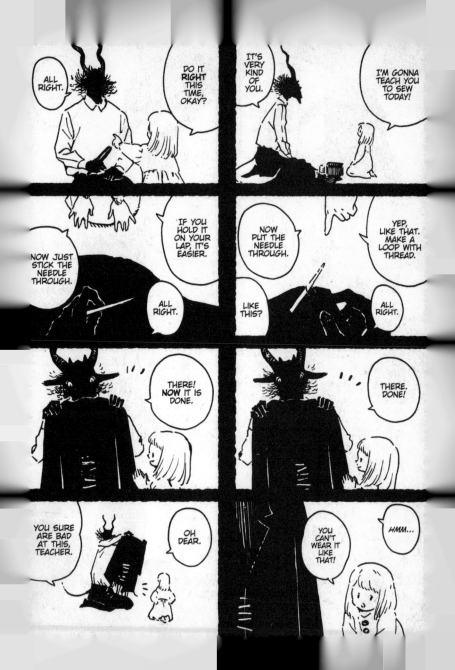

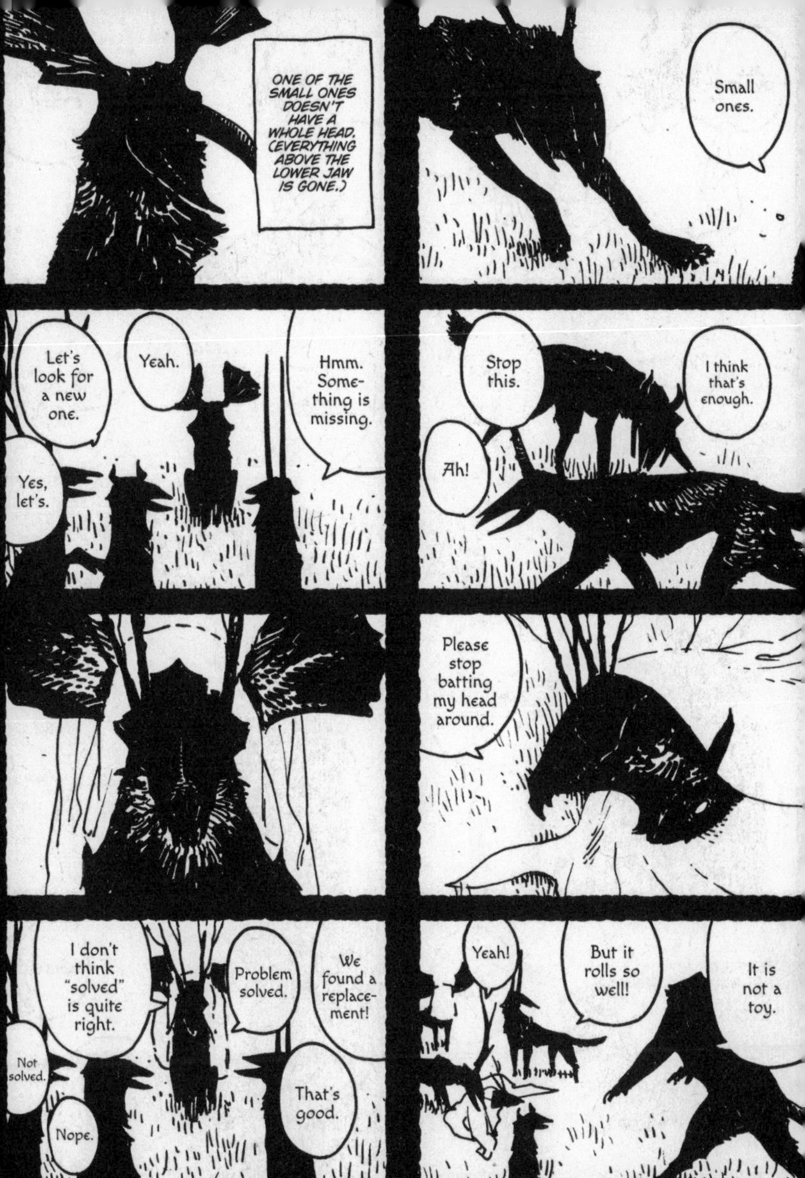
Small ones.
ONE OF THE SMALL ONES DOESN'T HAVE A WHOLE HEAD. (EVERYTHING ABOVE THE LOWER JAW IS GONE.)
I think that's enough.
Stop this.
Ah!
Hmm. Something is missing.
Yeah.
Let's look for a new one.
Yes, let's.
Please stop batting my head around.
It is not a toy.
But it rolls so well!
Yeah!
We found a replacement!
Problem solved.
I don't think "solved" is quite right.
That's good.
Not solved.
Nope.

Taken away to the Inside, the girl discovers--

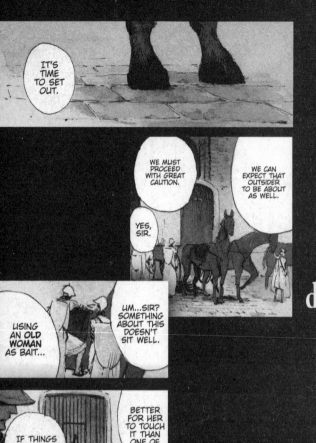

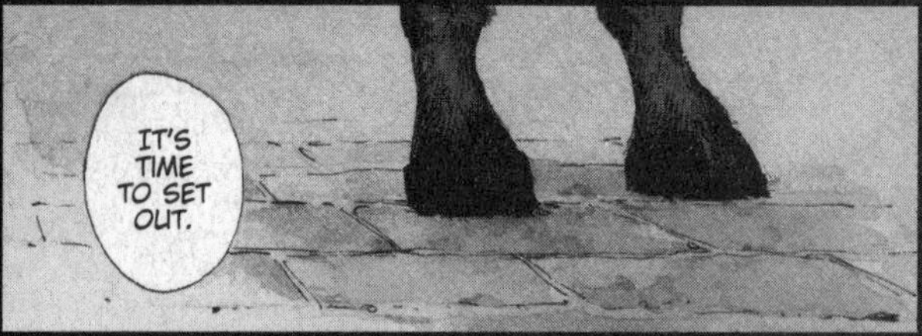
IT'S TIME TO SET OUT.

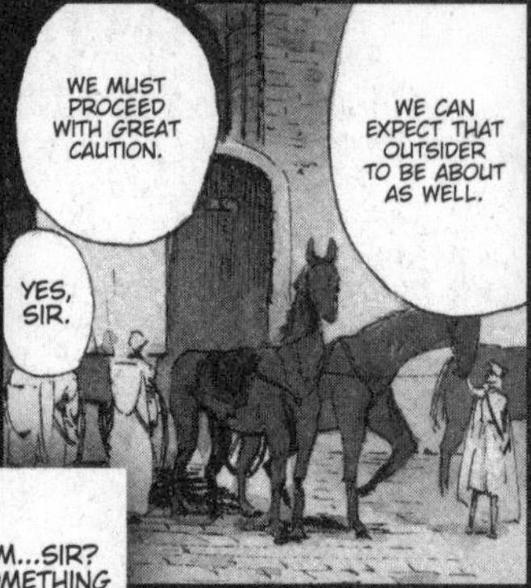
WE CAN EXPECT THAT OUTSIDER TO BE ABOUT AS WELL.
WE MUST PROCEED WITH GREAT CAUTION.
YES, SIR.

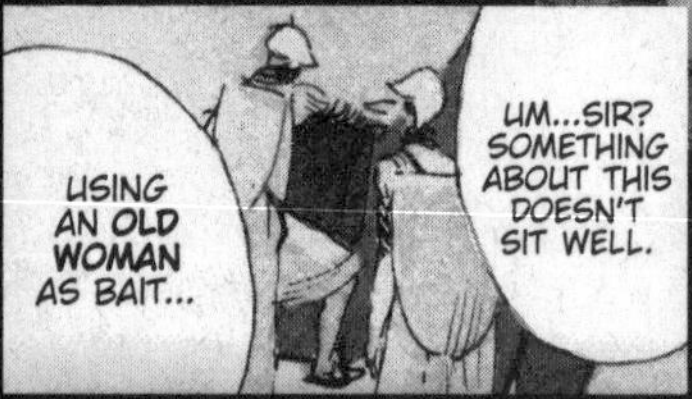
UM...SIR? SOMETHING ABOUT THIS DOESN'T SIT WELL.
USING AN **OLD WOMAN** AS BAIT...

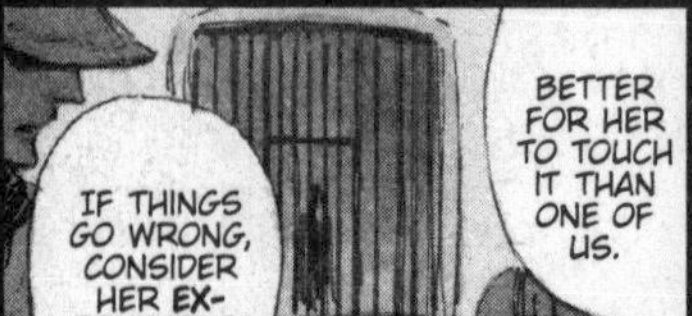
BETTER FOR HER TO TOUCH IT THAN ONE OF US.
IF THINGS GO WRONG, CONSIDER HER **EXPENDABLE.**
BESIDES...

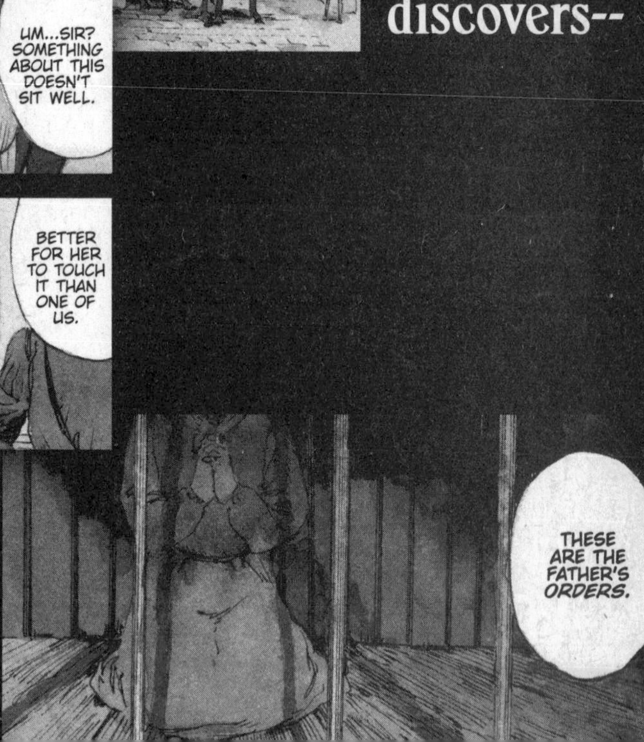
THESE ARE THE FATHER'S *ORDERS.*

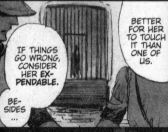

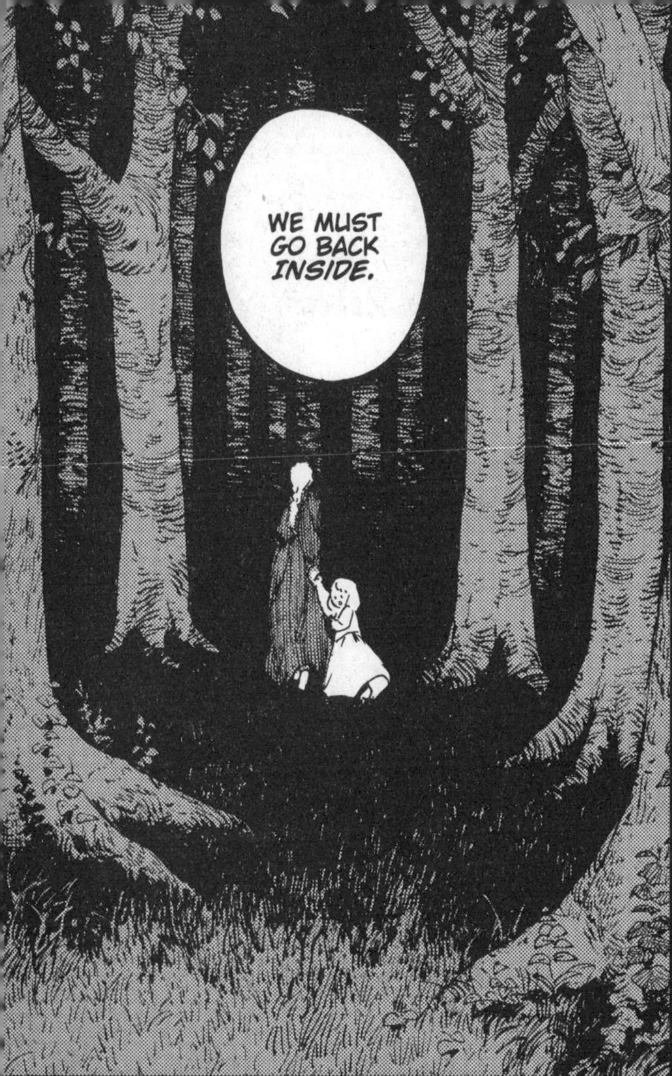
WE MUST GO BACK INSIDE.

Shiva is overjoyed to finally see her beloved aunt again, after worrying that they might never be together again. But the road before them leads to a horribly dark place. What fate awaits this child among stone streets that carry only the sounds of horses' hooves and cold voices...?

A tranquil fairy tale about those human and inhuman.

VOLUME 3 COMING SOON!

SEVEN SEAS ENTERTAINMENT PRESENTS

Siúil, a Rún
The Girl from the Other Side

•◦•

story and art by NAGABE   vol. 2

TRANSLATION
Adrienne Beck

ADAPTATION
Ysabet MacFarlane

LETTERING AND RETOUCH
Lys Blakeslee

LOGO DESIGN
Karis Page

COVER DESIGN
Nicky Lim

PROOFREADER
Shanti Whitesides
Jocelyne Allen

ASSISTANT EDITOR
Jenn Grunigen

PRODUCTION ASSISTANT
CK Russell

PRODUCTION MANAGER
Lissa Pattillo

EDITOR-IN-CHIEF
Adam Arnold

PUBLISHER
Jason DeAngelis

THE GIRL FROM THE OTHER SIDE: SIUIL, A RUN VOL. 2
©nagabe 2016
Originally published in Japan in 2016 by MAG Garden Corporation, Tokyo.
English translation rights arranged through TOHAN CORPORATION, Tokyo.

Seven Seas books may be purchased in bulk for educational, business, or promotional use. For information on bulk purchases, please contact Macmillan Corporate & Premium Sales Department at 1-800-221-7945 (ext 5442) or write specialmarkets@macmillan.com.

ISBN: 978-1-626925-23-6

Printed in Canada

First Printing: May 2017

10 9 8 7 6 5 4 3 2 1

FOLLOW US ONLINE: *www.gomanga.com*

READING DIRECTIONS

This book reads from *right to left*, Japanese style. If this is your first time reading manga, you start reading from the top right panel on each page and take it from there. If you get lost, just follow the numbered diag͏͏͏͏, first, but you'll

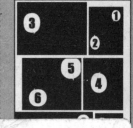